AWA UPSHOT PRESENTS

RED BORDER

JASON STARR
Writer

WILL CONRAD
Artist

IVAN NUNES
Colorist

SAL CIPRIANO
Letterer

TIM BRADSTREET
Cover Artist

 UPSHOT  AWA_studios AWAstudiosofficial   UPSHOT_studios UPSHOTstudiosofficial

Axel Alonso Chief Creative Officer
Chris Burns Production Editor
Stan Chou Art Director, Logo Designer
Michael Coast Senior Editor
Jaime Coyne Associate Editor
Frank Fochetta Senior Consultant, Sales & Distribution
William Graves Managing Editor
Bill Jemas CEO & Publisher

Amy Kim Events & Sales Associate
Bosung Kim Production & Design Assistant
Allison Mase Executive Assistant
Dulce Montoya Associate Editor
Kevin Park Associate General Counsel
Maureen Sullivan Controller
Lisa Y. Wu Marketing Manager

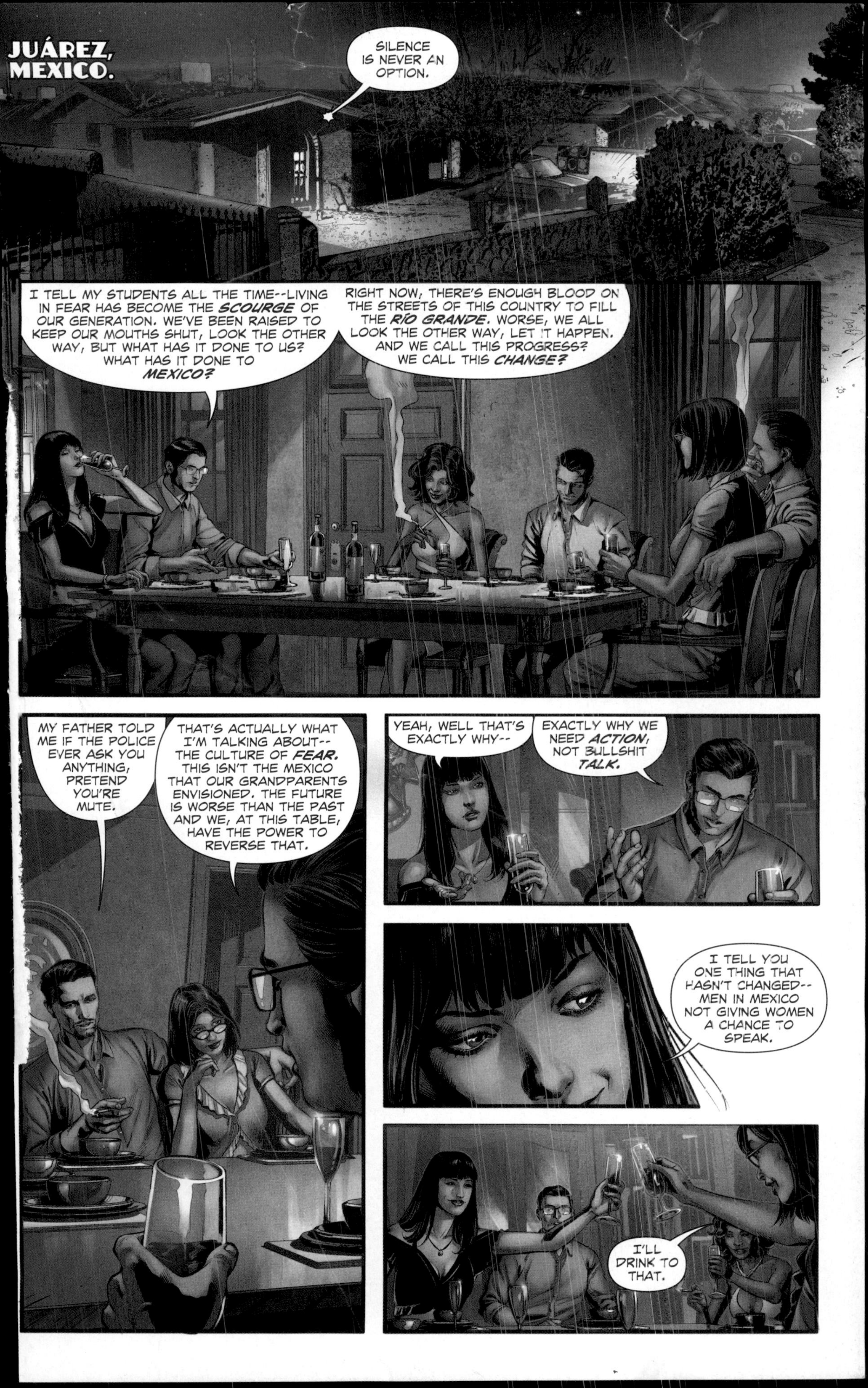
JUÁREZ, MEXICO.
SILENCE IS NEVER AN OPTION.
I TELL MY STUDENTS ALL THE TIME--LIVING IN FEAR HAS BECOME THE SCOURGE OF OUR GENERATION. WE'VE BEEN RAISED TO KEEP OUR MOUTHS SHUT, LOOK THE OTHER WAY, BUT WHAT HAS IT DONE TO US? WHAT HAS IT DONE TO MEXICO?
RIGHT NOW, THERE'S ENOUGH BLOOD ON THE STREETS OF THIS COUNTRY TO FILL THE RÍO GRANDE. WORSE, WE ALL LOOK THE OTHER WAY, LET IT HAPPEN. AND WE CALL THIS PROGRESS? WE CALL THIS CHANGE?
MY FATHER TOLD ME IF THE POLICE EVER ASK YOU ANYTHING, PRETEND YOU'RE MUTE.
THAT'S ACTUALLY WHAT I'M TALKING ABOUT-- THE CULTURE OF FEAR. THIS ISN'T THE MEXICO THAT OUR GRANDPARENTS ENVISIONED. THE FUTURE IS WORSE THAN THE PAST AND WE, AT THIS TABLE, HAVE THE POWER TO REVERSE THAT.
YEAH, WELL THAT'S EXACTLY WHY--
EXACTLY WHY WE NEED ACTION, NOT BULLSHIT TALK.
I TELL YOU ONE THING THAT HASN'T CHANGED-- MEN IN MEXICO NOT GIVING WOMEN A CHANCE TO SPEAK.
I'LL DRINK TO THAT.

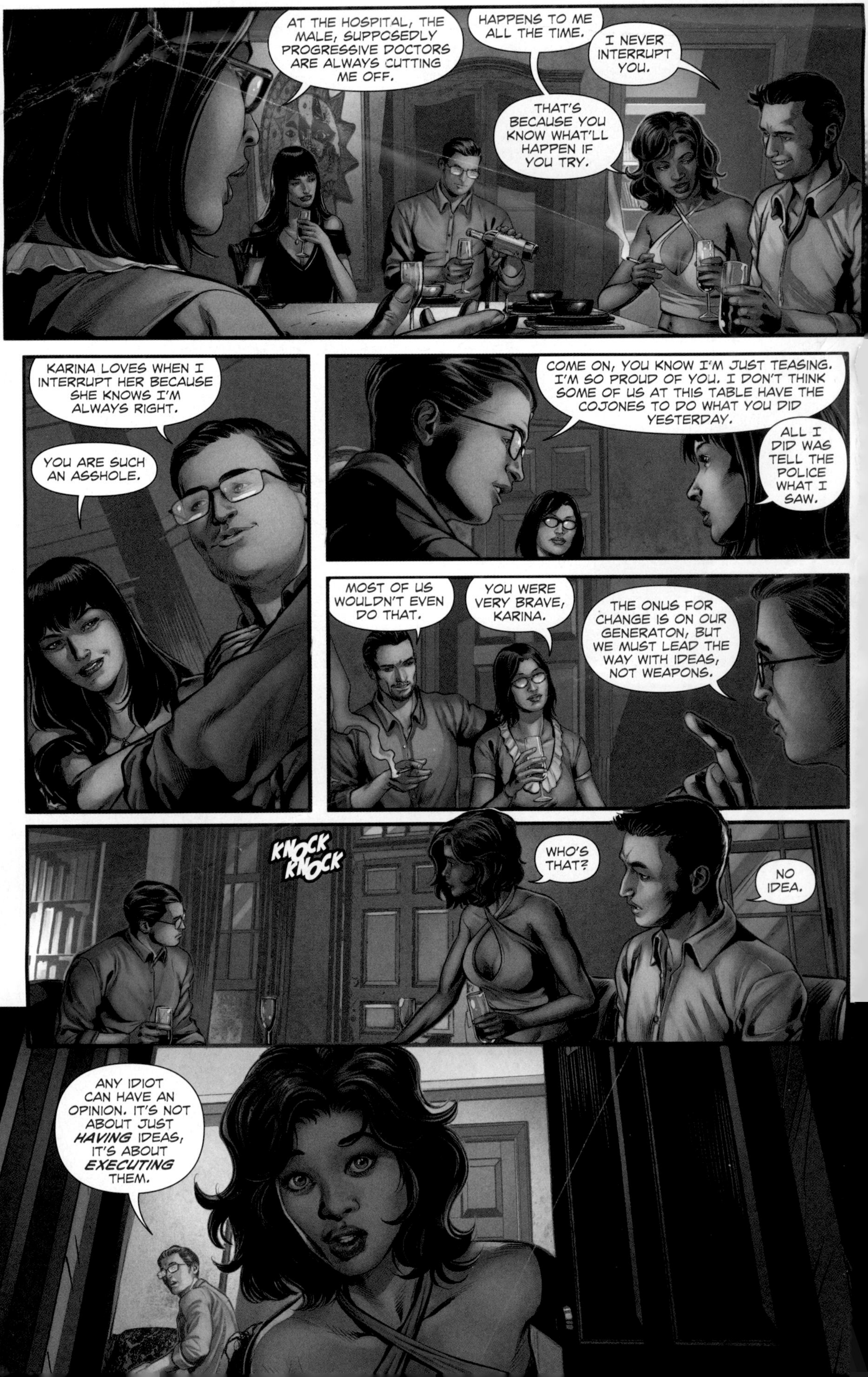
AT THE HOSPITAL, THE MALE, SUPPOSEDLY PROGRESSIVE DOCTORS ARE ALWAYS CUTTING ME OFF.
HAPPENS TO ME ALL THE TIME.
I NEVER INTERRUPT YOU.
THAT'S BECAUSE YOU KNOW WHAT'LL HAPPEN IF YOU TRY.
KARINA LOVES WHEN I INTERRUPT HER BECAUSE SHE KNOWS I'M ALWAYS RIGHT.
YOU ARE SUCH AN ASSHOLE.
COME ON, YOU KNOW I'M JUST TEASING. I'M SO PROUD OF YOU. I DON'T THINK SOME OF US AT THIS TABLE HAVE THE COJONES TO DO WHAT YOU DID YESTERDAY.
ALL I DID WAS TELL THE POLICE WHAT I SAW.
MOST OF US WOULDN'T EVEN DO THAT.
YOU WERE VERY BRAVE, KARINA.
THE ONUS FOR CHANGE IS ON OUR GENERATON, BUT WE MUST LEAD THE WAY WITH IDEAS, NOT WEAPONS.
KNOCK KNOCK
WHO'S THAT?
NO IDEA.
ANY IDIOT CAN HAVE AN OPINION. IT'S NOT ABOUT JUST *HAVING* IDEAS, IT'S ABOUT *EXECUTING* THEM.

WHAT THE FUCK?!

BLAM   BLAM

GET THE BITCH! SHE CAN'T GET AWAY!

BLAM BLAM BLAM

COME ON!

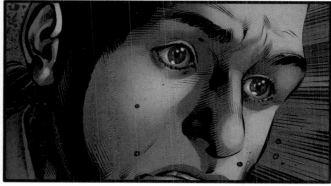

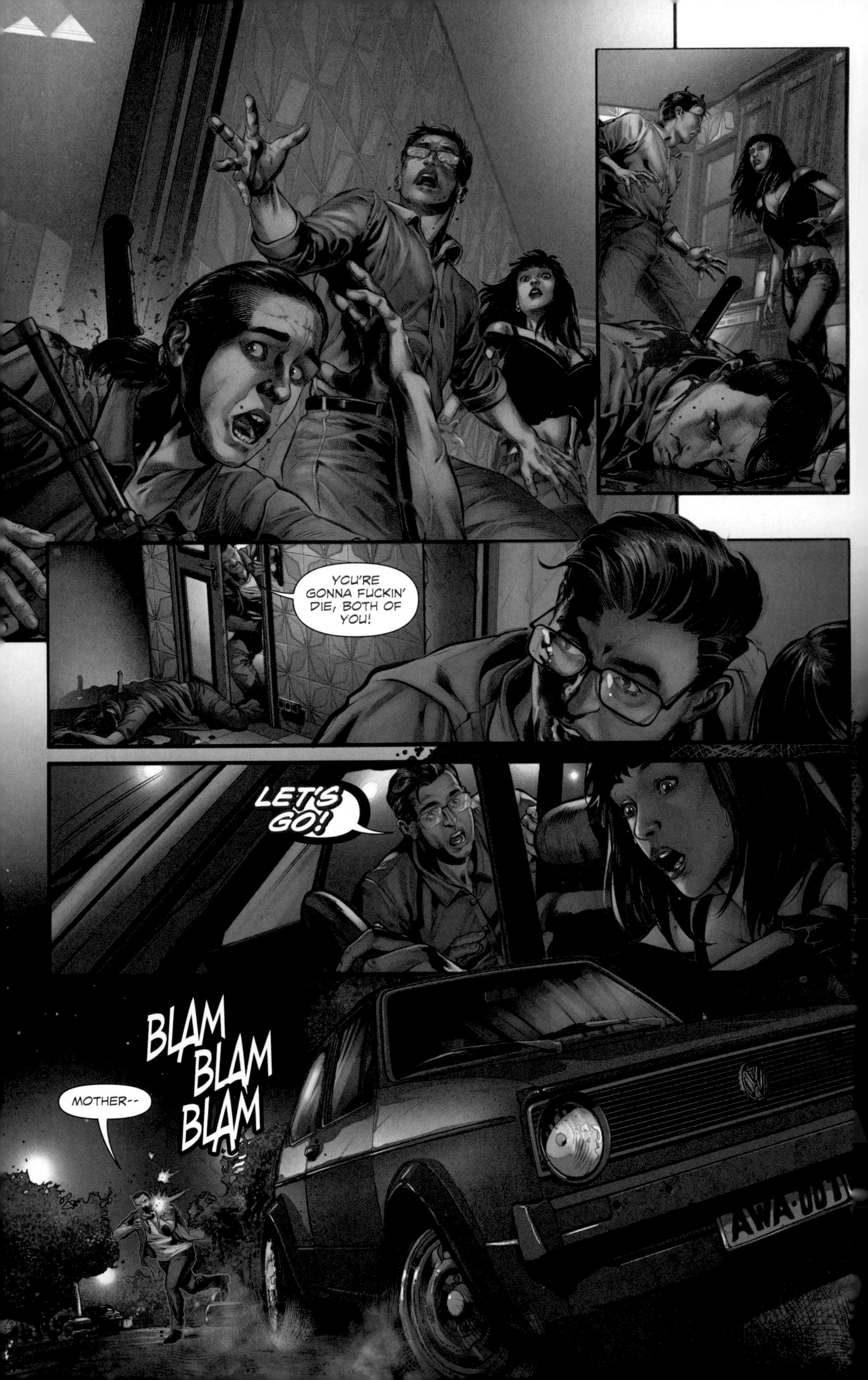
YOU'RE GONNA FUCKIN' DIE, BOTH OF YOU!
LET'S GO!
MOTHER--
BLAM BLAM BLAM

OH, YEAH, RIGHT THERE--
I FEEL ALL THAT TENSION. YOU'VE GOT A HUGE KNOT.
YOU SURE YOU KNOW WHAT THE FUCK YOU'RE DOING?
I WORKED AS A MASSEUSE IN GUADALAJARA FOR THREE YEARS, BUT MY SPECIALTY WAS *HAPPY ENDINGS.*
MAYBE THE PROBLEM IS *YOU.* YOU'RE NOT SEXY ENOUGH.
I GOT NO PROBLEM GETTING IT UP FOR BLONDES.
KNOCK KNOCK
THE FUCK IS IT?!
JEFE, WE HAVE TO TALK.
ABOUT WHAT?
IT'S IMPORTANT.

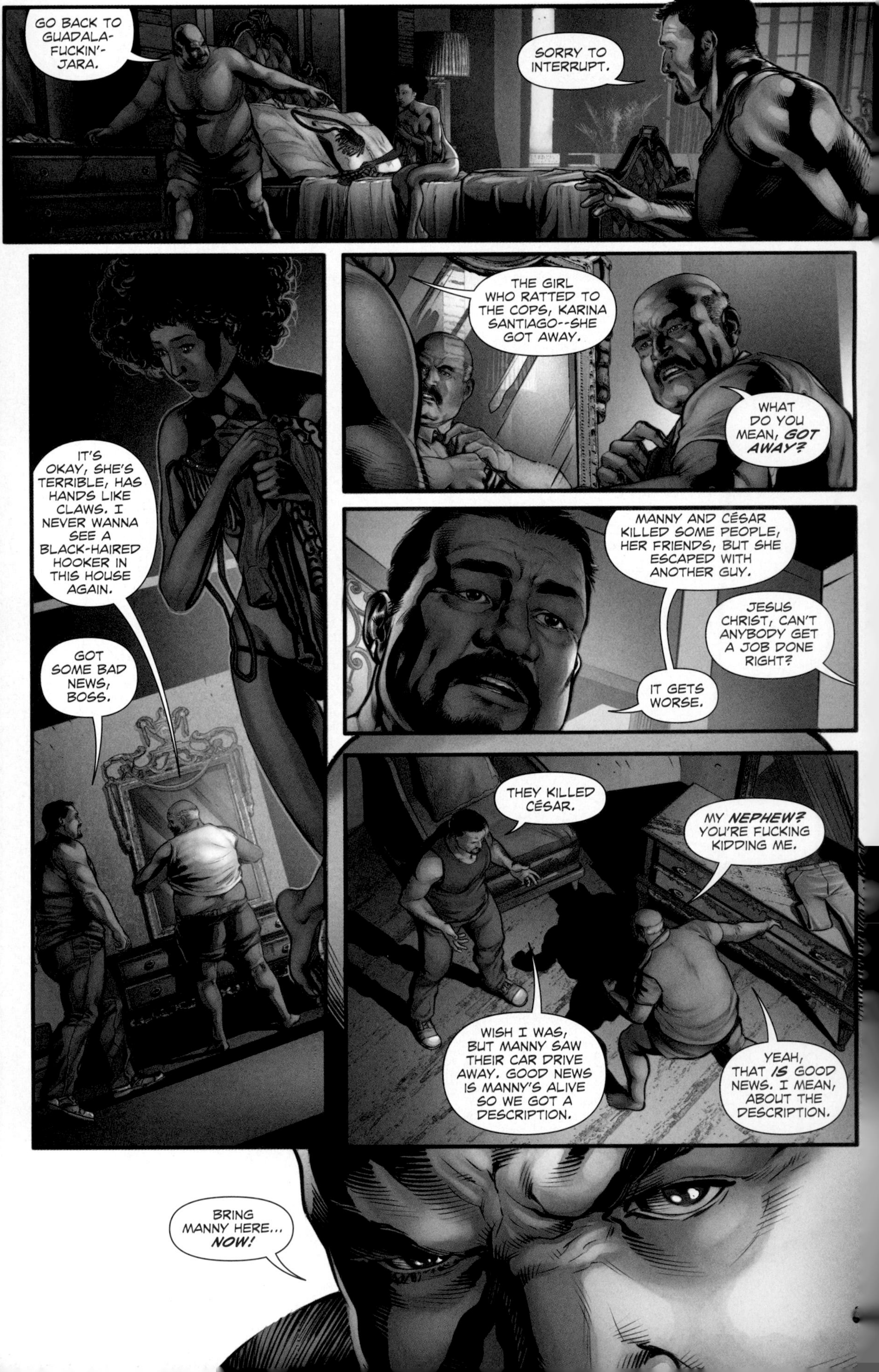
GO BACK TO GUADALA-FUCKIN'-JARA.
SORRY TO INTERRUPT.
IT'S OKAY, SHE'S TERRIBLE, HAS HANDS LIKE CLAWS. I NEVER WANNA SEE A BLACK-HAIRED HOOKER IN THIS HOUSE AGAIN.
GOT SOME BAD NEWS, BOSS.
THE GIRL WHO RATTED TO THE COPS, KARINA SANTIAGO--SHE GOT AWAY.
WHAT DO YOU MEAN, ***GOT AWAY?***
MANNY AND CÉSAR KILLED SOME PEOPLE, HER FRIENDS, BUT SHE ESCAPED WITH ANOTHER GUY.
JESUS CHRIST, CAN'T ANYBODY GET A JOB DONE RIGHT?
IT GETS WORSE.
THEY KILLED CÉSAR.
MY ***NEPHEW?*** YOU'RE FUCKING KIDDING ME.
WISH I WAS, BUT MANNY SAW THEIR CAR DRIVE AWAY. GOOD NEWS IS MANNY'S ALIVE SO WE GOT A DESCRIPTION.
YEAH, THAT ***IS*** GOOD NEWS. I MEAN, ABOUT THE DESCRIPTION.
BRING MANNY HERE... ***NOW!***

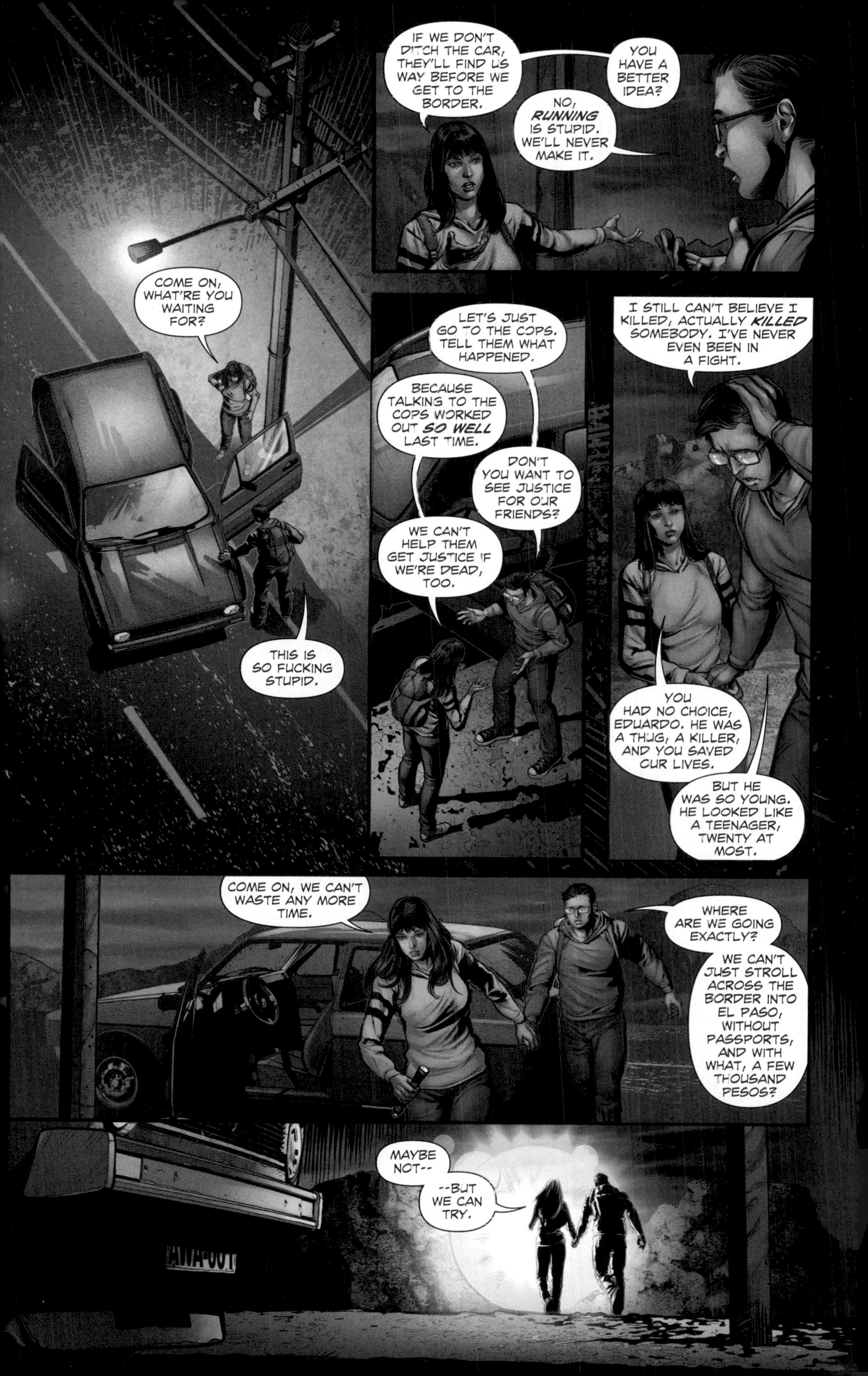
COME ON, WHAT'RE YOU WAITING FOR?
THIS IS SO FUCKING STUPID.
IF WE DON'T DITCH THE CAR, THEY'LL FIND US WAY BEFORE WE GET TO THE BORDER.
YOU HAVE A BETTER IDEA?
NO, RUNNING IS STUPID. WE'LL NEVER MAKE IT.
LET'S JUST GO TO THE COPS. TELL THEM WHAT HAPPENED.
BECAUSE TALKING TO THE COPS WORKED OUT SO WELL LAST TIME.
DON'T YOU WANT TO SEE JUSTICE FOR OUR FRIENDS?
WE CAN'T HELP THEM GET JUSTICE IF WE'RE DEAD, TOO.
I STILL CAN'T BELIEVE I KILLED, ACTUALLY KILLED SOMEBODY. I'VE NEVER EVEN BEEN IN A FIGHT.
YOU HAD NO CHOICE, EDUARDO. HE WAS A THUG, A KILLER, AND YOU SAVED OUR LIVES.
BUT HE WAS SO YOUNG. HE LOOKED LIKE A TEENAGER, TWENTY AT MOST.
COME ON, WE CAN'T WASTE ANY MORE TIME.
WHERE ARE WE GOING EXACTLY?
WE CAN'T JUST STROLL ACROSS THE BORDER INTO EL PASO, WITHOUT PASSPORTS, AND WITH WHAT, A FEW THOUSAND PESOS?
MAYBE NOT--
--BUT WE CAN TRY.

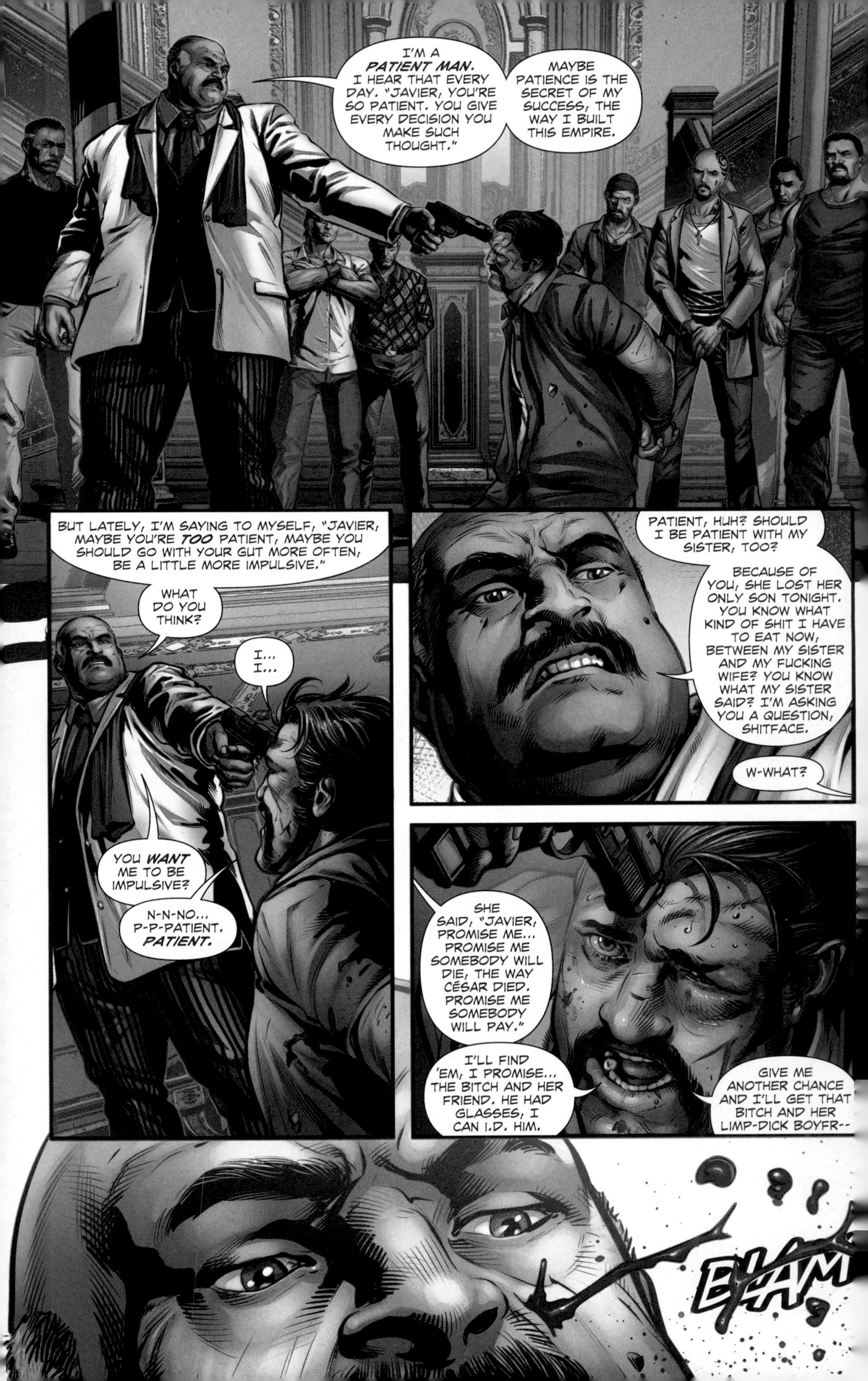

I'M A *PATIENT MAN.* I HEAR THAT EVERY DAY. "JAVIER, YOU'RE SO PATIENT. YOU GIVE EVERY DECISION YOU MAKE SUCH THOUGHT."
MAYBE PATIENCE IS THE SECRET OF MY SUCCESS, THE WAY I BUILT THIS EMPIRE.
BUT LATELY, I'M SAYING TO MYSELF, "JAVIER, MAYBE YOU'RE *TOO* PATIENT, MAYBE YOU SHOULD GO WITH YOUR GUT MORE OFTEN, BE A LITTLE MORE IMPULSIVE."
WHAT DO YOU THINK?
I... I...
YOU *WANT* ME TO BE IMPULSIVE?
N-N-NO... P-P-PATIENT. *PATIENT.*
PATIENT, HUH? SHOULD I BE PATIENT WITH MY SISTER, TOO?
BECAUSE OF YOU, SHE LOST HER ONLY SON TONIGHT. YOU KNOW WHAT KIND OF SHIT I HAVE TO EAT NOW, BETWEEN MY SISTER AND MY FUCKING WIFE? YOU KNOW WHAT MY SISTER SAID? I'M ASKING YOU A QUESTION, SHITFACE.
W-WHAT?
SHE SAID, "JAVIER, PROMISE ME... PROMISE ME SOMEBODY WILL DIE, THE WAY CÉSAR DIED. PROMISE ME SOMEBODY WILL PAY."
I'LL FIND 'EM, I PROMISE... THE BITCH AND HER FRIEND. HE HAD GLASSES, I CAN I.D. HIM.
GIVE ME ANOTHER CHANCE AND I'LL GET THAT BITCH AND HER LIMP-DICK BOYFR--
BLAM

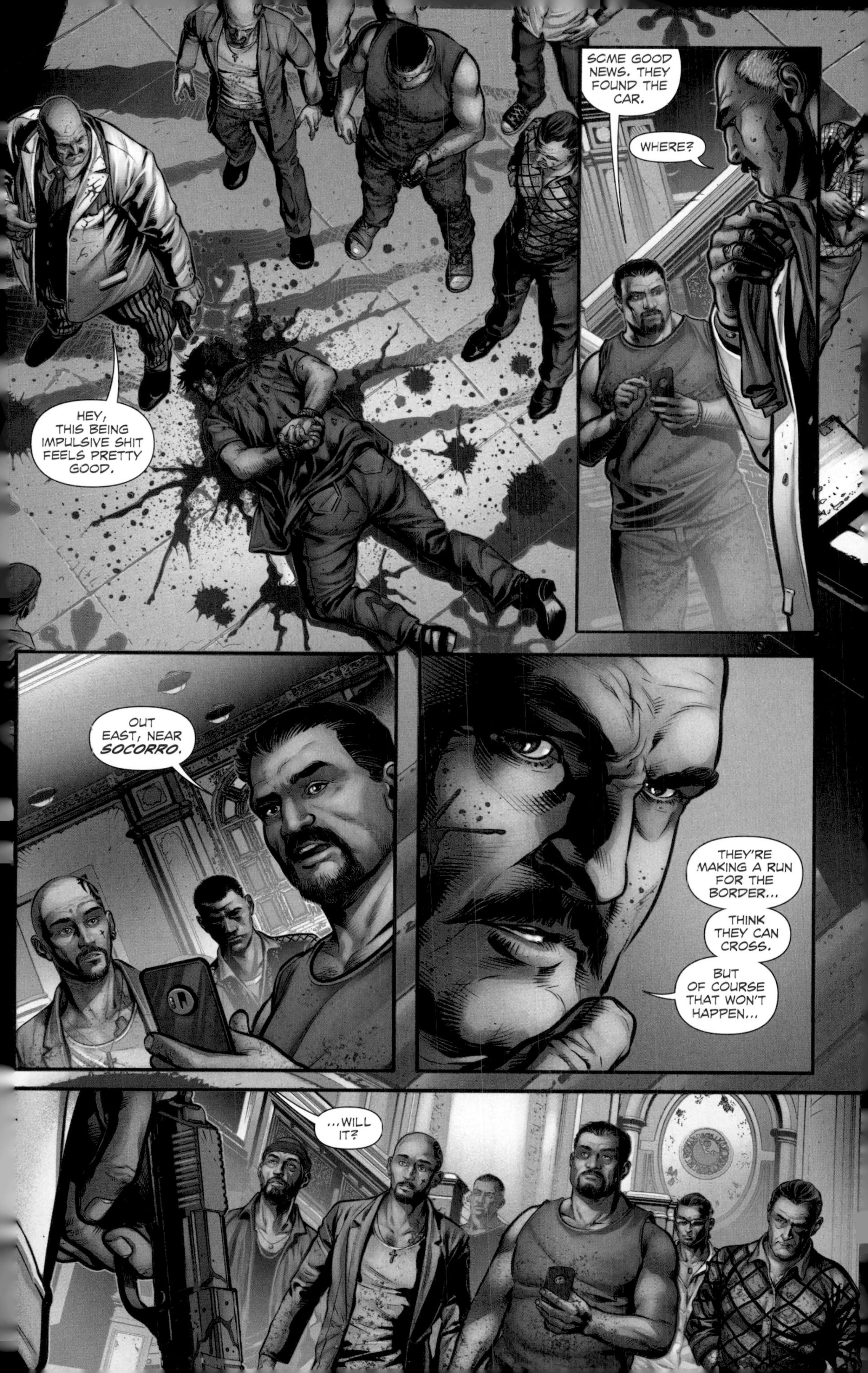
HEY, THIS BEING IMPULSIVE SHIT FEELS PRETTY GOOD.
SOME GOOD NEWS. THEY FOUND THE CAR.
WHERE?
OUT EAST, NEAR *SOCORRO.*
THEY'RE MAKING A RUN FOR THE BORDER...
THINK THEY CAN CROSS.
BUT OF COURSE THAT WON'T HAPPEN...
...WILL IT?

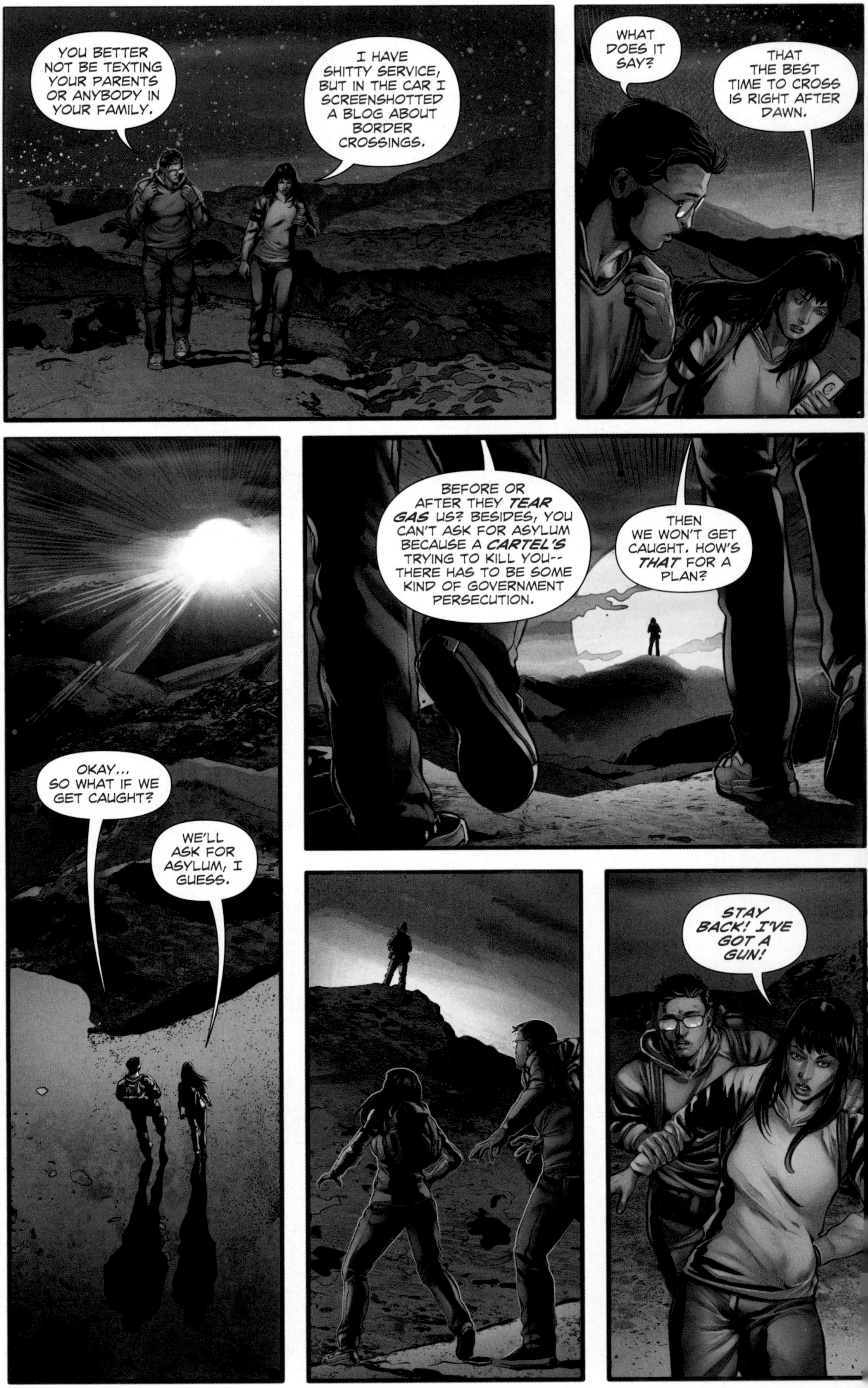
YOU BETTER NOT BE TEXTING YOUR PARENTS OR ANYBODY IN YOUR FAMILY.
I HAVE SHITTY SERVICE, BUT IN THE CAR I SCREENSHOTTED A BLOG ABOUT BORDER CROSSINGS.
WHAT DOES IT SAY?
THAT THE BEST TIME TO CROSS IS RIGHT AFTER DAWN.
OKAY... SO WHAT IF WE GET CAUGHT?
WE'LL ASK FOR ASYLUM, I GUESS.
BEFORE OR AFTER THEY *TEAR GAS* US? BESIDES, YOU CAN'T ASK FOR ASYLUM BECAUSE A *CARTEL'S* TRYING TO KILL YOU-- THERE HAS TO BE SOME KIND OF GOVERNMENT PERSECUTION.
THEN WE WON'T GET CAUGHT. HOW'S *THAT* FOR A PLAN?
STAY BACK! I'VE GOT A GUN!

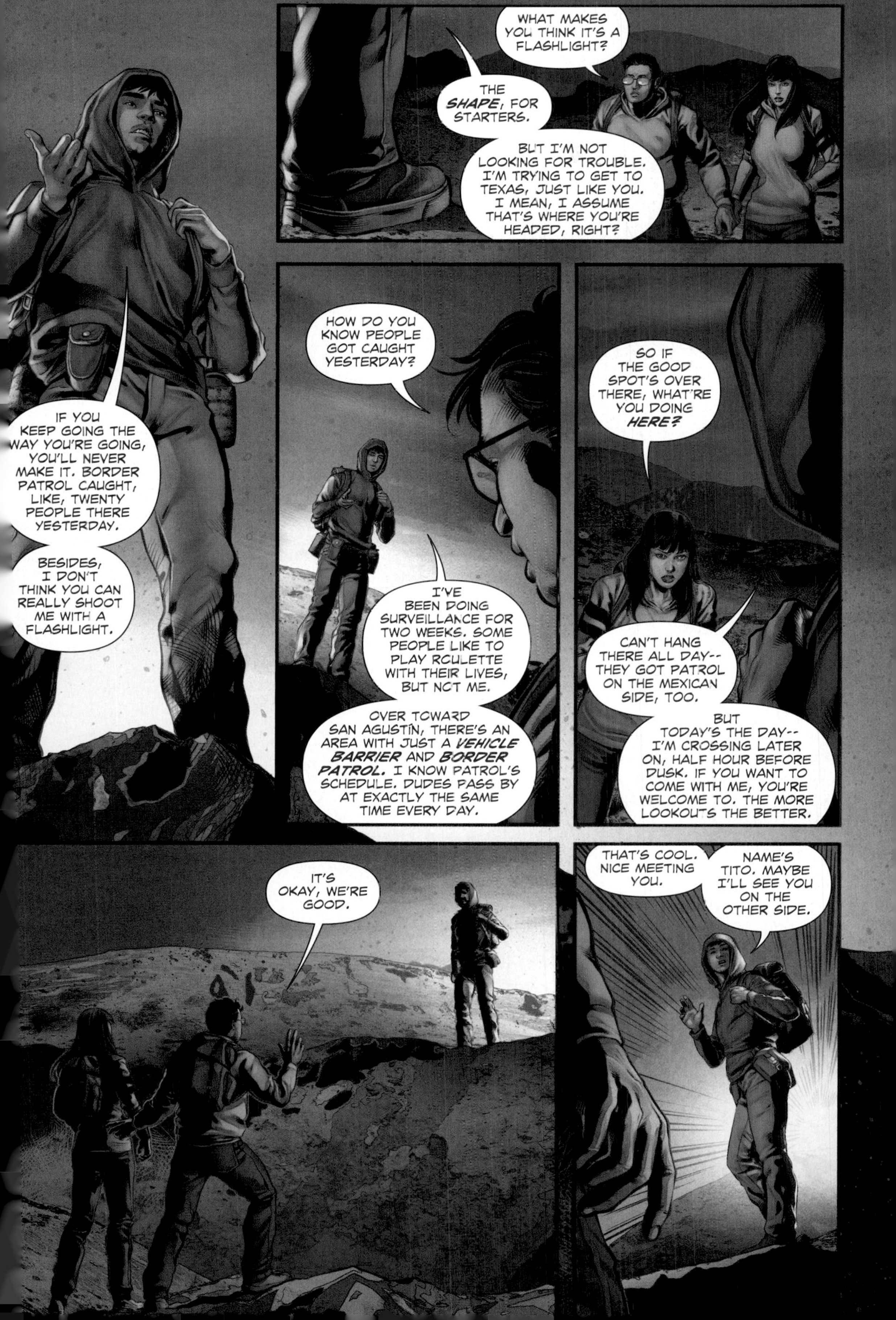
WHAT MAKES YOU THINK IT'S A FLASHLIGHT?
THE SHAPE, FOR STARTERS.
BUT I'M NOT LOOKING FOR TROUBLE. I'M TRYING TO GET TO TEXAS, JUST LIKE YOU. I MEAN, I ASSUME THAT'S WHERE YOU'RE HEADED, RIGHT?
IF YOU KEEP GOING THE WAY YOU'RE GOING, YOU'LL NEVER MAKE IT. BORDER PATROL CAUGHT, LIKE, TWENTY PEOPLE THERE YESTERDAY.
BESIDES, I DON'T THINK YOU CAN REALLY SHOOT ME WITH A FLASHLIGHT.
HOW DO YOU KNOW PEOPLE GOT CAUGHT YESTERDAY?
I'VE BEEN DOING SURVEILLANCE FOR TWO WEEKS. SOME PEOPLE LIKE TO PLAY ROULETTE WITH THEIR LIVES, BUT NOT ME.
OVER TOWARD SAN AGUSTÍN, THERE'S AN AREA WITH JUST A VEHICLE BARRIER AND BORDER PATROL. I KNOW PATROL'S SCHEDULE. DUDES PASS BY AT EXACTLY THE SAME TIME EVERY DAY.
SO IF THE GOOD SPOT'S OVER THERE, WHAT'RE YOU DOING HERE?
CAN'T HANG THERE ALL DAY-- THEY GOT PATROL ON THE MEXICAN SIDE, TOO.
BUT TODAY'S THE DAY-- I'M CROSSING LATER ON, HALF HOUR BEFORE DUSK. IF YOU WANT TO COME WITH ME, YOU'RE WELCOME TO. THE MORE LOOKOUTS THE BETTER.
IT'S OKAY, WE'RE GOOD.
THAT'S COOL. NICE MEETING YOU.
NAME'S TITO. MAYBE I'LL SEE YOU ON THE OTHER SIDE.

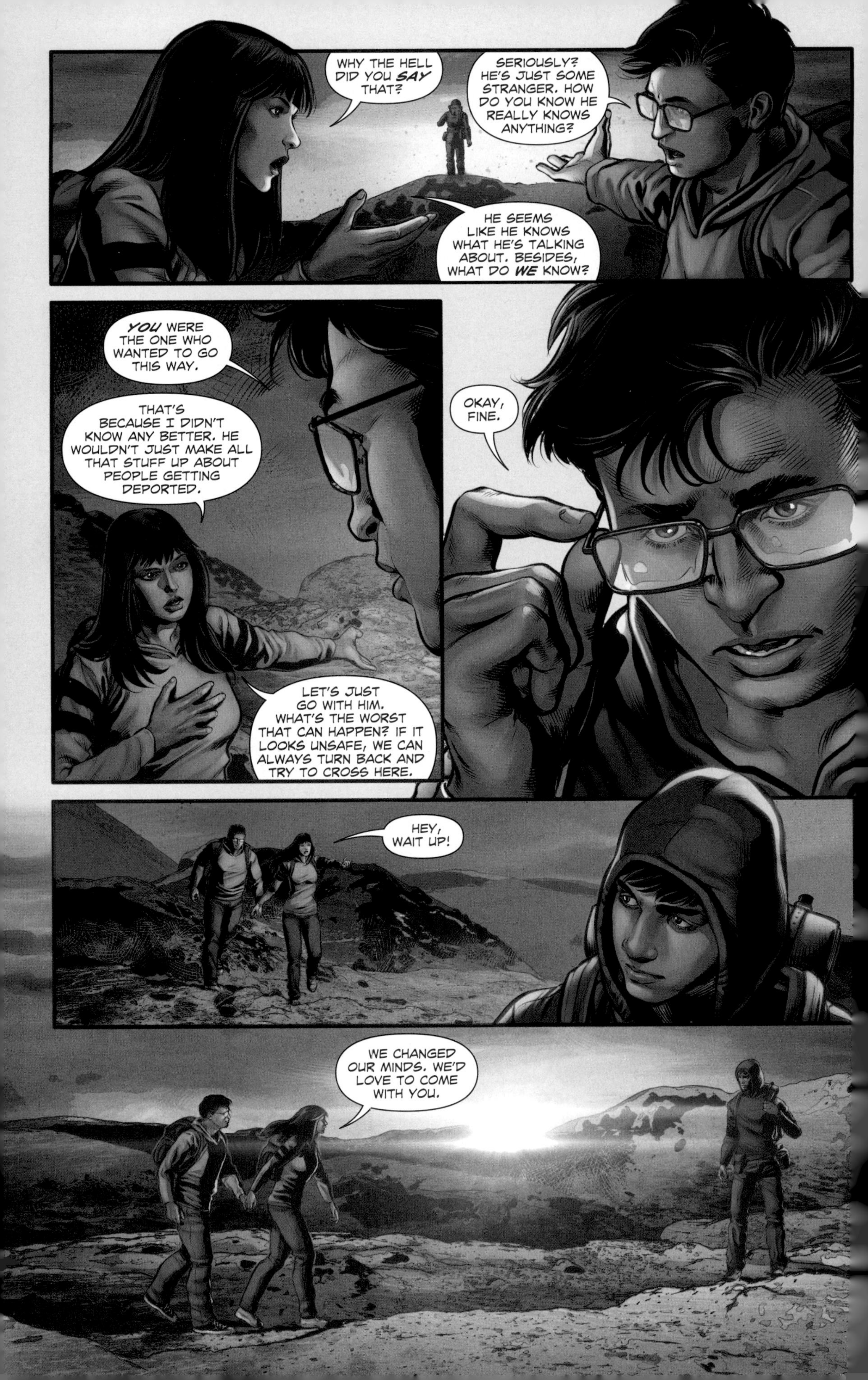
WHY THE HELL DID YOU *SAY* THAT?
SERIOUSLY? HE'S JUST SOME STRANGER. HOW DO YOU KNOW HE REALLY KNOWS ANYTHING?
HE SEEMS LIKE HE KNOWS WHAT HE'S TALKING ABOUT. BESIDES, WHAT DO *WE* KNOW?
YOU WERE THE ONE WHO WANTED TO GO THIS WAY.
THAT'S BECAUSE I DIDN'T KNOW ANY BETTER. HE WOULDN'T JUST MAKE ALL THAT STUFF UP ABOUT PEOPLE GETTING DEPORTED.
LET'S JUST GO WITH HIM. WHAT'S THE WORST THAT CAN HAPPEN? IF IT LOOKS UNSAFE, WE CAN ALWAYS TURN BACK AND TRY TO CROSS HERE.
OKAY, FINE.
HEY, WAIT UP!
WE CHANGED OUR MINDS. WE'D LOVE TO COME WITH YOU.

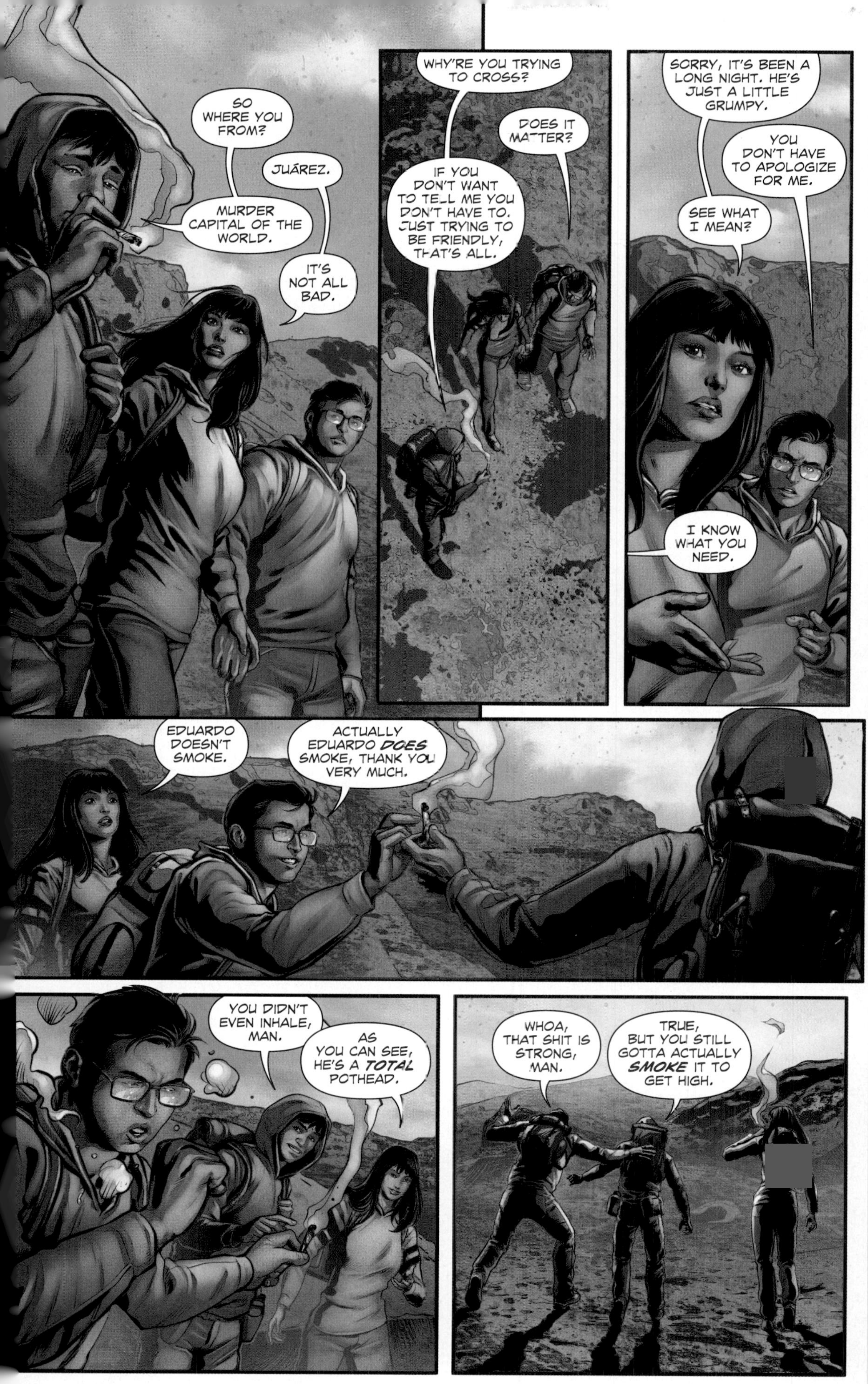
SO WHERE YOU FROM?
JUÁREZ.
MURDER CAPITAL OF THE WORLD.
IT'S NOT ALL BAD.
WHY'RE YOU TRYING TO CROSS?
DOES IT MATTER?
IF YOU DON'T WANT TO TELL ME YOU DON'T HAVE TO. JUST TRYING TO BE FRIENDLY, THAT'S ALL.
SORRY, IT'S BEEN A LONG NIGHT. HE'S JUST A LITTLE GRUMPY.
YOU DON'T HAVE TO APOLOGIZE FOR ME.
SEE WHAT I MEAN?
I KNOW WHAT YOU NEED.
EDUARDO DOESN'T SMOKE.
ACTUALLY EDUARDO *DOES* SMOKE, THANK YOU VERY MUCH.
YOU DIDN'T EVEN INHALE, MAN.
AS YOU CAN SEE, HE'S A *TOTAL* POTHEAD.
WHOA, THAT SHIT IS STRONG, MAN.
TRUE, BUT YOU STILL GOTTA ACTUALLY *SMOKE* IT TO GET HIGH.

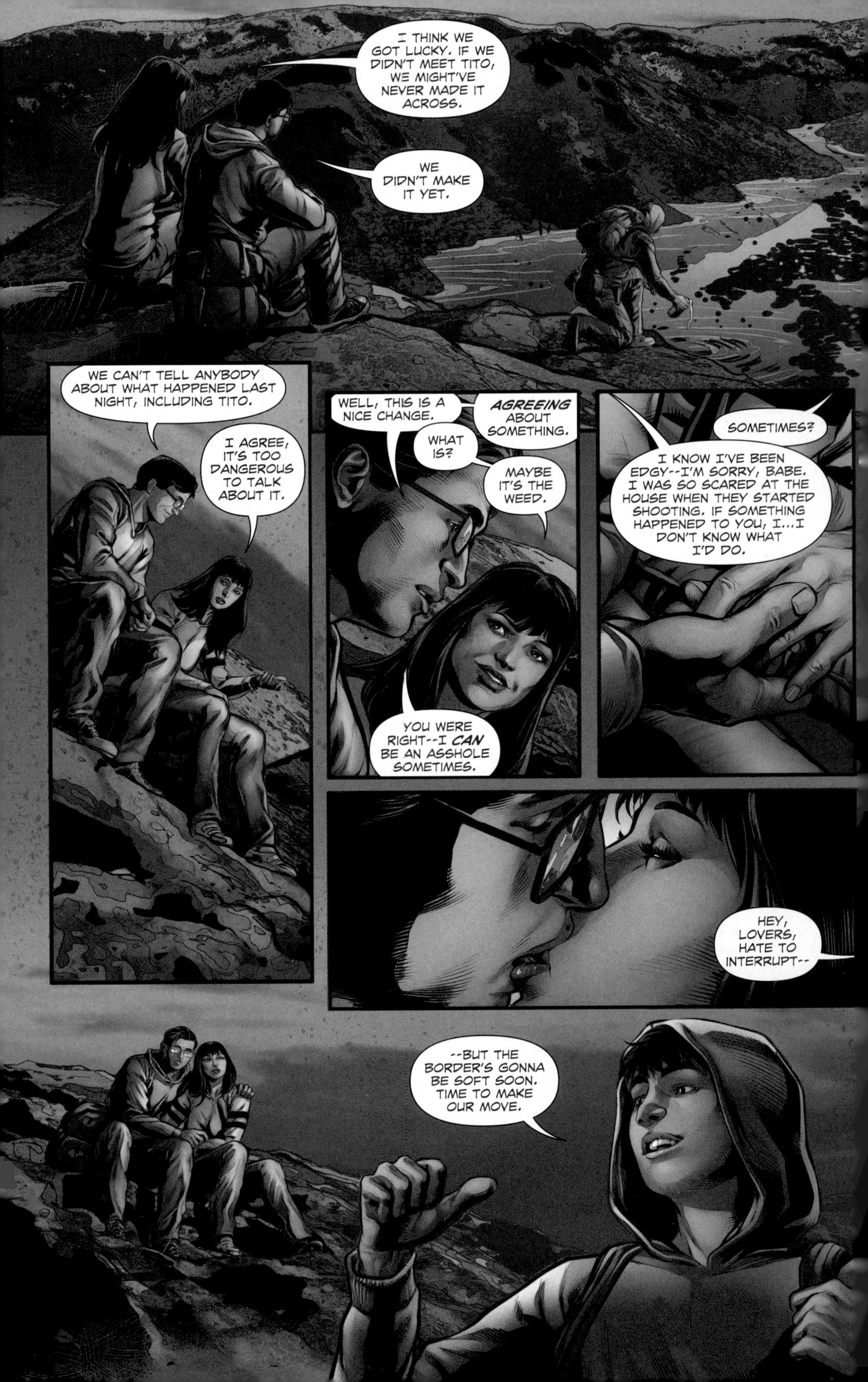

I THINK WE GOT LUCKY. IF WE DIDN'T MEET TITO, WE MIGHT'VE NEVER MADE IT ACROSS.
WE DIDN'T MAKE IT YET.
WE CAN'T TELL ANYBODY ABOUT WHAT HAPPENED LAST NIGHT, INCLUDING TITO.
I AGREE, IT'S TOO DANGEROUS TO TALK ABOUT IT.
WELL, THIS IS A NICE CHANGE.
WHAT IS?
AGREEING ABOUT SOMETHING.
MAYBE IT'S THE WEED.
YOU WERE RIGHT--I *CAN* BE AN ASSHOLE SOMETIMES.
SOMETIMES?
I KNOW I'VE BEEN EDGY--I'M SORRY, BABE. I WAS SO SCARED AT THE HOUSE WHEN THEY STARTED SHOOTING. IF SOMETHING HAPPENED TO YOU, I...I DON'T KNOW WHAT I'D DO.
HEY, LOVERS, HATE TO INTERRUPT--
--BUT THE BORDER'S GONNA BE SOFT SOON. TIME TO MAKE OUR MOVE.

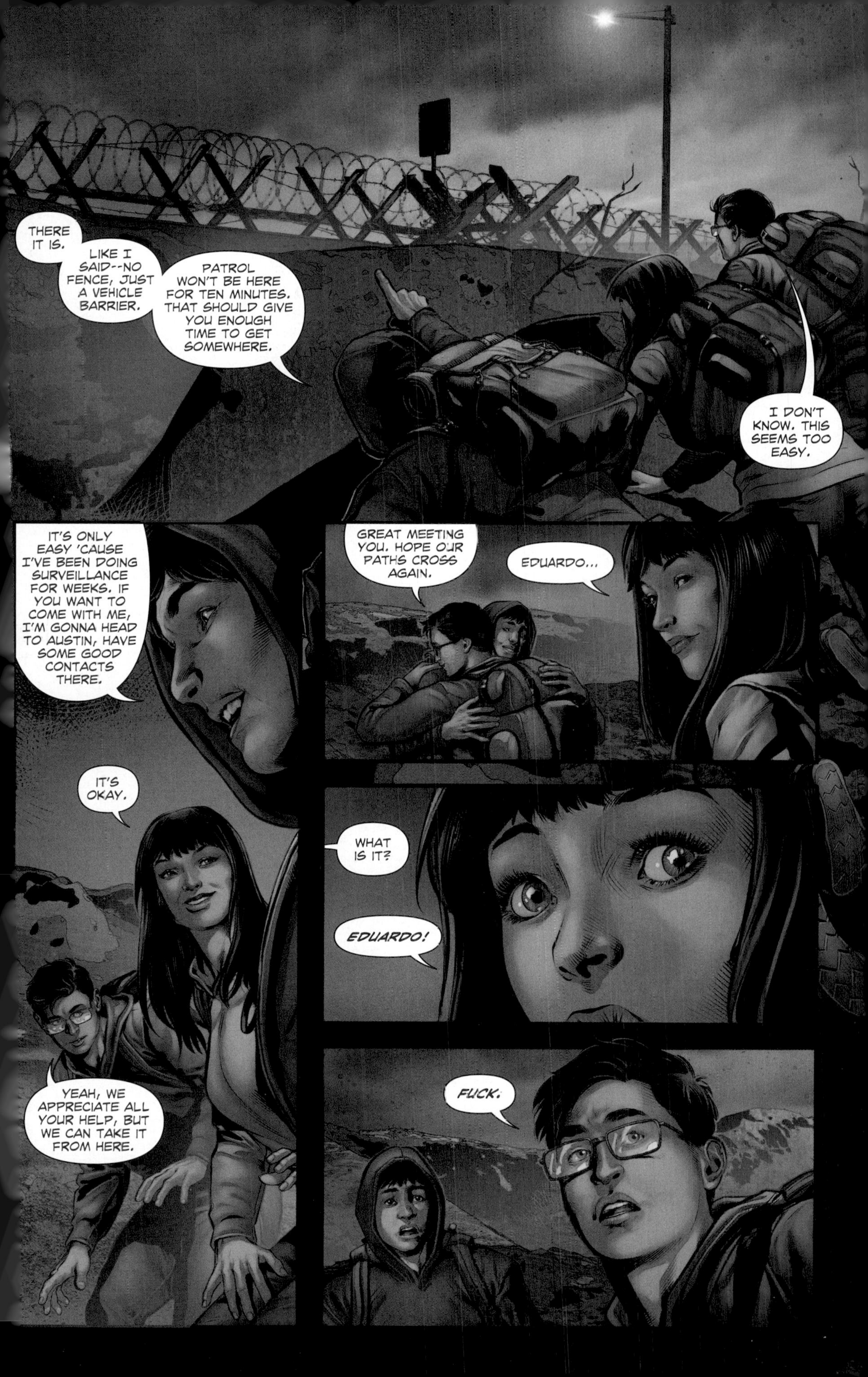
THERE IT IS.
LIKE I SAID--NO FENCE, JUST A VEHICLE BARRIER.
PATROL WON'T BE HERE FOR TEN MINUTES. THAT SHOULD GIVE YOU ENOUGH TIME TO GET SOMEWHERE.
I DON'T KNOW. THIS SEEMS TOO EASY.
IT'S ONLY EASY 'CAUSE I'VE BEEN DOING SURVEILLANCE FOR WEEKS. IF YOU WANT TO COME WITH ME, I'M GONNA HEAD TO AUSTIN, HAVE SOME GOOD CONTACTS THERE.
IT'S OKAY.
YEAH, WE APPRECIATE ALL YOUR HELP, BUT WE CAN TAKE IT FROM HERE.
GREAT MEETING YOU. HOPE OUR PATHS CROSS AGAIN.
EDUARDO...
WHAT IS IT?
EDUARDO!
FUCK.

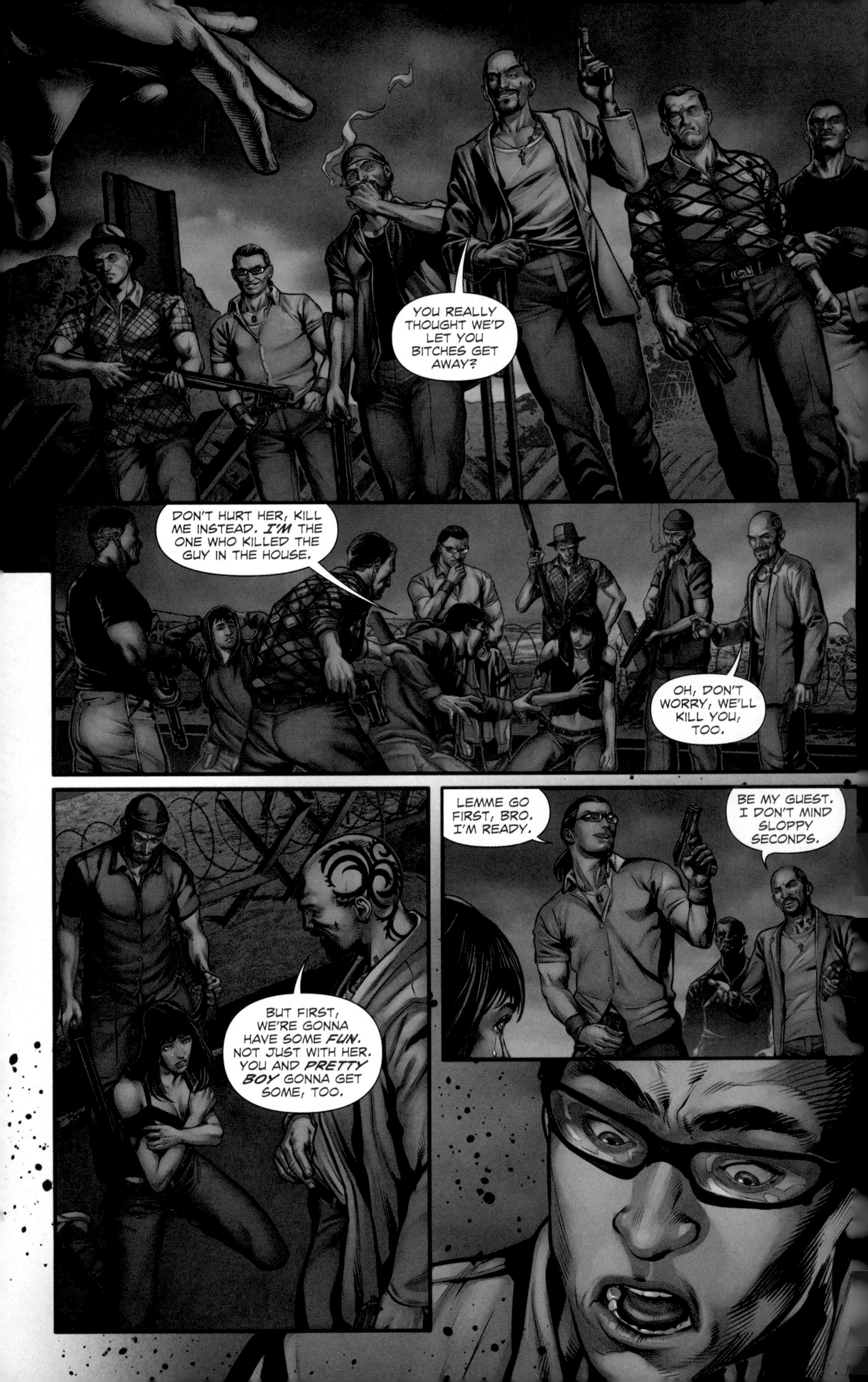
YOU REALLY THOUGHT WE'D LET YOU BITCHES GET AWAY?
DON'T HURT HER, KILL ME INSTEAD. *I'M* THE ONE WHO KILLED THE GUY IN THE HOUSE.
OH, DON'T WORRY, WE'LL KILL YOU, TOO.
BUT FIRST, WE'RE GONNA HAVE SOME *FUN*. NOT JUST WITH HER. YOU AND *PRETTY BOY* GONNA GET SOME, TOO.
LEMME GO FIRST, BRO. I'M READY.
BE MY GUEST. I DON'T MIND SLOPPY SECONDS.

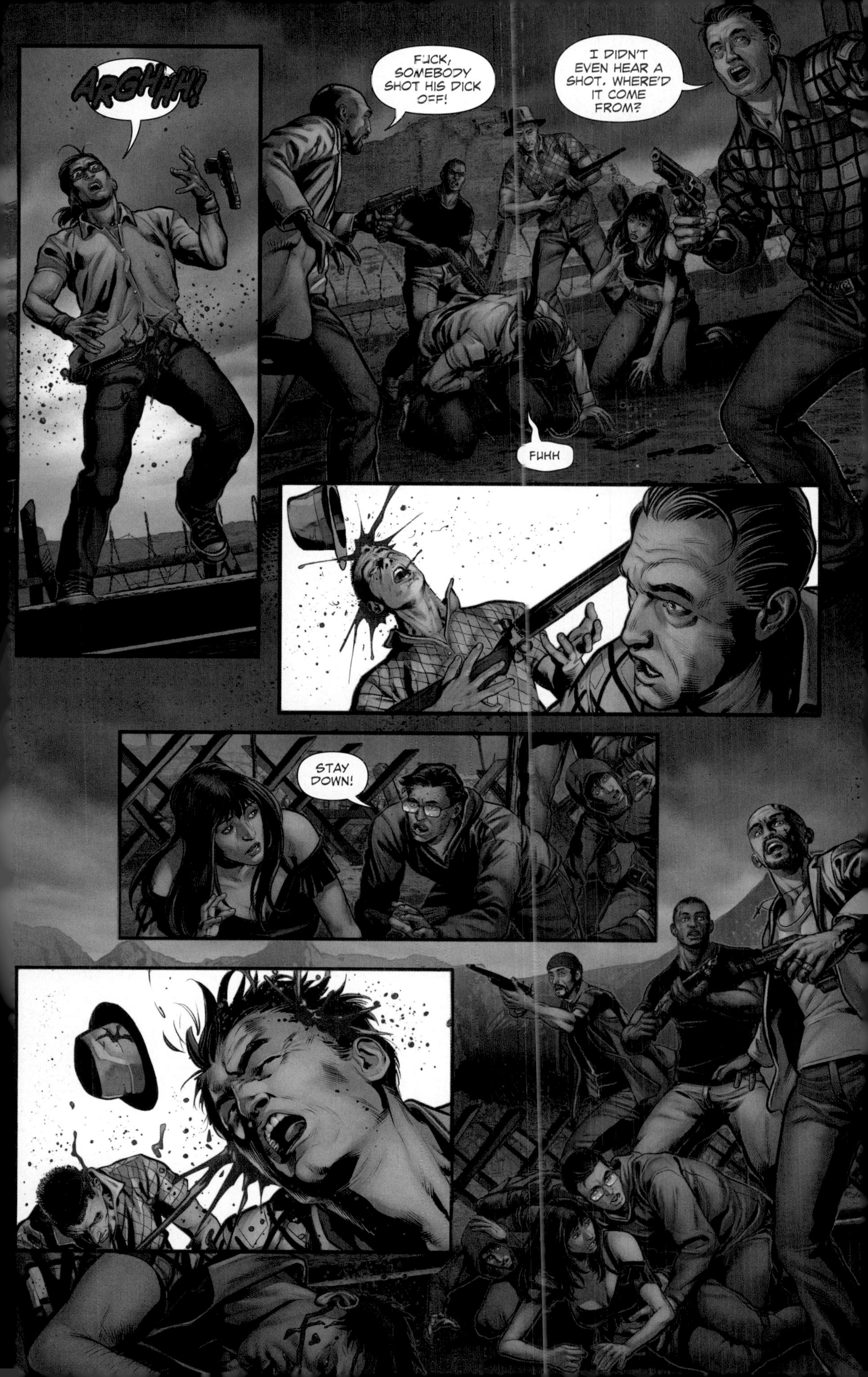
ARGHHH!
FUCK, SOMEBODY SHOT HIS DICK OFF!
I DIDN'T EVEN HEAR A SHOT. WHERE'D IT COME FROM?
FUHH
STAY DOWN!

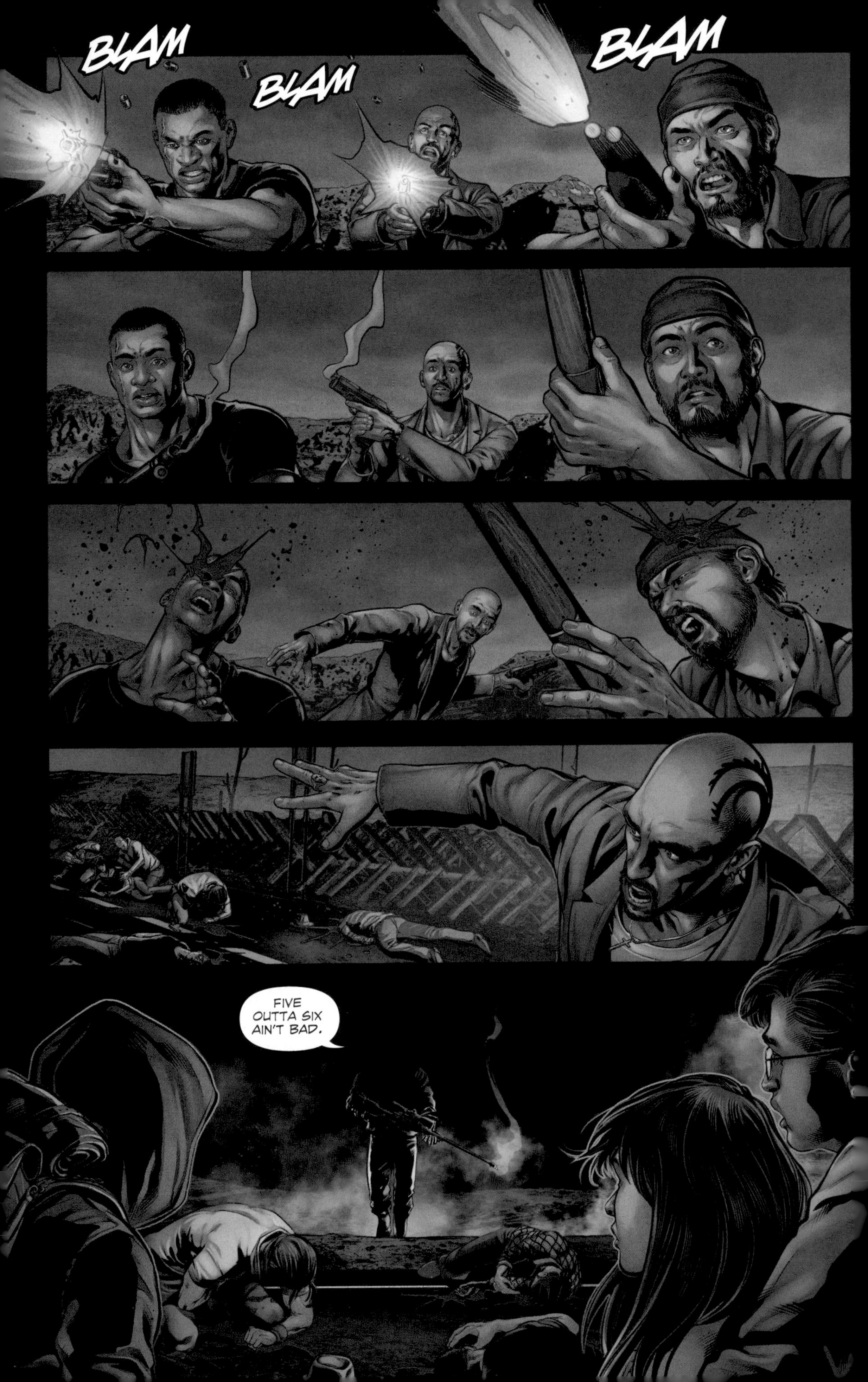
BLAM
BLAM
BLAM
FIVE OUTTA SIX AIN'T BAD.

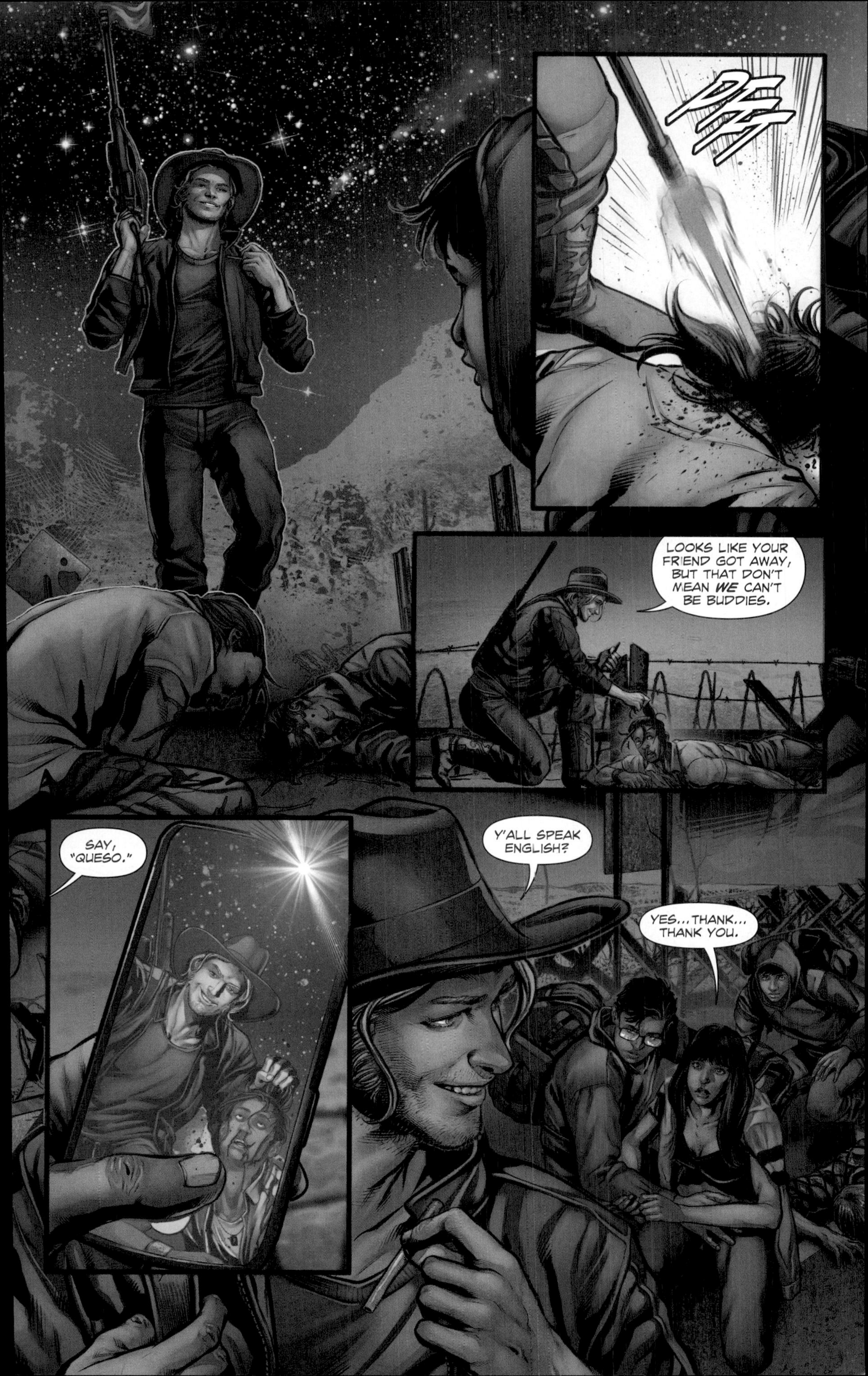
PFFT
LOOKS LIKE YOUR FRIEND GOT AWAY, BUT THAT DON'T MEAN WE CAN'T BE BUDDIES.
SAY, "QUESO."
Y'ALL SPEAK ENGLISH?
YES...THANK... THANK YOU.

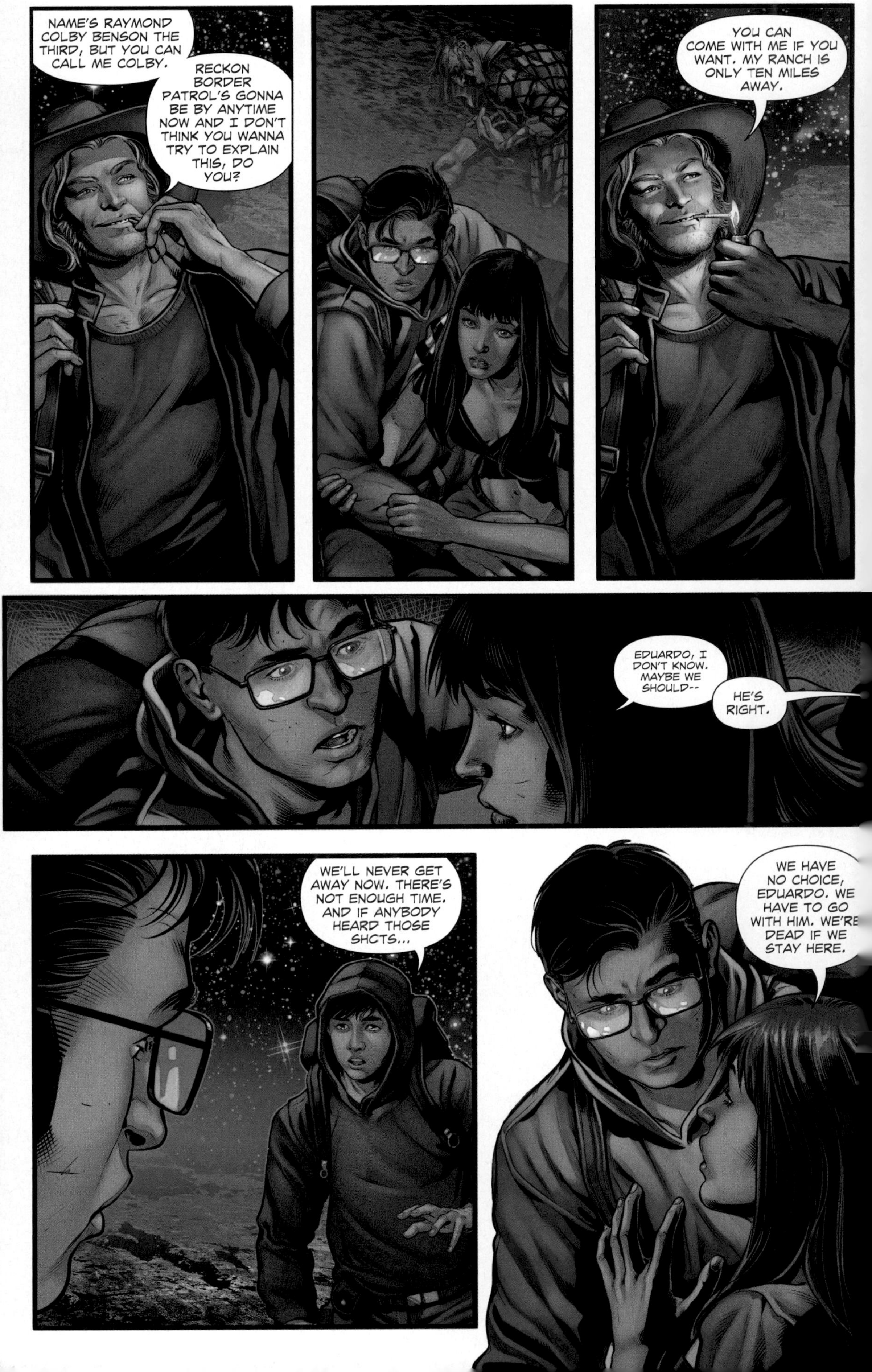
NAME'S RAYMOND COLBY BENSON THE THIRD, BUT YOU CAN CALL ME COLBY.
RECKON BORDER PATROL'S GONNA BE BY ANYTIME NOW AND I DON'T THINK YOU WANNA TRY TO EXPLAIN THIS, DO YOU?
YOU CAN COME WITH ME IF YOU WANT. MY RANCH IS ONLY TEN MILES AWAY.
EDUARDO, I DON'T KNOW. MAYBE WE SHOULD--
HE'S RIGHT.
WE'LL NEVER GET AWAY NOW. THERE'S NOT ENOUGH TIME. AND IF ANYBODY HEARD THOSE SHCTS...
WE HAVE NO CHOICE, EDUARDO. WE HAVE TO GO WITH HIM. WE'RE DEAD IF WE STAY HERE.

I HAVE TO SAY, I CONSIDER THIS HERE AN HONOR.
'ROUND THESE PARTS, WE ALWAYS WELCOME AN OPPORTUNITY TO SHOW OUR SOUTHERN FRIENDS SOME AMERICAN HOSPITALITY.
TRUST ME, FOLKS--
--Y'ALL GONNA LOVE MY FAMILY.
TO BE CONTINUED

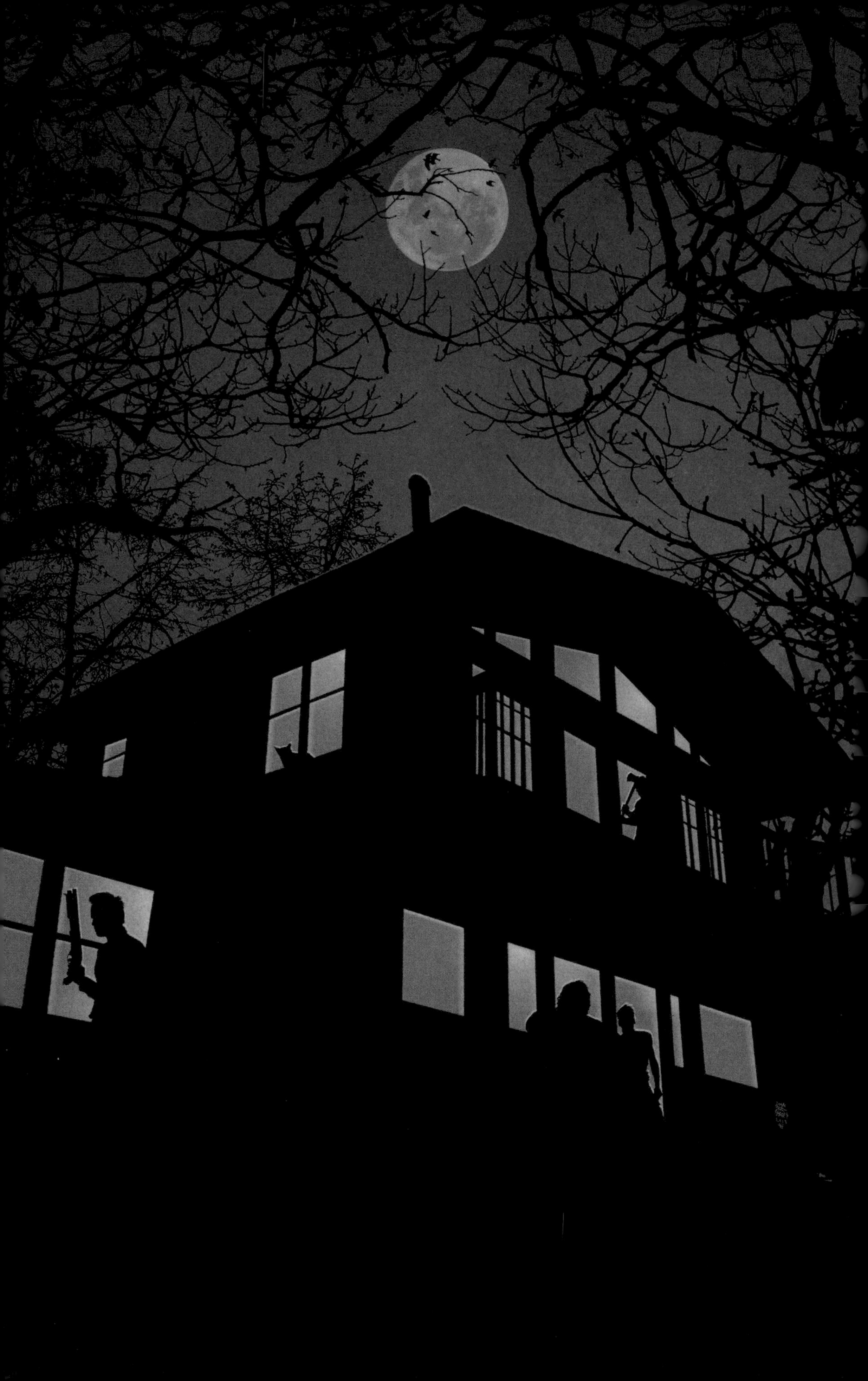

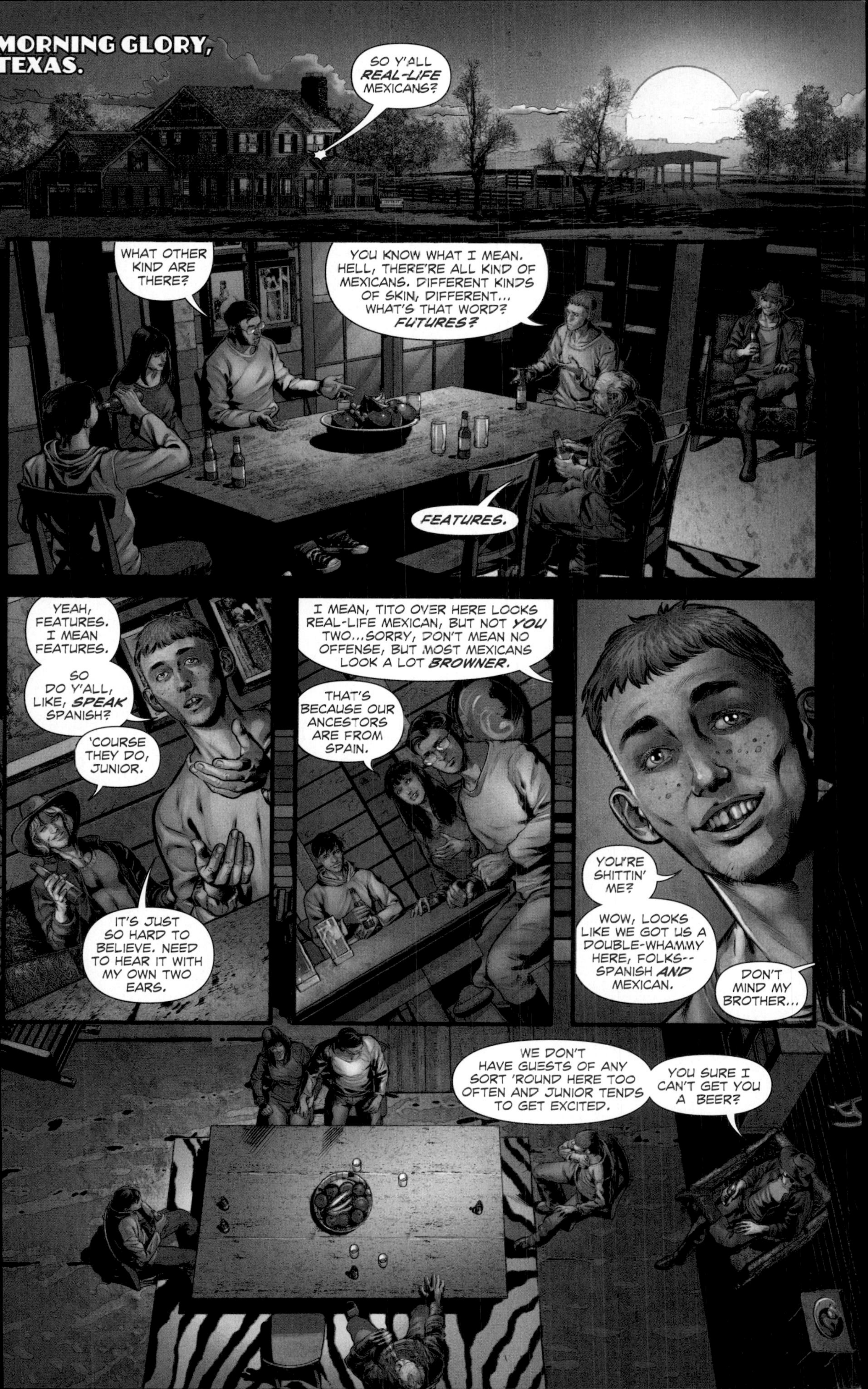
MORNING GLORY, TEXAS.
SO Y'ALL REAL-LIFE MEXICANS?
WHAT OTHER KIND ARE THERE?
YOU KNOW WHAT I MEAN. HELL, THERE'RE ALL KIND OF MEXICANS. DIFFERENT KINDS OF SKIN, DIFFERENT... WHAT'S THAT WORD? FUTURES?
FEATURES.
YEAH, FEATURES. I MEAN FEATURES.
SO DO Y'ALL, LIKE, SPEAK SPANISH?
'COURSE THEY DO, JUNIOR.
IT'S JUST SO HARD TO BELIEVE. NEED TO HEAR IT WITH MY OWN TWO EARS.
I MEAN, TITO OVER HERE LOOKS REAL-LIFE MEXICAN, BUT NOT YOU TWO...SORRY, DON'T MEAN NO OFFENSE, BUT MOST MEXICANS LOOK A LOT BROWNER.
THAT'S BECAUSE OUR ANCESTORS ARE FROM SPAIN.
YOU'RE SHITTIN' ME?
WOW, LOOKS LIKE WE GOT US A DOUBLE-WHAMMY HERE, FOLKS-- SPANISH AND MEXICAN.
DON'T MIND MY BROTHER...
WE DON'T HAVE GUESTS OF ANY SORT 'ROUND HERE TOO OFTEN AND JUNIOR TENDS TO GET EXCITED.
YOU SURE I CAN'T GET YOU A BEER?

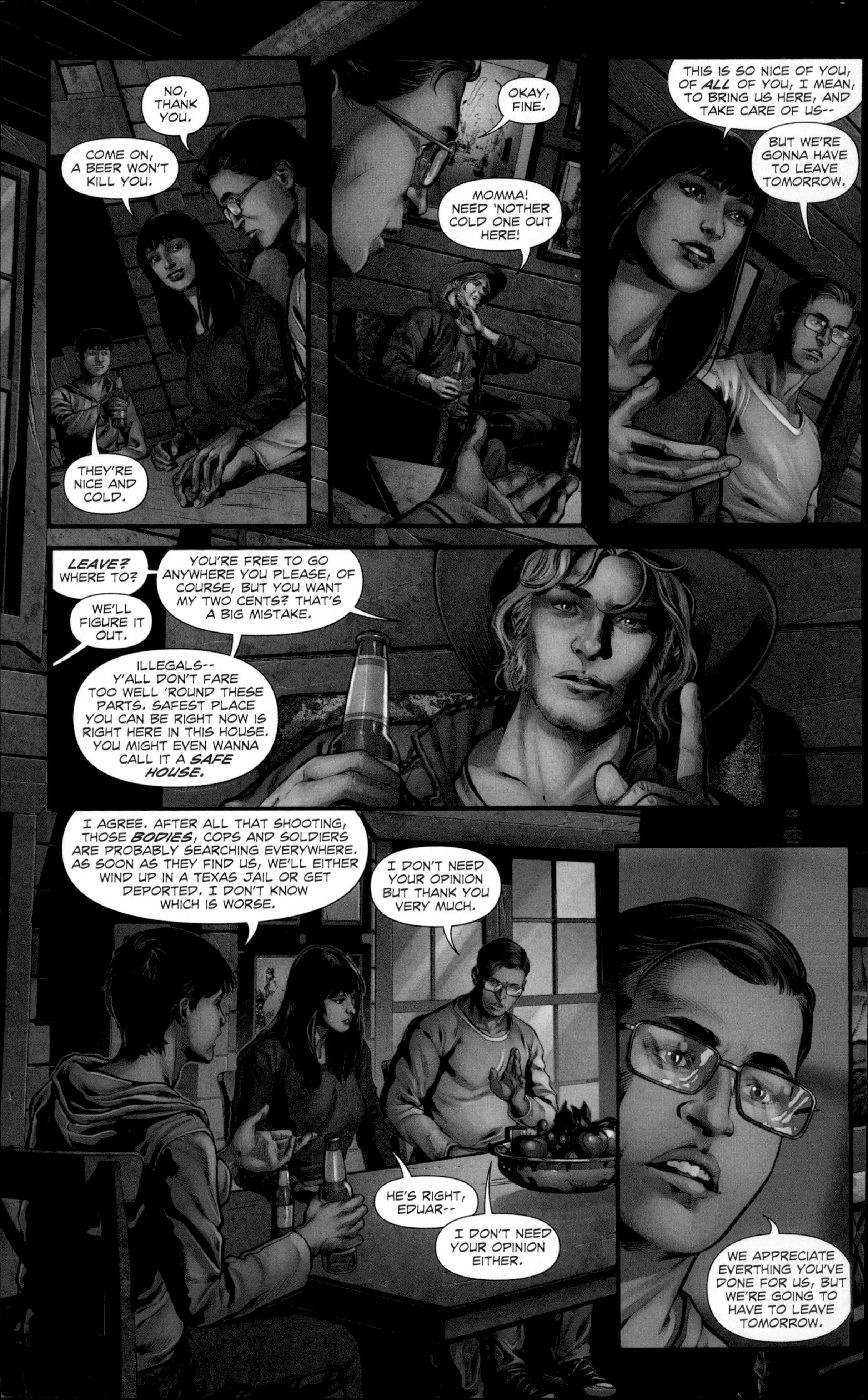
NO, THANK YOU.
COME ON, A BEER WON'T KILL YOU.
THEY'RE NICE AND COLD.
OKAY, FINE.
MOMMA! NEED 'NOTHER COLD ONE OUT HERE!
THIS IS SO NICE OF YOU, OF ALL OF YOU, I MEAN, TO BRING US HERE, AND TAKE CARE OF US--
BUT WE'RE GONNA HAVE TO LEAVE TOMORROW.
LEAVE? WHERE TO?
WE'LL FIGURE IT OUT.
YOU'RE FREE TO GO ANYWHERE YOU PLEASE, OF COURSE, BUT YOU WANT MY TWO CENTS? THAT'S A BIG MISTAKE.
ILLEGALS-- Y'ALL DON'T FARE TOO WELL 'ROUND THESE PARTS. SAFEST PLACE YOU CAN BE RIGHT NOW IS RIGHT HERE IN THIS HOUSE. YOU MIGHT EVEN WANNA CALL IT A SAFE HOUSE.
I AGREE. AFTER ALL THAT SHOOTING, THOSE BODIES, COPS AND SOLDIERS ARE PROBABLY SEARCHING EVERYWHERE. AS SOON AS THEY FIND US, WE'LL EITHER WIND UP IN A TEXAS JAIL OR GET DEPORTED. I DON'T KNOW WHICH IS WORSE.
I DON'T NEED YOUR OPINION BUT THANK YOU VERY MUCH.
HE'S RIGHT, EDUAR--
I DON'T NEED YOUR OPINION EITHER.
WE APPRECIATE EVERTHING YOU'VE DONE FOR US, BUT WE'RE GOING TO HAVE TO LEAVE TOMORROW.

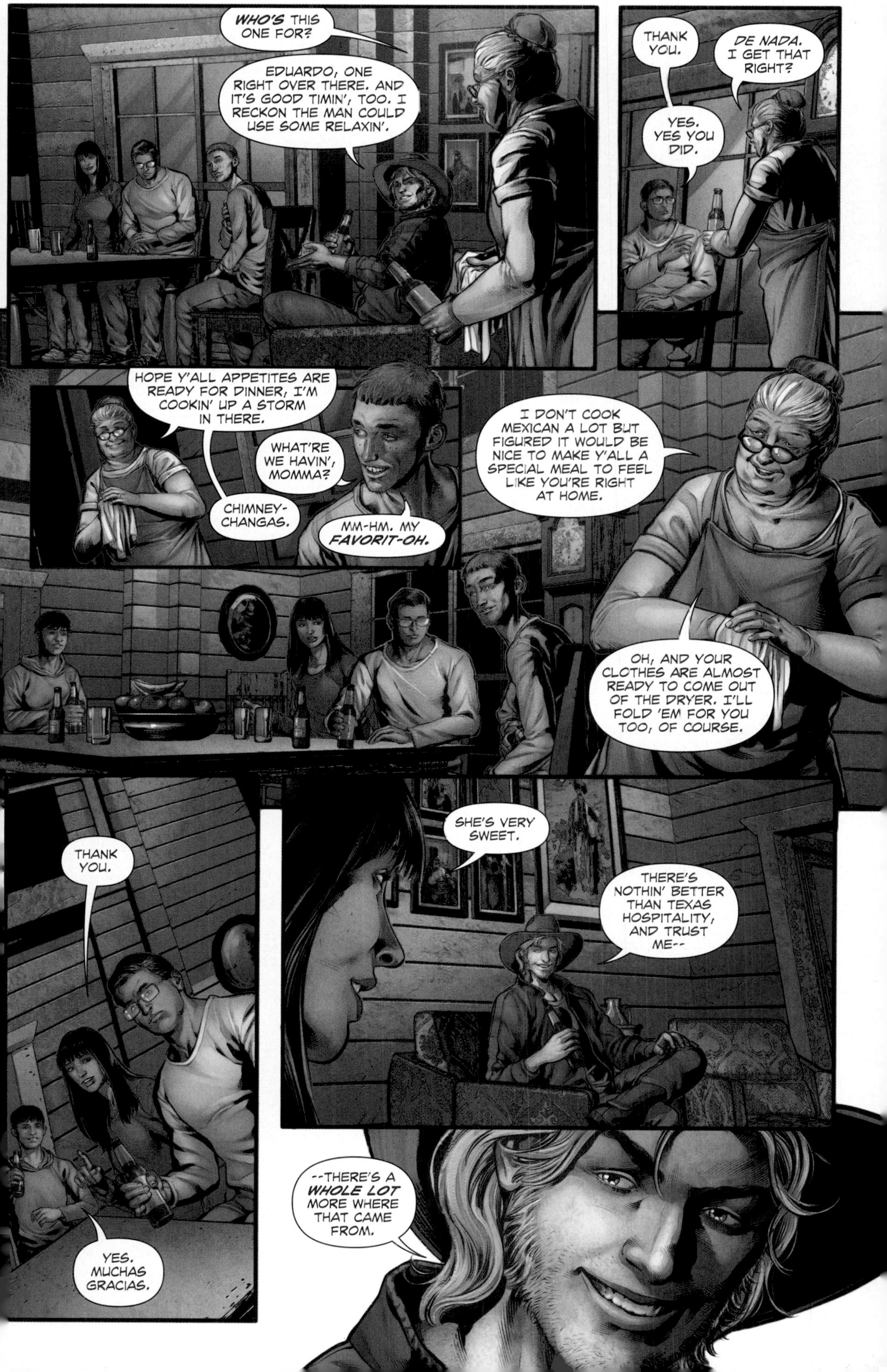
WHO'S THIS ONE FOR?
EDUARDO, ONE RIGHT OVER THERE. AND IT'S GOOD TIMIN', TOO. I RECKON THE MAN COULD USE SOME RELAXIN'.
THANK YOU.
DE NADA. I GET THAT RIGHT?
YES. YES YOU DID.
HOPE Y'ALL APPETITES ARE READY FOR DINNER, I'M COOKIN' UP A STORM IN THERE.
WHAT'RE WE HAVIN', MOMMA?
CHIMNEY-CHANGAS.
MM-HM. MY FAVORIT-OH.
I DON'T COOK MEXICAN A LOT BUT FIGURED IT WOULD BE NICE TO MAKE Y'ALL A SPECIAL MEAL TO FEEL LIKE YOU'RE RIGHT AT HOME.
OH, AND YOUR CLOTHES ARE ALMOST READY TO COME OUT OF THE DRYER. I'LL FOLD 'EM FOR YOU TOO, OF COURSE.
THANK YOU.
YES. MUCHAS GRACIAS.
SHE'S VERY SWEET.
THERE'S NOTHIN' BETTER THAN TEXAS HOSPITALITY, AND TRUST ME--
--THERE'S A WHOLE LOT MORE WHERE THAT CAME FROM.

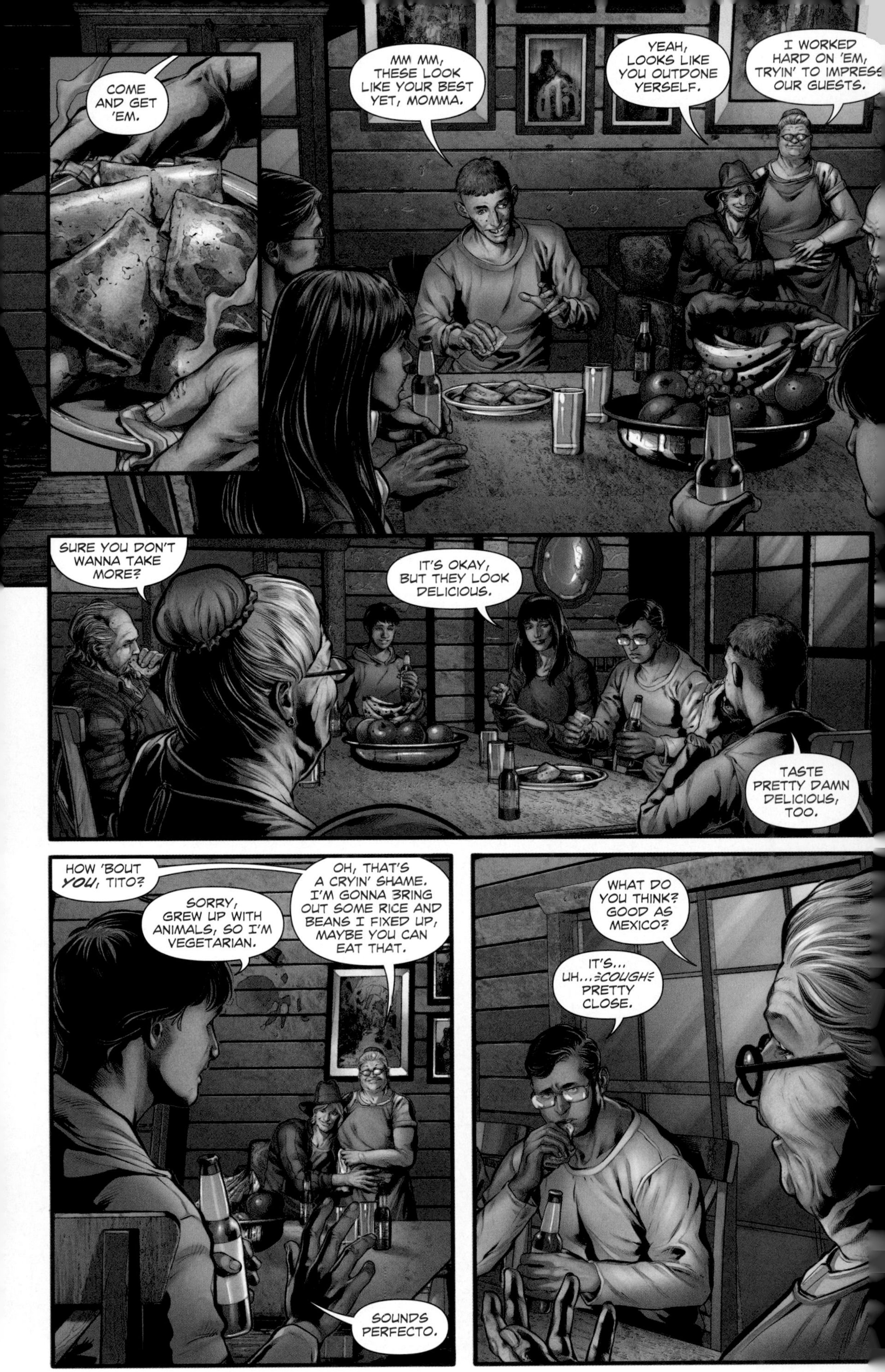
COME AND GET 'EM.
MM MM, THESE LOOK LIKE YOUR BEST YET, MOMMA.
YEAH, LOOKS LIKE YOU OUTDONE YERSELF.
I WORKED HARD ON 'EM, TRYIN' TO IMPRESS OUR GUESTS.
SURE YOU DON'T WANNA TAKE MORE?
IT'S OKAY, BUT THEY LOOK DELICIOUS.
TASTE PRETTY DAMN DELICIOUS, TOO.
HOW 'BOUT *YOU*, TITO?
SORRY, GREW UP WITH ANIMALS, SO I'M VEGETARIAN.
OH, THAT'S A CRYIN' SHAME. I'M GONNA BRING OUT SOME RICE AND BEANS I FIXED UP, MAYBE YOU CAN EAT THAT.
SOUNDS PERFECTO.
WHAT DO YOU THINK? GOOD AS MEXICO?
IT'S... UH... *COUGH* PRETTY CLOSE.

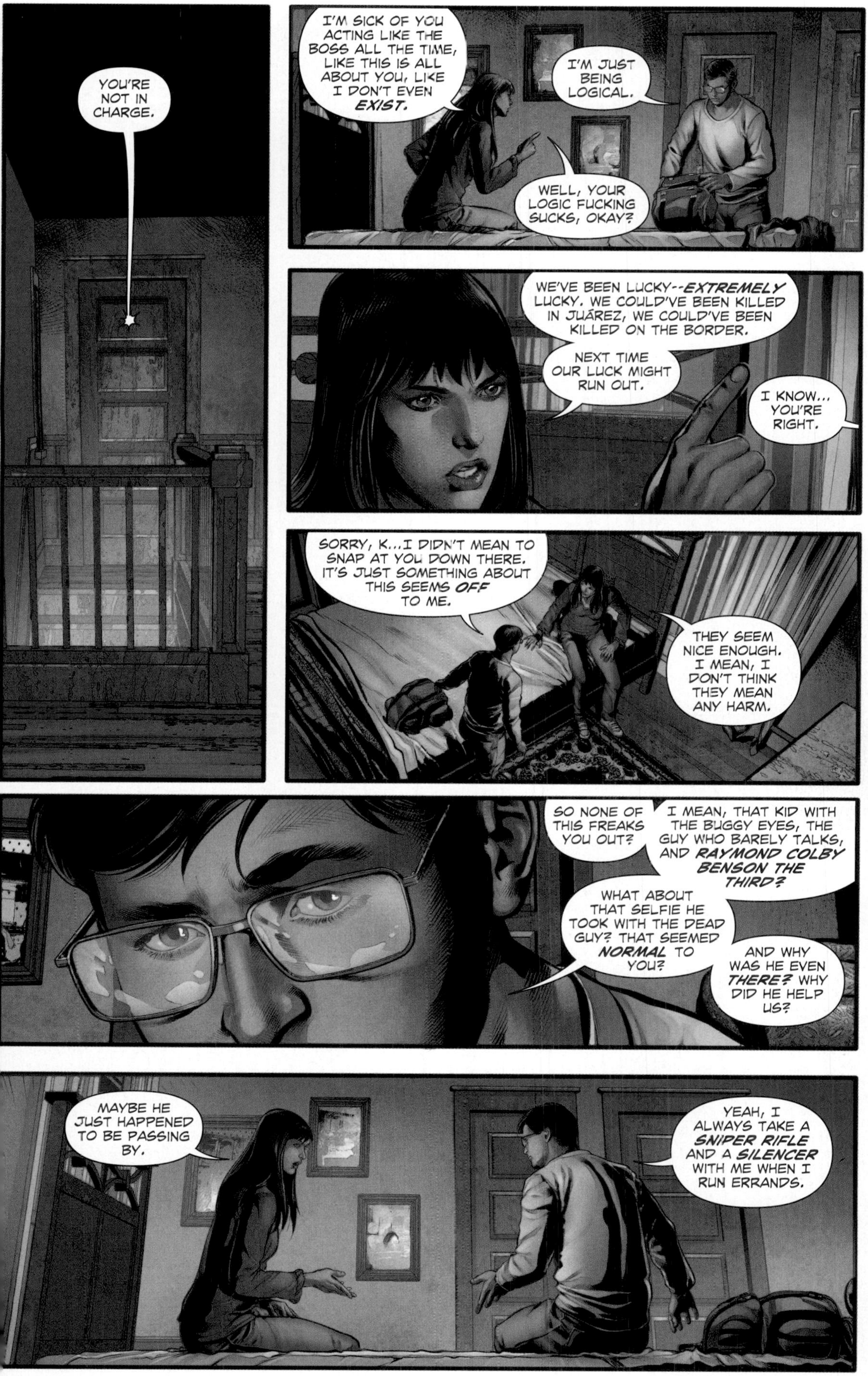
YOU'RE NOT IN CHARGE.
I'M SICK OF YOU ACTING LIKE THE BOSS ALL THE TIME, LIKE THIS IS ALL ABOUT YOU, LIKE I DON'T EVEN EXIST.
I'M JUST BEING LOGICAL.
WELL, YOUR LOGIC FUCKING SUCKS, OKAY?
WE'VE BEEN LUCKY--EXTREMELY LUCKY. WE COULD'VE BEEN KILLED IN JUÁREZ, WE COULD'VE BEEN KILLED ON THE BORDER.
NEXT TIME OUR LUCK MIGHT RUN OUT.
I KNOW... YOU'RE RIGHT.
SORRY, K...I DIDN'T MEAN TO SNAP AT YOU DOWN THERE. IT'S JUST SOMETHING ABOUT THIS SEEMS OFF TO ME.
THEY SEEM NICE ENOUGH. I MEAN, I DON'T THINK THEY MEAN ANY HARM.
SO NONE OF THIS FREAKS YOU OUT?
I MEAN, THAT KID WITH THE BUGGY EYES, THE GUY WHO BARELY TALKS, AND RAYMOND COLBY BENSON THE THIRD?
WHAT ABOUT THAT SELFIE HE TOOK WITH THE DEAD GUY? THAT SEEMED NORMAL TO YOU?
AND WHY WAS HE EVEN THERE? WHY DID HE HELP US?
MAYBE HE JUST HAPPENED TO BE PASSING BY.
YEAH, I ALWAYS TAKE A SNIPER RIFLE AND A SILENCER WITH ME WHEN I RUN ERRANDS.

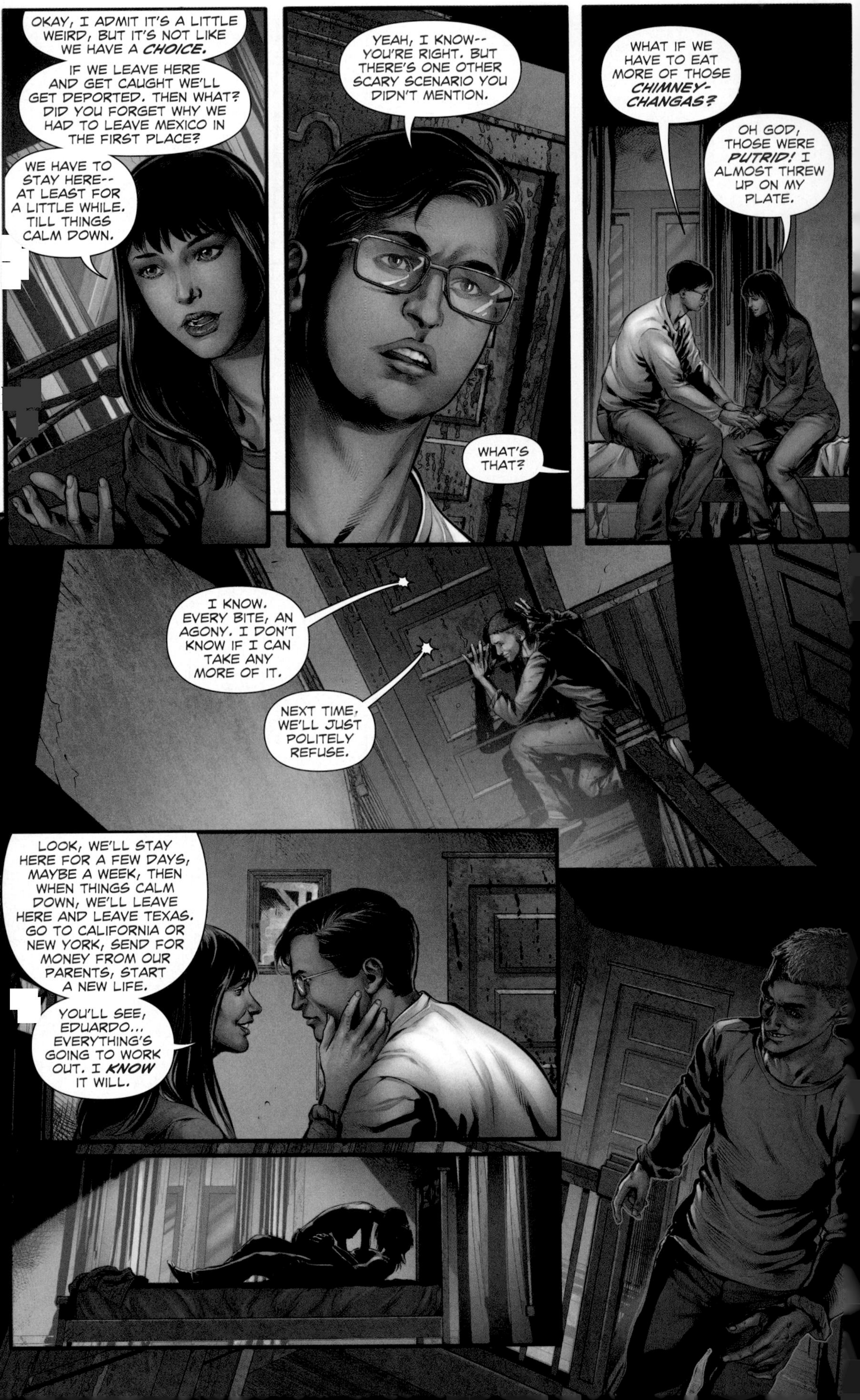

OKAY, I ADMIT IT'S A LITTLE WEIRD, BUT IT'S NOT LIKE WE HAVE A *CHOICE.*
IF WE LEAVE HERE AND GET CAUGHT WE'LL GET DEPORTED. THEN WHAT? DID YOU FORGET WHY WE HAD TO LEAVE MEXICO IN THE FIRST PLACE?
WE HAVE TO STAY HERE-- AT LEAST FOR A LITTLE WHILE. TILL THINGS CALM DOWN.
YEAH, I KNOW-- YOU'RE RIGHT. BUT THERE'S ONE OTHER SCARY SCENARIO YOU DIDN'T MENTION.
WHAT'S THAT?
WHAT IF WE HAVE TO EAT MORE OF THOSE *CHIMNEY-CHANGAS?*
OH GOD, THOSE WERE *PUTRID!* I ALMOST THREW UP ON MY PLATE.
I KNOW. EVERY BITE, AN AGONY. I DON'T KNOW IF I CAN TAKE ANY MORE OF IT.
NEXT TIME, WE'LL JUST POLITELY REFUSE.
LOOK, WE'LL STAY HERE FOR A FEW DAYS, MAYBE A WEEK, THEN WHEN THINGS CALM DOWN, WE'LL LEAVE HERE AND LEAVE TEXAS. GO TO CALIFORNIA OR NEW YORK, SEND FOR MONEY FROM OUR PARENTS, START A NEW LIFE.
YOU'LL SEE, EDUARDO... EVERYTHING'S GOING TO WORK OUT. I *KNOW* IT WILL.

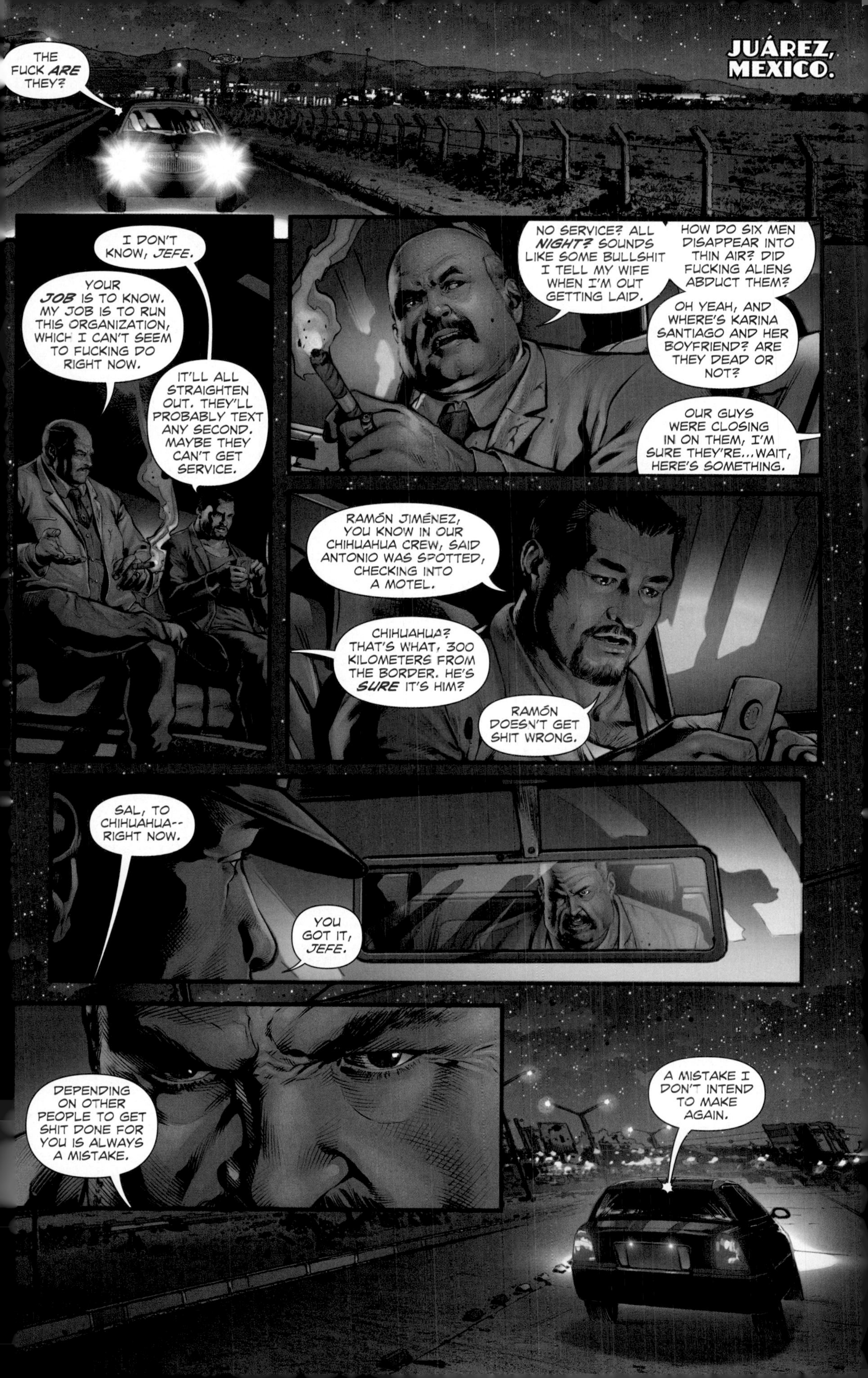
JUÁREZ, MEXICO.
THE FUCK ARE THEY?
I DON'T KNOW, JEFE.
YOUR JOB IS TO KNOW. MY JOB IS TO RUN THIS ORGANIZATION, WHICH I CAN'T SEEM TO FUCKING DO RIGHT NOW.
IT'LL ALL STRAIGHTEN OUT. THEY'LL PROBABLY TEXT ANY SECOND. MAYBE THEY CAN'T GET SERVICE.
NO SERVICE? ALL NIGHT? SOUNDS LIKE SOME BULLSHIT I TELL MY WIFE WHEN I'M OUT GETTING LAID.
HOW DO SIX MEN DISAPPEAR INTO THIN AIR? DID FUCKING ALIENS ABDUCT THEM?
OH YEAH, AND WHERE'S KARINA SANTIAGO AND HER BOYFRIEND? ARE THEY DEAD OR NOT?
OUR GUYS WERE CLOSING IN ON THEM, I'M SURE THEY'RE...WAIT, HERE'S SOMETHING.
RAMÓN JIMÉNEZ, YOU KNOW IN OUR CHIHUAHUA CREW, SAID ANTONIO WAS SPOTTED, CHECKING INTO A MOTEL.
CHIHUAHUA? THAT'S WHAT, 300 KILOMETERS FROM THE BORDER. HE'S SURE IT'S HIM?
RAMÓN DOESN'T GET SHIT WRONG.
SAL, TO CHIHUAHUA-- RIGHT NOW.
YOU GOT IT, JEFE.
DEPENDING ON OTHER PEOPLE TO GET SHIT DONE FOR YOU IS ALWAYS A MISTAKE.
A MISTAKE I DON'T INTEND TO MAKE AGAIN.

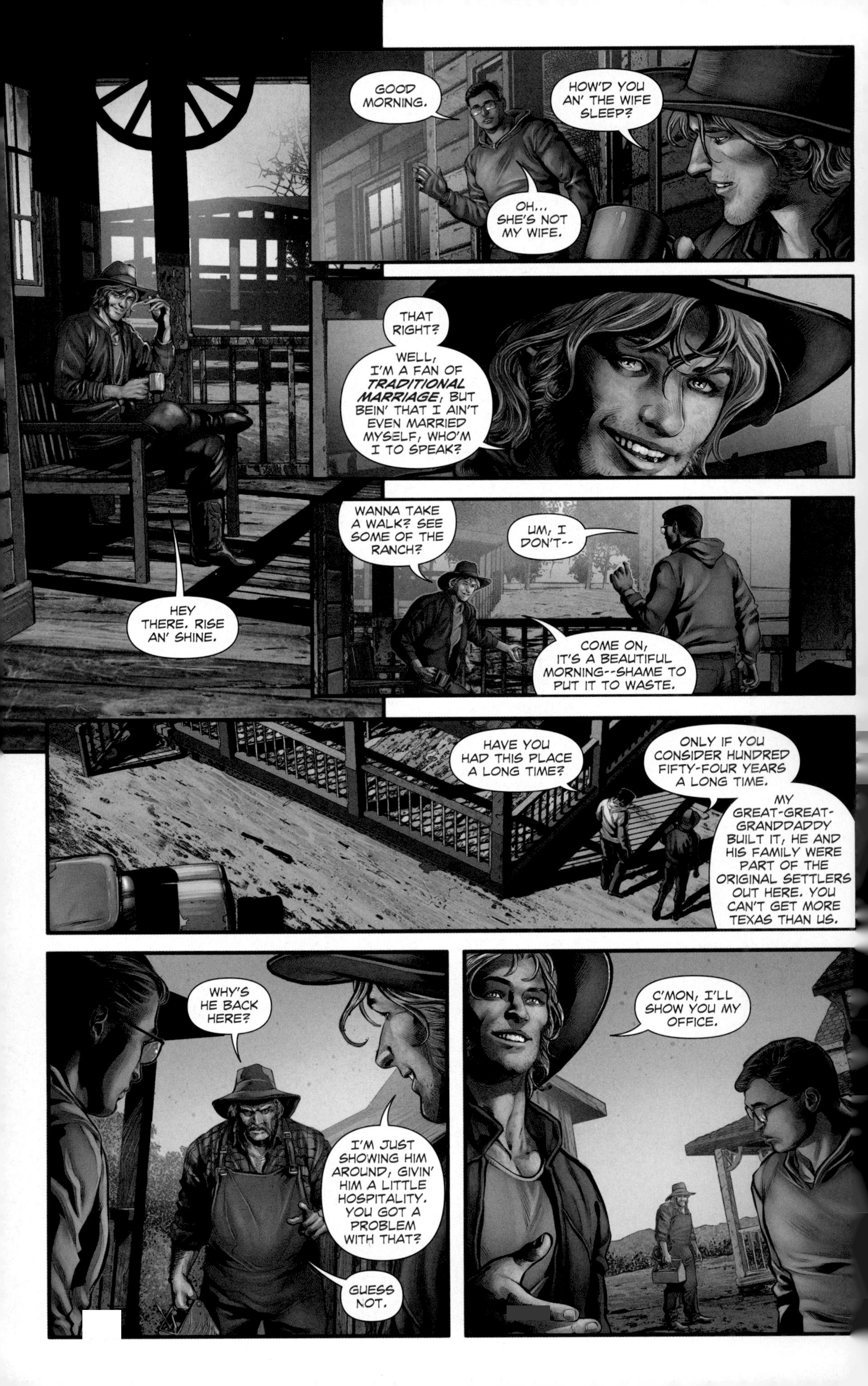
HEY THERE. RISE AN' SHINE.
GOOD MORNING.
HOW'D YOU AN' THE WIFE SLEEP?
OH... SHE'S NOT MY WIFE.
THAT RIGHT?
WELL, I'M A FAN OF TRADITIONAL MARRIAGE, BUT BEIN' THAT I AIN'T EVEN MARRIED MYSELF, WHO'M I TO SPEAK?
WANNA TAKE A WALK? SEE SOME OF THE RANCH?
UM, I DON'T--
COME ON, IT'S A BEAUTIFUL MORNING--SHAME TO PUT IT TO WASTE.
HAVE YOU HAD THIS PLACE A LONG TIME?
ONLY IF YOU CONSIDER HUNDRED FIFTY-FOUR YEARS A LONG TIME.
MY GREAT-GREAT-GRANDDADDY BUILT IT, HE AND HIS FAMILY WERE PART OF THE ORIGINAL SETTLERS OUT HERE. YOU CAN'T GET MORE TEXAS THAN US.
WHY'S HE BACK HERE?
I'M JUST SHOWING HIM AROUND, GIVIN' HIM A LITTLE HOSPITALITY. YOU GOT A PROBLEM WITH THAT?
GUESS NOT.
C'MON, I'LL SHOW YOU MY OFFICE.

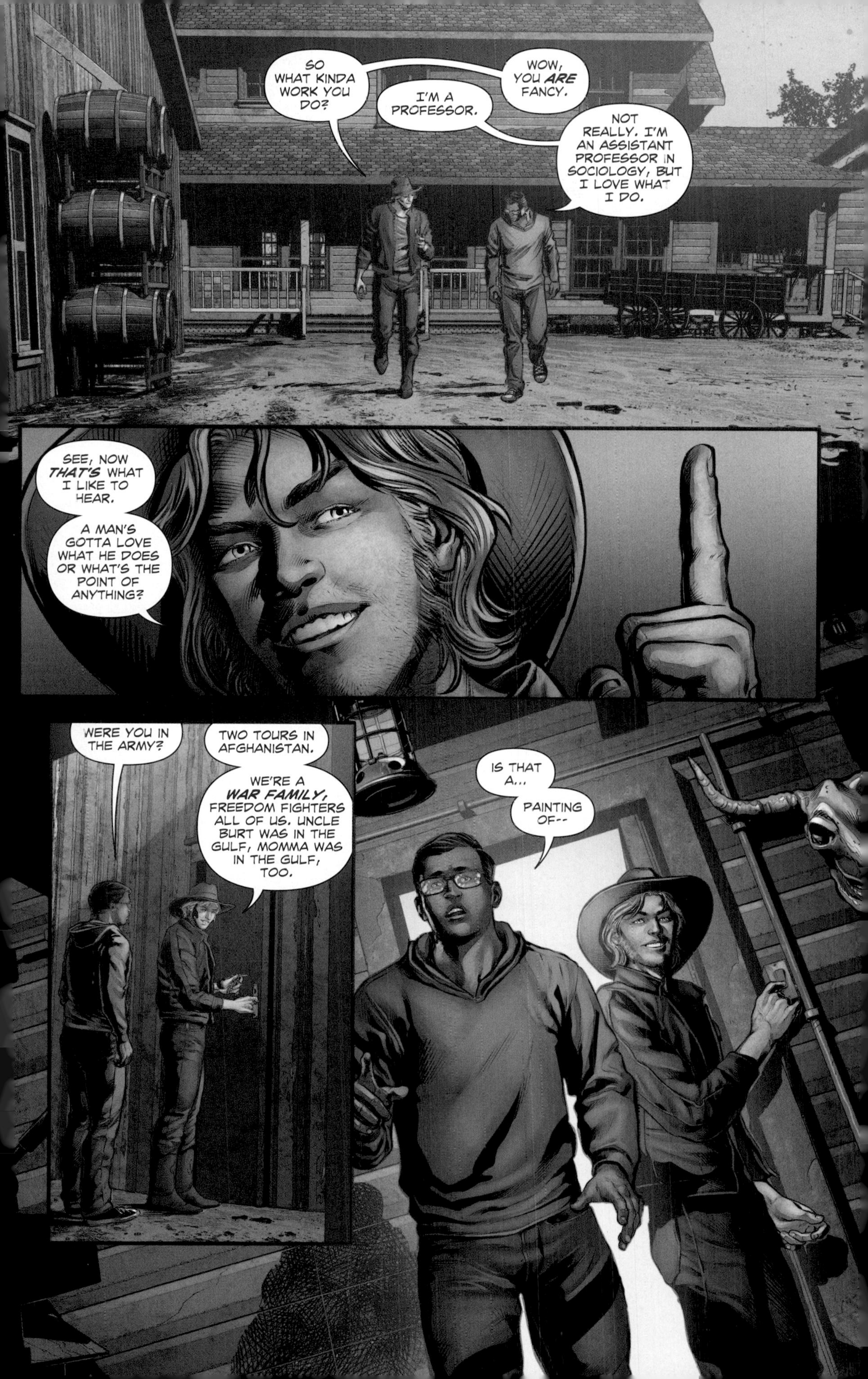
SO WHAT KINDA WORK YOU DO?
I'M A PROFESSOR.
WOW, YOU ARE FANCY.
NOT REALLY. I'M AN ASSISTANT PROFESSOR IN SOCIOLOGY, BUT I LOVE WHAT I DO.
SEE, NOW THAT'S WHAT I LIKE TO HEAR.
A MAN'S GOTTA LOVE WHAT HE DOES OR WHAT'S THE POINT OF ANYTHING?
WERE YOU IN THE ARMY?
TWO TOURS IN AFGHANISTAN.
WE'RE A WAR FAMILY, FREEDOM FIGHTERS ALL OF US. UNCLE BURT WAS IN THE GULF, MOMMA WAS IN THE GULF, TOO.
IS THAT A...
PAINTING OF--

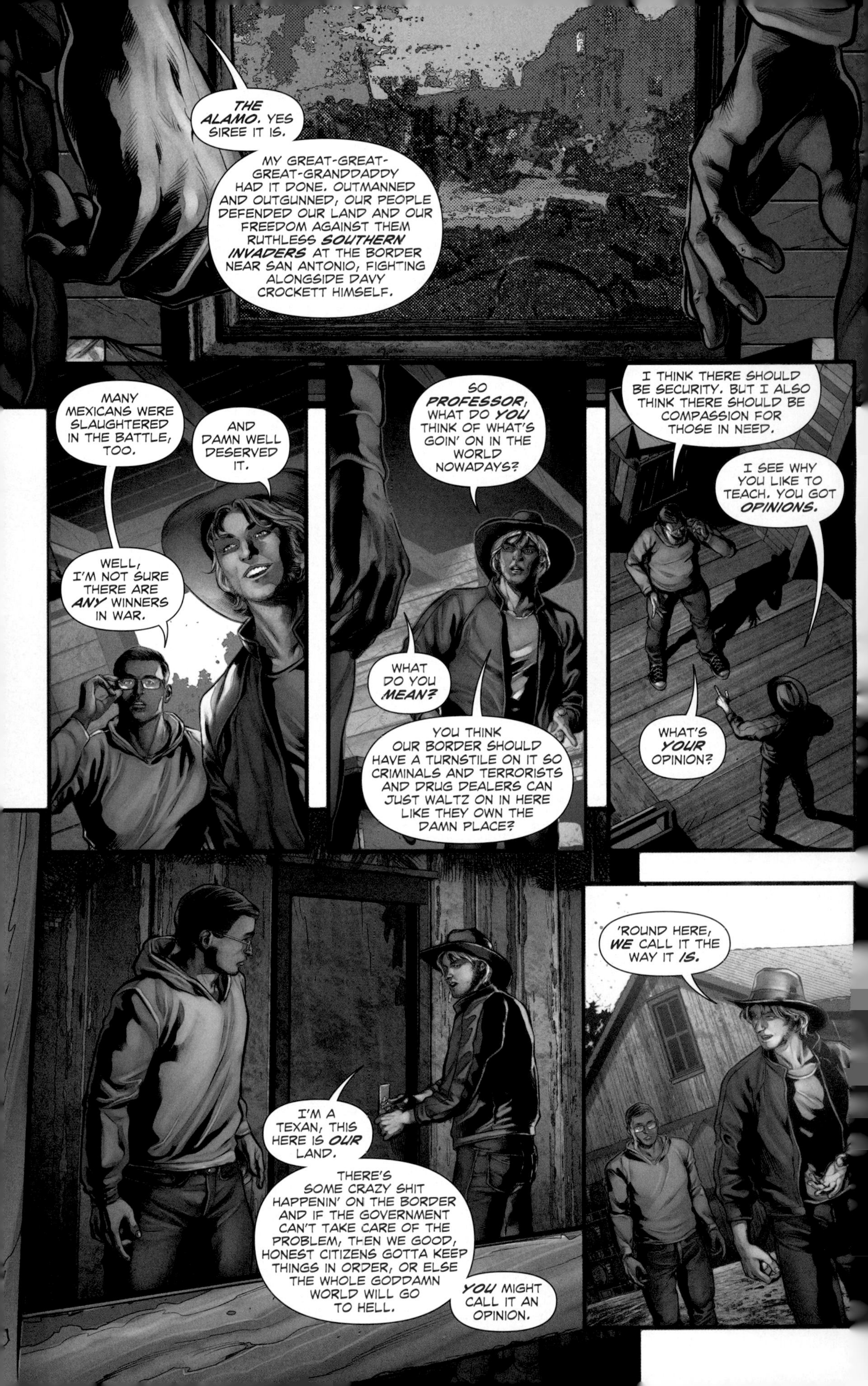
THE ALAMO. YES SIREE IT IS.
MY GREAT-GREAT-GREAT-GRANDDADDY HAD IT DONE. OUTMANNED AND OUTGUNNED, OUR PEOPLE DEFENDED OUR LAND AND OUR FREEDOM AGAINST THEM RUTHLESS SOUTHERN INVADERS AT THE BORDER NEAR SAN ANTONIO, FIGHTING ALONGSIDE DAVY CROCKETT HIMSELF.
MANY MEXICANS WERE SLAUGHTERED IN THE BATTLE, TOO.
AND DAMN WELL DESERVED IT.
WELL, I'M NOT SURE THERE ARE ANY WINNERS IN WAR.
SO PROFESSOR, WHAT DO YOU THINK OF WHAT'S GOIN' ON IN THE WORLD NOWADAYS?
WHAT DO YOU MEAN?
YOU THINK OUR BORDER SHOULD HAVE A TURNSTILE ON IT SO CRIMINALS AND TERRORISTS AND DRUG DEALERS CAN JUST WALTZ ON IN HERE LIKE THEY OWN THE DAMN PLACE?
I THINK THERE SHOULD BE SECURITY. BUT I ALSO THINK THERE SHOULD BE COMPASSION FOR THOSE IN NEED.
I SEE WHY YOU LIKE TO TEACH. YOU GOT OPINIONS.
WHAT'S YOUR OPINION?
I'M A TEXAN, THIS HERE IS OUR LAND.
THERE'S SOME CRAZY SHIT HAPPENIN' ON THE BORDER AND IF THE GOVERNMENT CAN'T TAKE CARE OF THE PROBLEM, THEN WE GOOD, HONEST CITIZENS GOTTA KEEP THINGS IN ORDER, OR ELSE THE WHOLE GODDAMN WORLD WILL GO TO HELL.
YOU MIGHT CALL IT AN OPINION.
'ROUND HERE, WE CALL IT THE WAY IT IS.

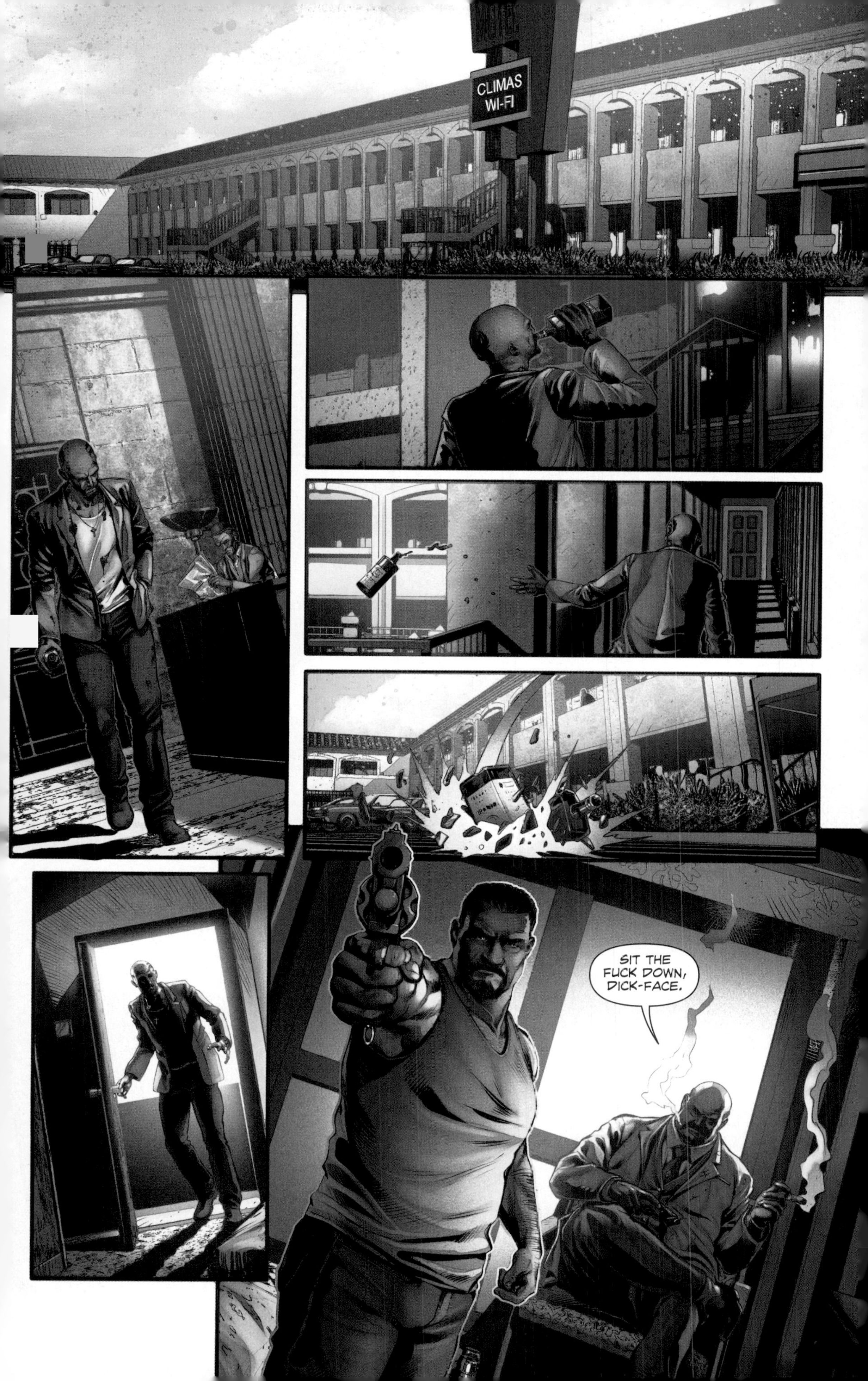
CLIMAS
WI-FI
SIT THE FUCK DOWN, DICK-FACE.

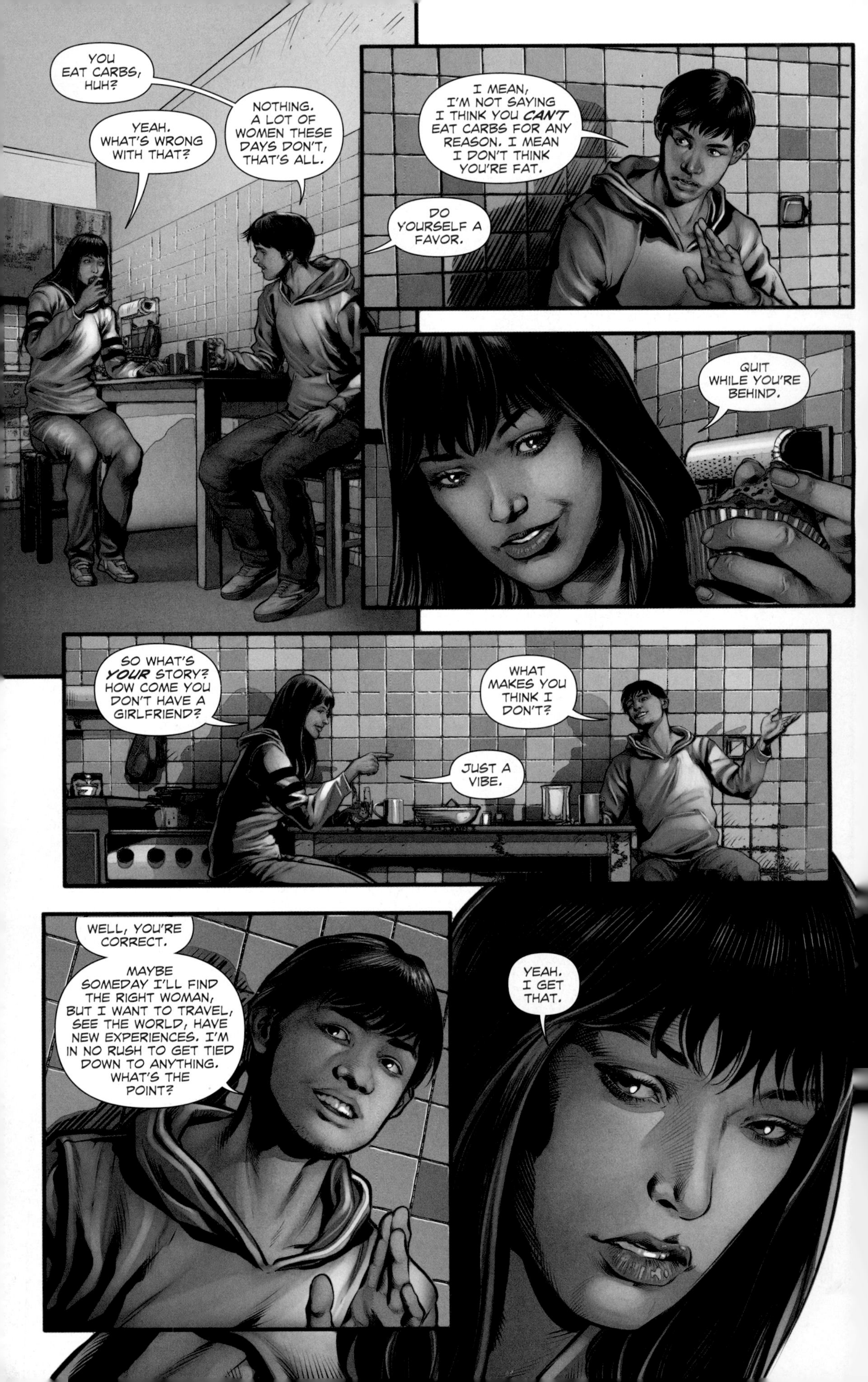
YOU EAT CARBS, HUH?
YEAH. WHAT'S WRONG WITH THAT?
NOTHING. A LOT OF WOMEN THESE DAYS DON'T, THAT'S ALL.
I MEAN, I'M NOT SAYING I THINK YOU CAN'T EAT CARBS FOR ANY REASON. I MEAN I DON'T THINK YOU'RE FAT.
DO YOURSELF A FAVOR.
QUIT WHILE YOU'RE BEHIND.
SO WHAT'S YOUR STORY? HOW COME YOU DON'T HAVE A GIRLFRIEND?
WHAT MAKES YOU THINK I DON'T?
JUST A VIBE.
WELL, YOU'RE CORRECT.
MAYBE SOMEDAY I'LL FIND THE RIGHT WOMAN, BUT I WANT TO TRAVEL, SEE THE WORLD, HAVE NEW EXPERIENCES. I'M IN NO RUSH TO GET TIED DOWN TO ANYTHING. WHAT'S THE POINT?
YEAH. I GET THAT.

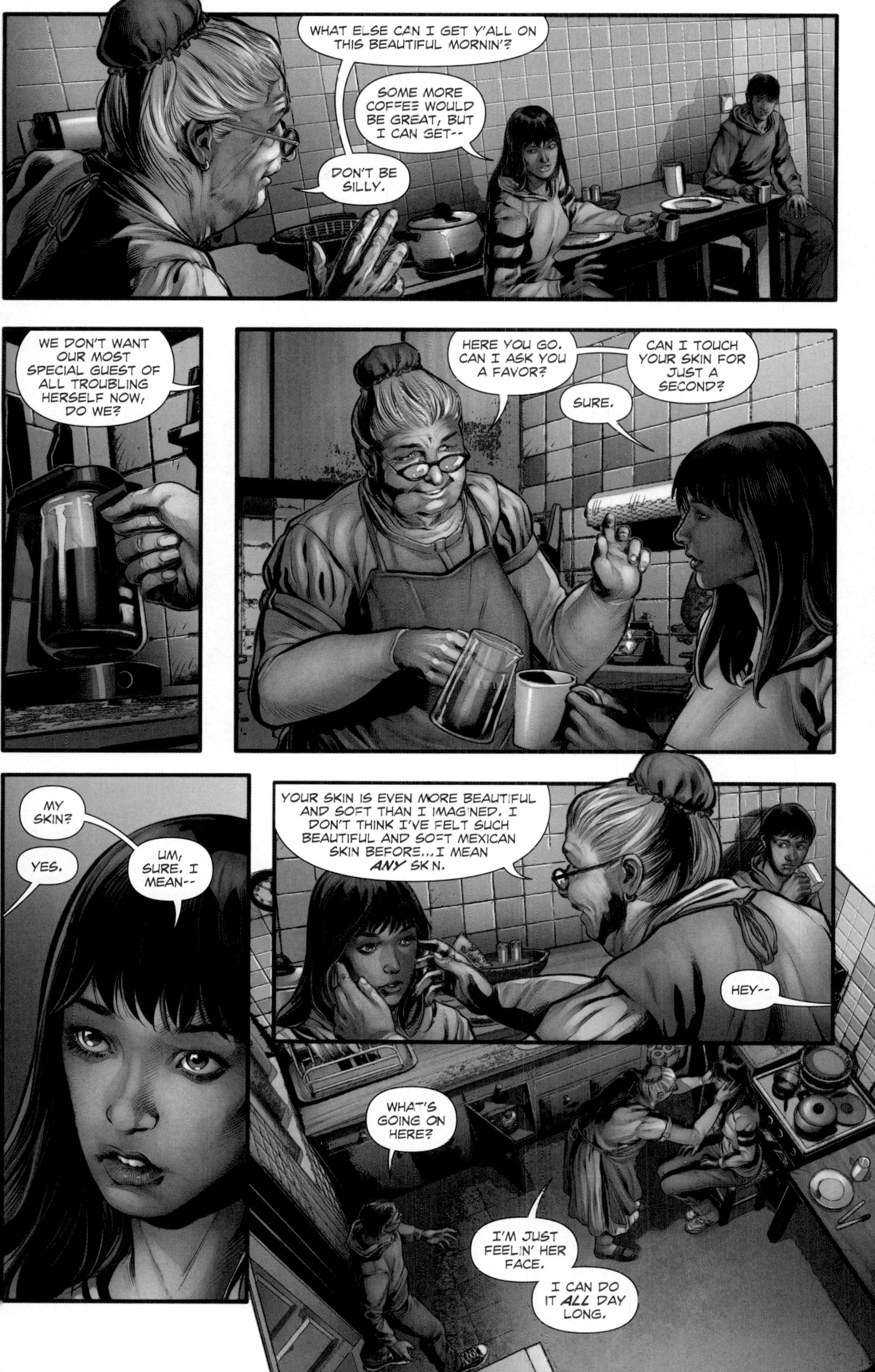
WHAT ELSE CAN I GET Y'ALL ON THIS BEAUTIFUL MORNIN'?
SOME MORE COFFEE WOULD BE GREAT, BUT I CAN GET--
DON'T BE SILLY.
WE DON'T WANT OUR MOST SPECIAL GUEST OF ALL TROUBLING HERSELF NOW, DO WE?
HERE YOU GO. CAN I ASK YOU A FAVOR?
CAN I TOUCH YOUR SKIN FOR JUST A SECOND?
SURE.
MY SKIN?
YES.
UM, SURE. I MEAN--
YOUR SKIN IS EVEN MORE BEAUTIFUL AND SOFT THAN I IMAGINED. I DON'T THINK I'VE FELT SUCH BEAUTIFUL AND SOFT MEXICAN SKIN BEFORE...I MEAN *ANY* SKIN.
HEY--
WHAT'S GOING ON HERE?
I'M JUST FEELIN' HER FACE.
I CAN DO IT *ALL* DAY LONG.

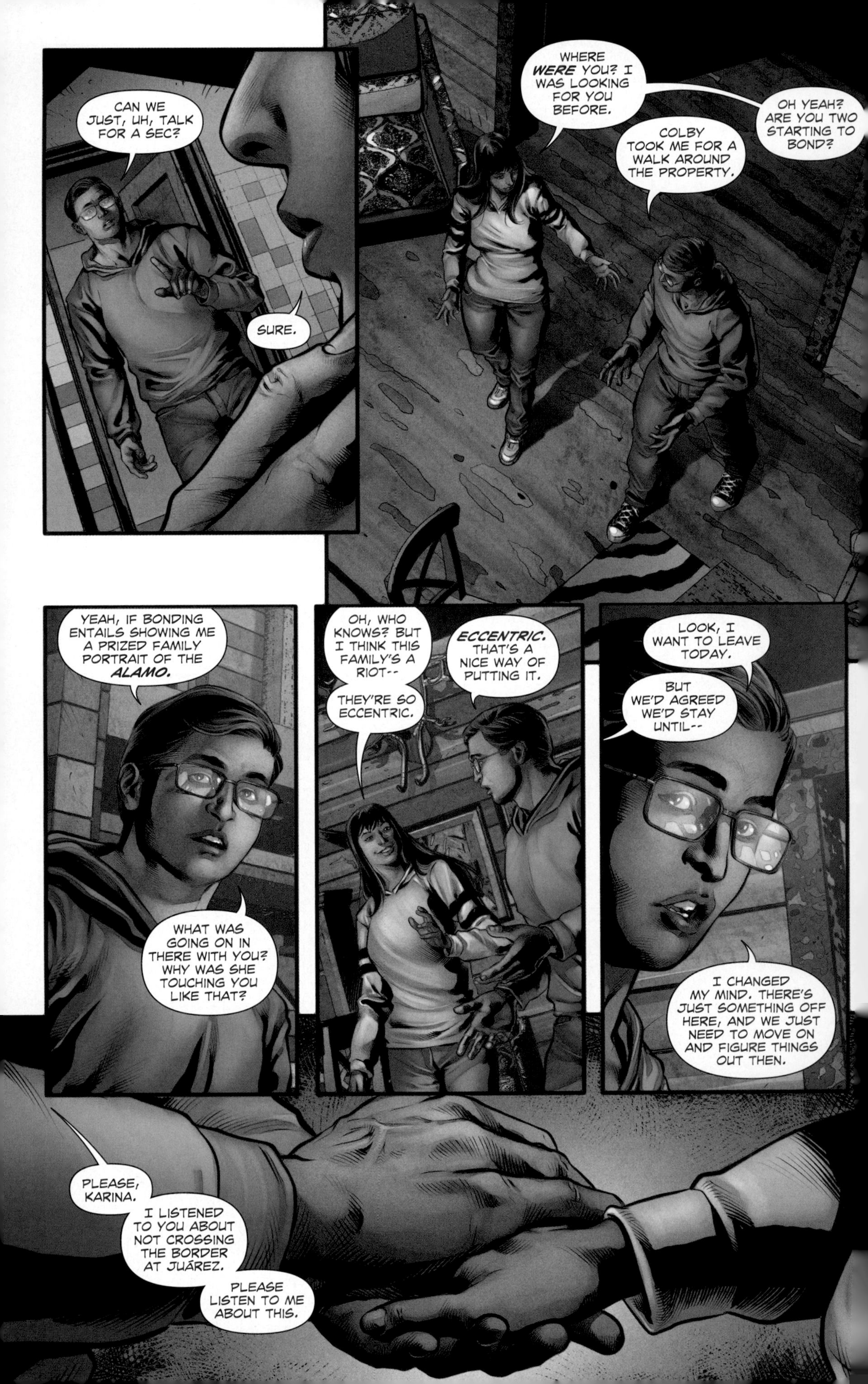
CAN WE JUST, UH, TALK FOR A SEC?
SURE.
WHERE *WERE* YOU? I WAS LOOKING FOR YOU BEFORE.
COLBY TOOK ME FOR A WALK AROUND THE PROPERTY.
OH YEAH? ARE YOU TWO STARTING TO BOND?
YEAH, IF BONDING ENTAILS SHOWING ME A PRIZED FAMILY PORTRAIT OF THE *ALAMO.*
WHAT WAS GOING ON IN THERE WITH YOU? WHY WAS SHE TOUCHING YOU LIKE THAT?
OH, WHO KNOWS? BUT I THINK THIS FAMILY'S A RIOT--
THEY'RE SO ECCENTRIC.
ECCENTRIC. THAT'S A NICE WAY OF PUTTING IT.
LOOK, I WANT TO LEAVE TODAY.
BUT WE'D AGREED WE'D STAY UNTIL--
I CHANGED MY MIND. THERE'S JUST SOMETHING OFF HERE, AND WE JUST NEED TO MOVE ON AND FIGURE THINGS OUT THEN.
PLEASE, KARINA.
I LISTENED TO YOU ABOUT NOT CROSSING THE BORDER AT JUÁREZ.
PLEASE LISTEN TO ME ABOUT THIS.

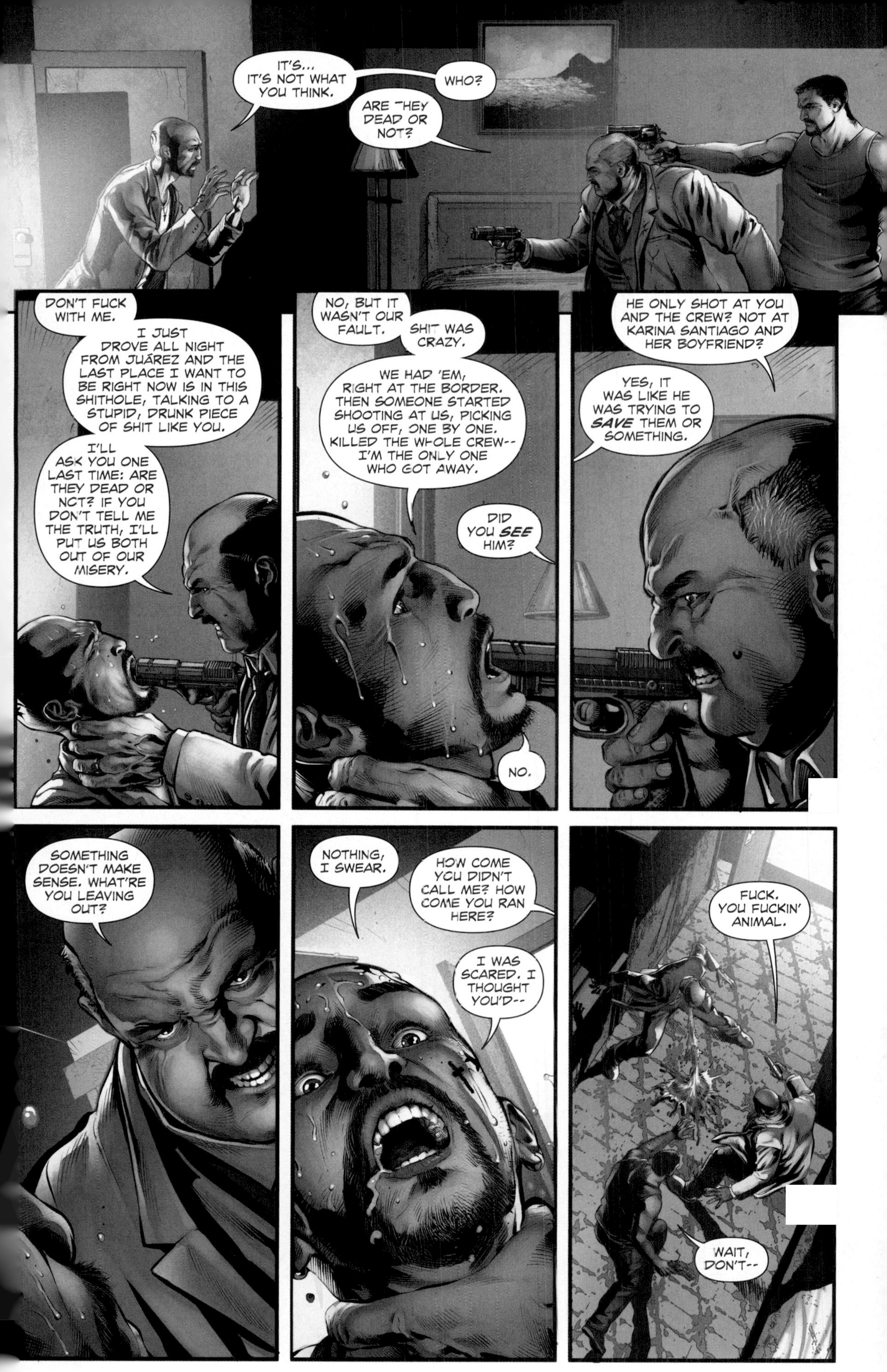
IT'S... IT'S NOT WHAT YOU THINK.
WHO?
ARE THEY DEAD OR NOT?
DON'T FUCK WITH ME.
I JUST DROVE ALL NIGHT FROM JUÁREZ AND THE LAST PLACE I WANT TO BE RIGHT NOW IS IN THIS SHITHOLE, TALKING TO A STUPID, DRUNK PIECE OF SHIT LIKE YOU.
I'LL ASK YOU ONE LAST TIME: ARE THEY DEAD OR NOT? IF YOU DON'T TELL ME THE TRUTH, I'LL PUT US BOTH OUT OF OUR MISERY.
NO, BUT IT WASN'T OUR FAULT.
SHIT WAS CRAZY.
WE HAD 'EM, RIGHT AT THE BORDER. THEN SOMEONE STARTED SHOOTING AT US, PICKING US OFF, ONE BY ONE. KILLED THE WHOLE CREW-- I'M THE ONLY ONE WHO GOT AWAY.
DID YOU SEE HIM?
NO.
HE ONLY SHOT AT YOU AND THE CREW? NOT AT KARINA SANTIAGO AND HER BOYFRIEND?
YES, IT WAS LIKE HE WAS TRYING TO SAVE THEM OR SOMETHING.
SOMETHING DOESN'T MAKE SENSE. WHAT'RE YOU LEAVING OUT?
NOTHING, I SWEAR.
HOW COME YOU DIDN'T CALL ME? HOW COME YOU RAN HERE?
I WAS SCARED. I THOUGHT YOU'D--
FUCK. YOU FUCKIN' ANIMAL.
WAIT, DON'T--

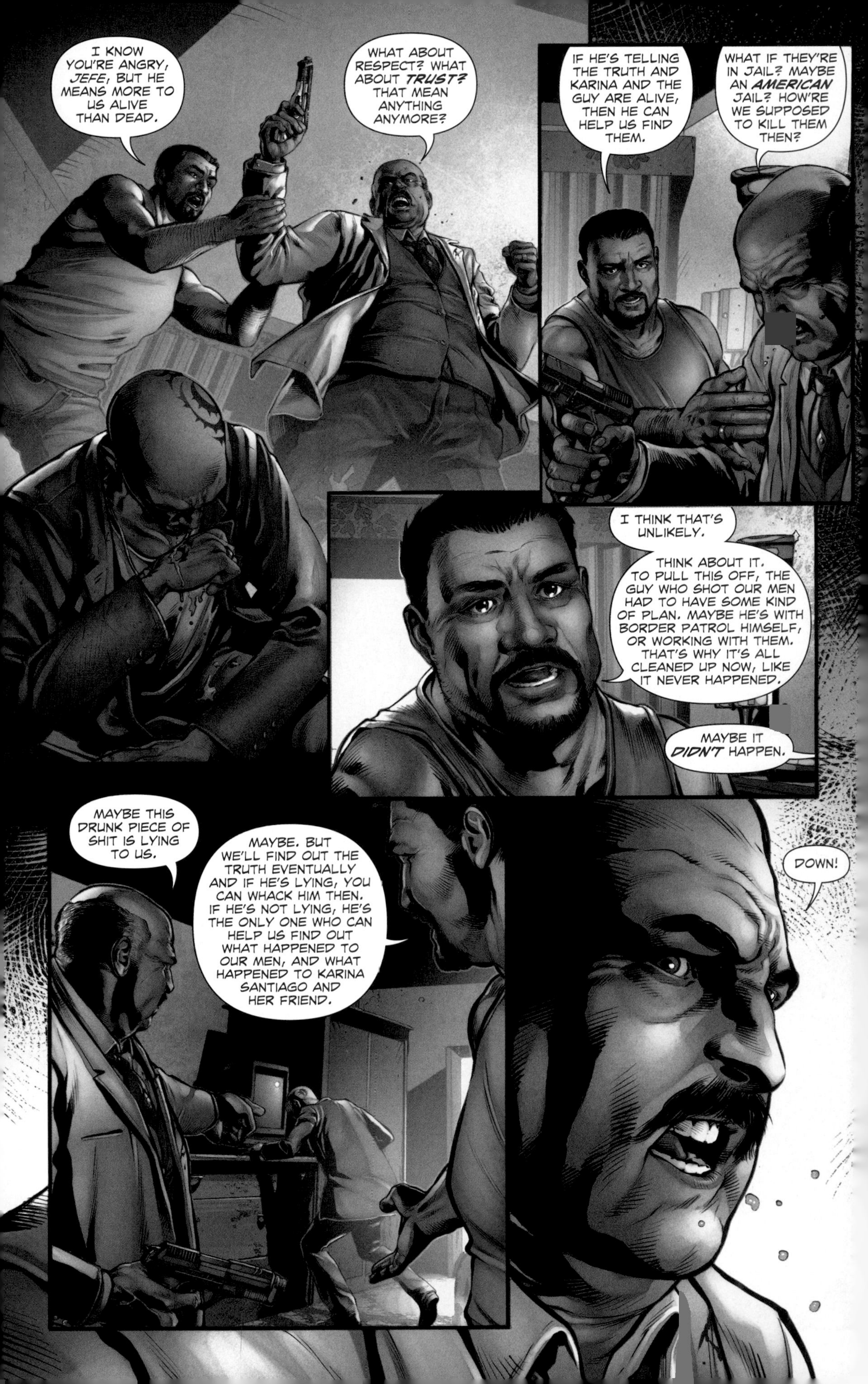
I KNOW YOU'RE ANGRY, *JEFE*, BUT HE MEANS MORE TO US ALIVE THAN DEAD.
WHAT ABOUT RESPECT? WHAT ABOUT ***TRUST?*** THAT MEAN ANYTHING ANYMORE?
IF HE'S TELLING THE TRUTH AND KARINA AND THE GUY ARE ALIVE, THEN HE CAN HELP US FIND THEM.
WHAT IF THEY'RE IN JAIL? MAYBE AN ***AMERICAN*** JAIL? HOW'RE WE SUPPOSED TO KILL THEM THEN?
I THINK THAT'S UNLIKELY.
THINK ABOUT IT. TO PULL THIS OFF, THE GUY WHO SHOT OUR MEN HAD TO HAVE SOME KIND OF PLAN. MAYBE HE'S WITH BORDER PATROL HIMSELF, OR WORKING WITH THEM. THAT'S WHY IT'S ALL CLEANED UP NOW, LIKE IT NEVER HAPPENED.
MAYBE IT ***DIDN'T*** HAPPEN.
MAYBE THIS DRUNK PIECE OF SHIT IS LYING TO US.
MAYBE. BUT WE'LL FIND OUT THE TRUTH EVENTUALLY AND IF HE'S LYING, YOU CAN WHACK HIM THEN. IF HE'S NOT LYING, HE'S THE ONLY ONE WHO CAN HELP US FIND OUT WHAT HAPPENED TO OUR MEN, AND WHAT HAPPENED TO KARINA SANTIAGO AND HER FRIEND.
DOWN!

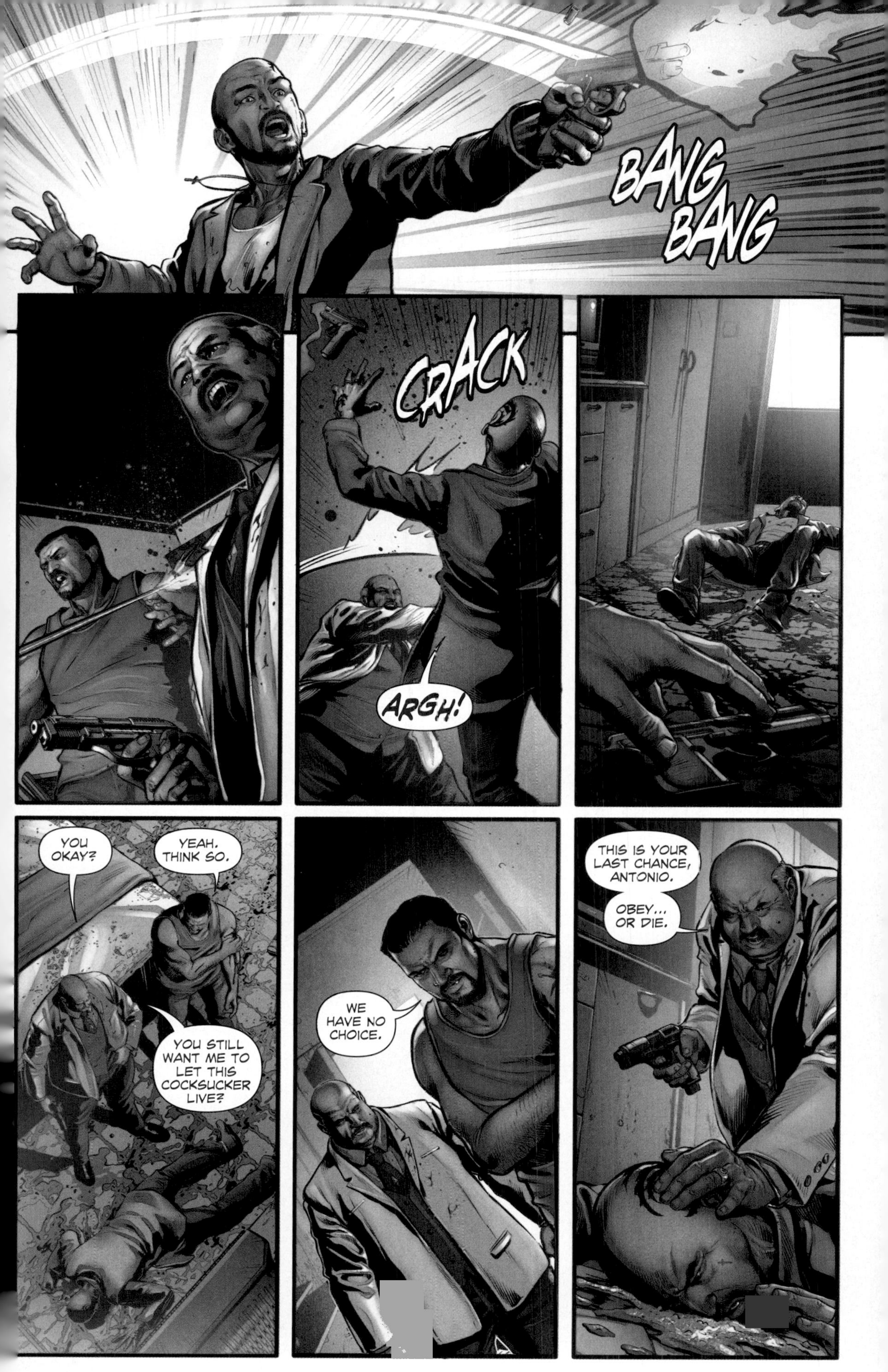
BANG BANG
CRACK
ARGH!
YOU OKAY?
YEAH. THINK SO.
YOU STILL WANT ME TO LET THIS COCKSUCKER LIVE?
WE HAVE NO CHOICE.
THIS IS YOUR LAST CHANCE, ANTONIO.
OBEY... OR DIE.

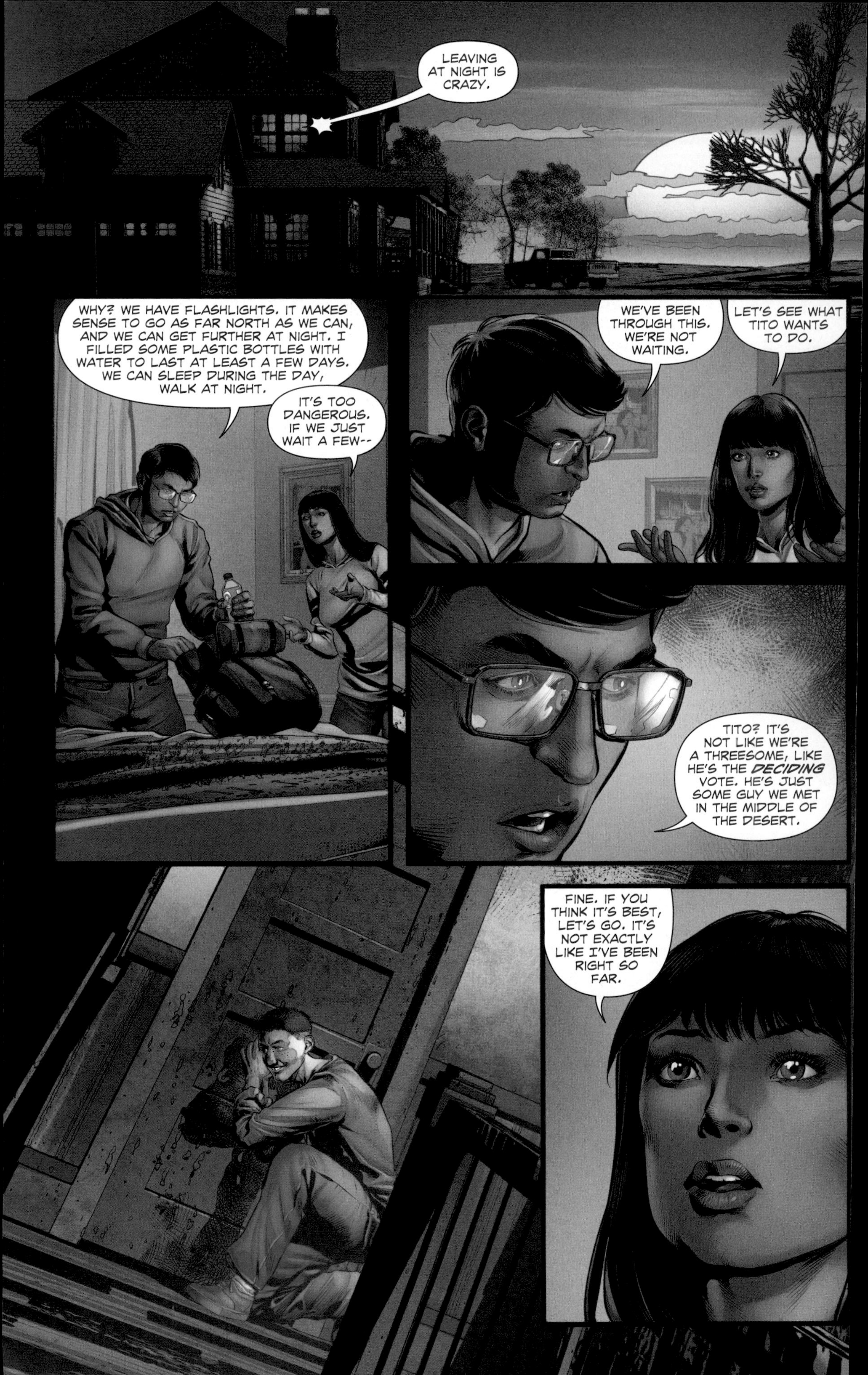
LEAVING AT NIGHT IS CRAZY.
WHY? WE HAVE FLASHLIGHTS. IT MAKES SENSE TO GO AS FAR NORTH AS WE CAN, AND WE CAN GET FURTHER AT NIGHT. I FILLED SOME PLASTIC BOTTLES WITH WATER TO LAST AT LEAST A FEW DAYS. WE CAN SLEEP DURING THE DAY, WALK AT NIGHT.
IT'S TOO DANGEROUS. IF WE JUST WAIT A FEW--
WE'VE BEEN THROUGH THIS. WE'RE NOT WAITING.
LET'S SEE WHAT TITO WANTS TO DO.
TITO? IT'S NOT LIKE WE'RE A THREESOME, LIKE HE'S THE *DECIDING* VOTE. HE'S JUST SOME GUY WE MET IN THE MIDDLE OF THE DESERT.
FINE. IF YOU THINK IT'S BEST, LET'S GO. IT'S NOT EXACTLY LIKE I'VE BEEN RIGHT SO FAR.

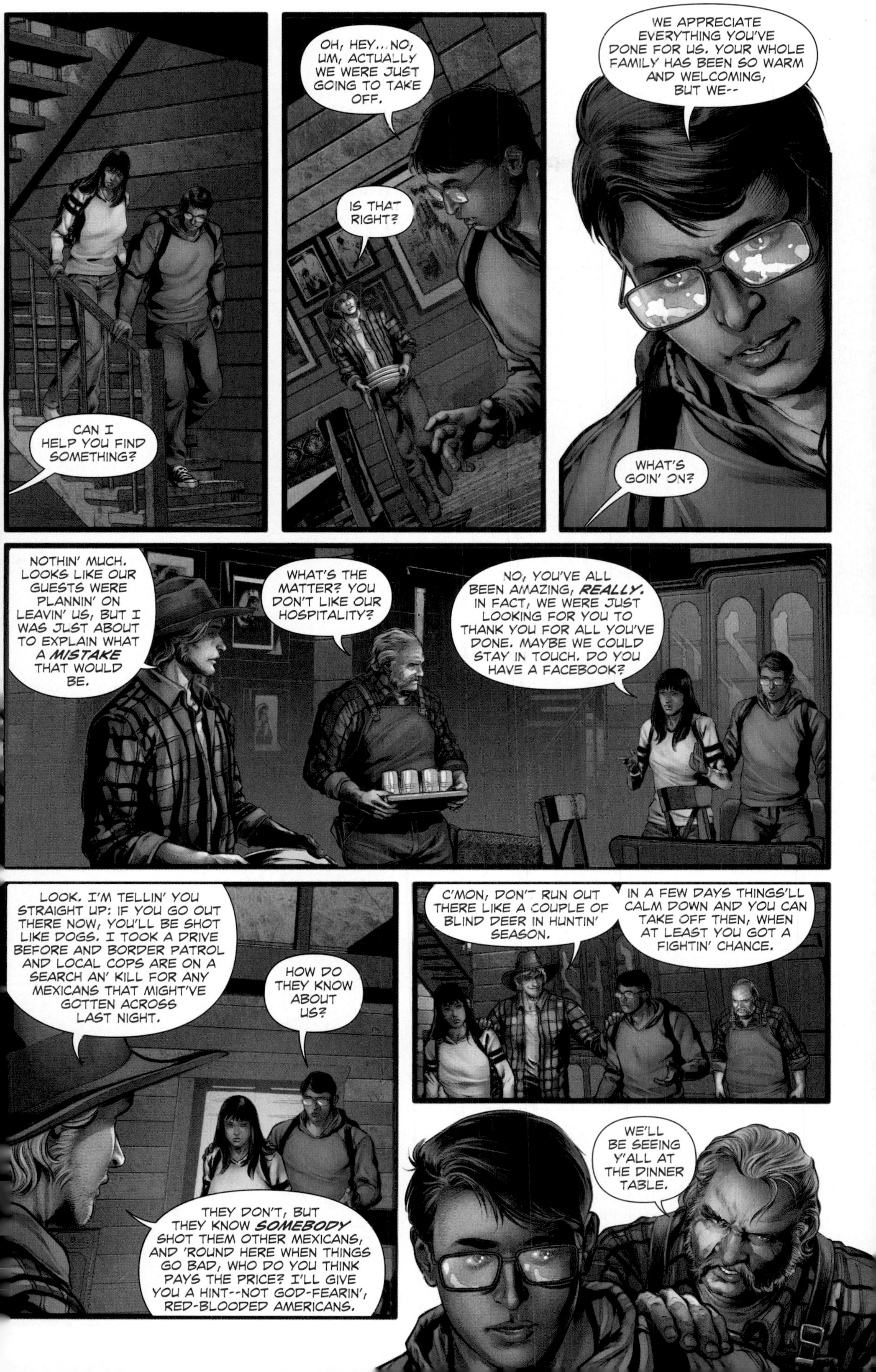

CAN I HELP YOU FIND SOMETHING?
OH, HEY... NO, UM, ACTUALLY WE WERE JUST GOING TO TAKE OFF.
IS THAT RIGHT?
WE APPRECIATE EVERYTHING YOU'VE DONE FOR US. YOUR WHOLE FAMILY HAS BEEN SO WARM AND WELCOMING, BUT WE--
WHAT'S GOIN' ON?
NOTHIN' MUCH. LOOKS LIKE OUR GUESTS WERE PLANNIN' ON LEAVIN' US, BUT I WAS JUST ABOUT TO EXPLAIN WHAT A MISTAKE THAT WOULD BE.
WHAT'S THE MATTER? YOU DON'T LIKE OUR HOSPITALITY?
NO, YOU'VE ALL BEEN AMAZING, REALLY. IN FACT, WE WERE JUST LOOKING FOR YOU TO THANK YOU FOR ALL YOU'VE DONE. MAYBE WE COULD STAY IN TOUCH. DO YOU HAVE A FACEBOOK?
LOOK. I'M TELLIN' YOU STRAIGHT UP: IF YOU GO OUT THERE NOW, YOU'LL BE SHOT LIKE DOGS. I TOOK A DRIVE BEFORE AND BORDER PATROL AND LOCAL COPS ARE ON A SEARCH AN' KILL FOR ANY MEXICANS THAT MIGHT'VE GOTTEN ACROSS LAST NIGHT.
HOW DO THEY KNOW ABOUT US?
THEY DON'T, BUT THEY KNOW SOMEBODY SHOT THEM OTHER MEXICANS, AND 'ROUND HERE WHEN THINGS GO BAD, WHO DO YOU THINK PAYS THE PRICE? I'LL GIVE YOU A HINT--NOT GOD-FEARIN', RED-BLOODED AMERICANS.
C'MON, DON'T RUN OUT THERE LIKE A COUPLE OF BLIND DEER IN HUNTIN' SEASON.
IN A FEW DAYS THINGS'LL CALM DOWN AND YOU CAN TAKE OFF THEN, WHEN AT LEAST YOU GOT A FIGHTIN' CHANCE.
WE'LL BE SEEING Y'ALL AT THE DINNER TABLE.

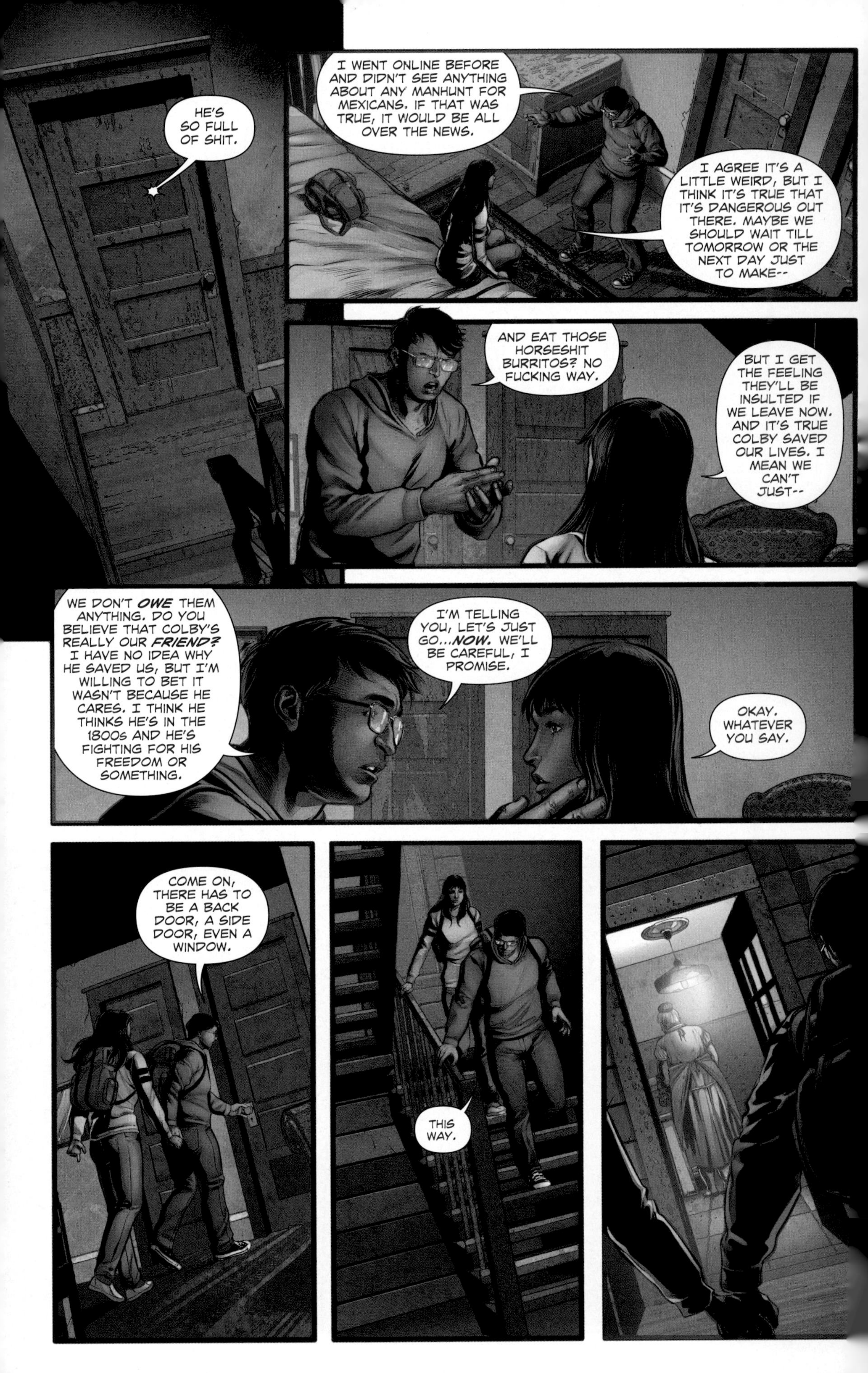
HE'S SO FULL OF SHIT.
I WENT ONLINE BEFORE AND DIDN'T SEE ANYTHING ABOUT ANY MANHUNT FOR MEXICANS. IF THAT WAS TRUE, IT WOULD BE ALL OVER THE NEWS.
I AGREE IT'S A LITTLE WEIRD, BUT I THINK IT'S TRUE THAT IT'S DANGEROUS OUT THERE. MAYBE WE SHOULD WAIT TILL TOMORROW OR THE NEXT DAY JUST TO MAKE--
AND EAT THOSE HORSESHIT BURRITOS? NO FUCKING WAY.
BUT I GET THE FEELING THEY'LL BE INSULTED IF WE LEAVE NOW. AND IT'S TRUE COLBY SAVED OUR LIVES. I MEAN WE CAN'T JUST--
WE DON'T ***OWE*** THEM ANYTHING. DO YOU BELIEVE THAT COLBY'S REALLY OUR ***FRIEND?*** I HAVE NO IDEA WHY HE SAVED US, BUT I'M WILLING TO BET IT WASN'T BECAUSE HE CARES. I THINK HE THINKS HE'S IN THE 1800s AND HE'S FIGHTING FOR HIS FREEDOM OR SOMETHING.
I'M TELLING YOU, LET'S JUST GO...***NOW.*** WE'LL BE CAREFUL, I PROMISE.
OKAY. WHATEVER YOU SAY.
COME ON, THERE HAS TO BE A BACK DOOR, A SIDE DOOR, EVEN A WINDOW.
THIS WAY.

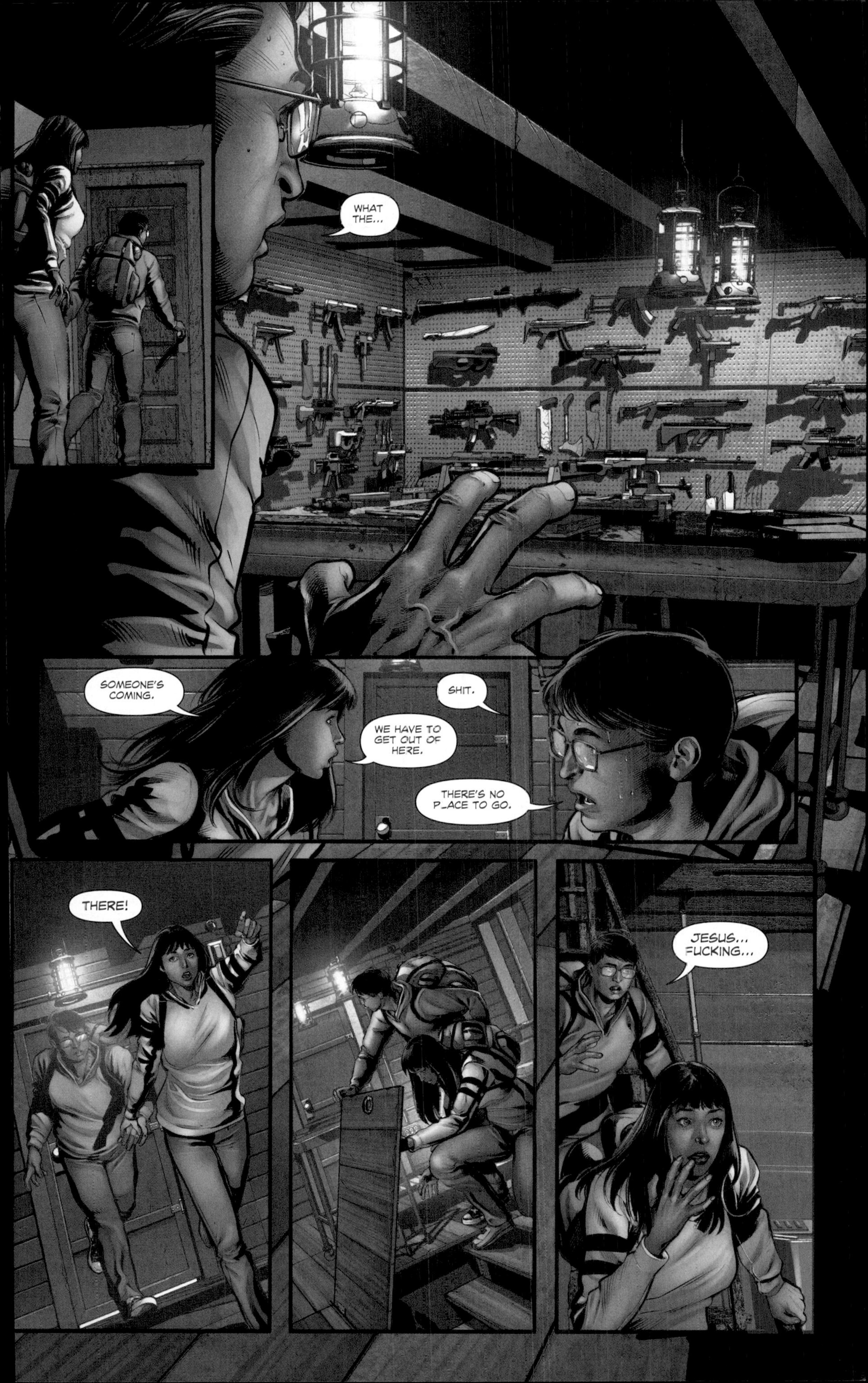
WHAT THE...
SOMEONE'S COMING.
SHIT.
WE HAVE TO GET OUT OF HERE.
THERE'S NO PLACE TO GO.
THERE!
JESUS... FUCKING...

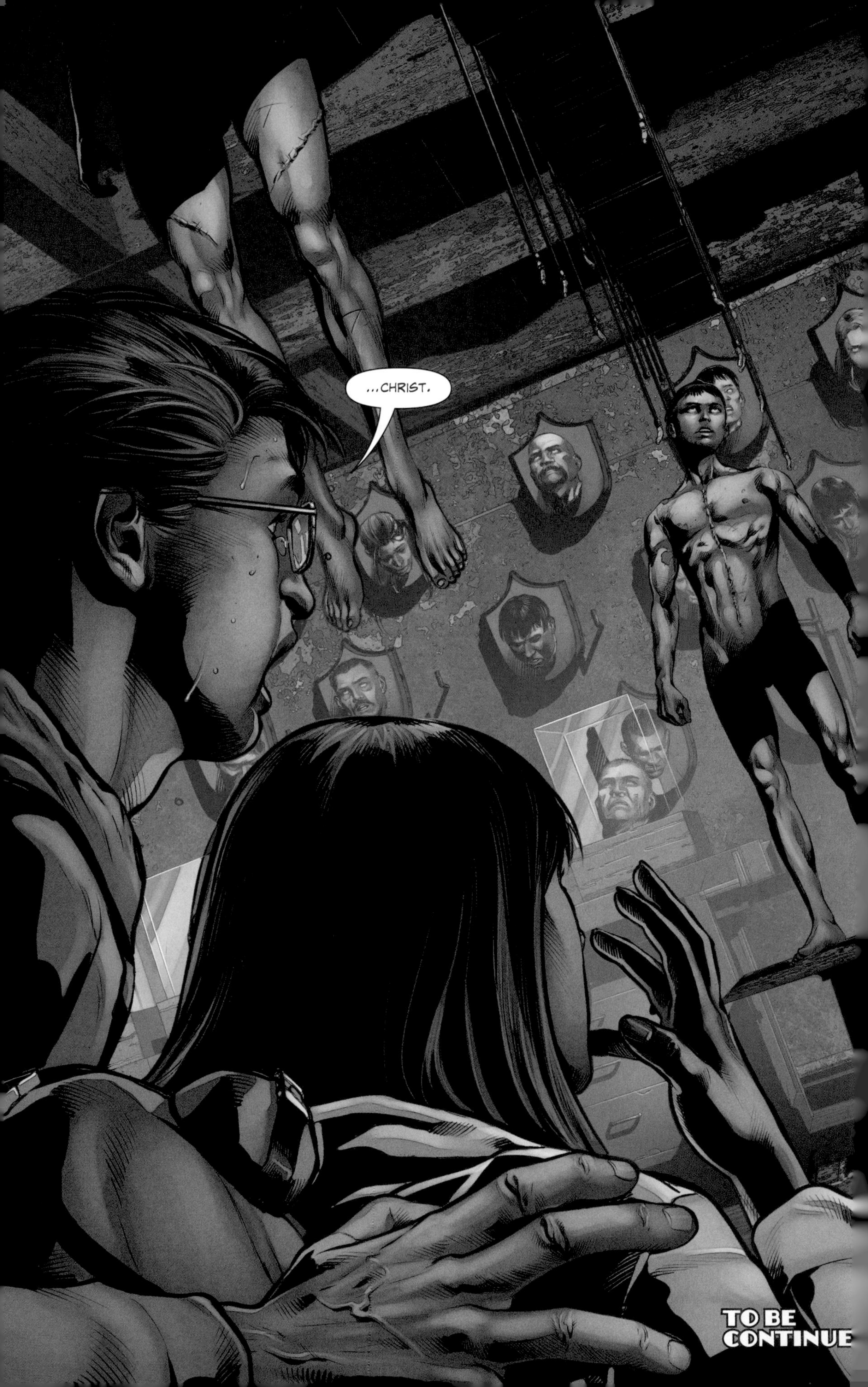
...CHRIST.
TO BE
CONTINUE

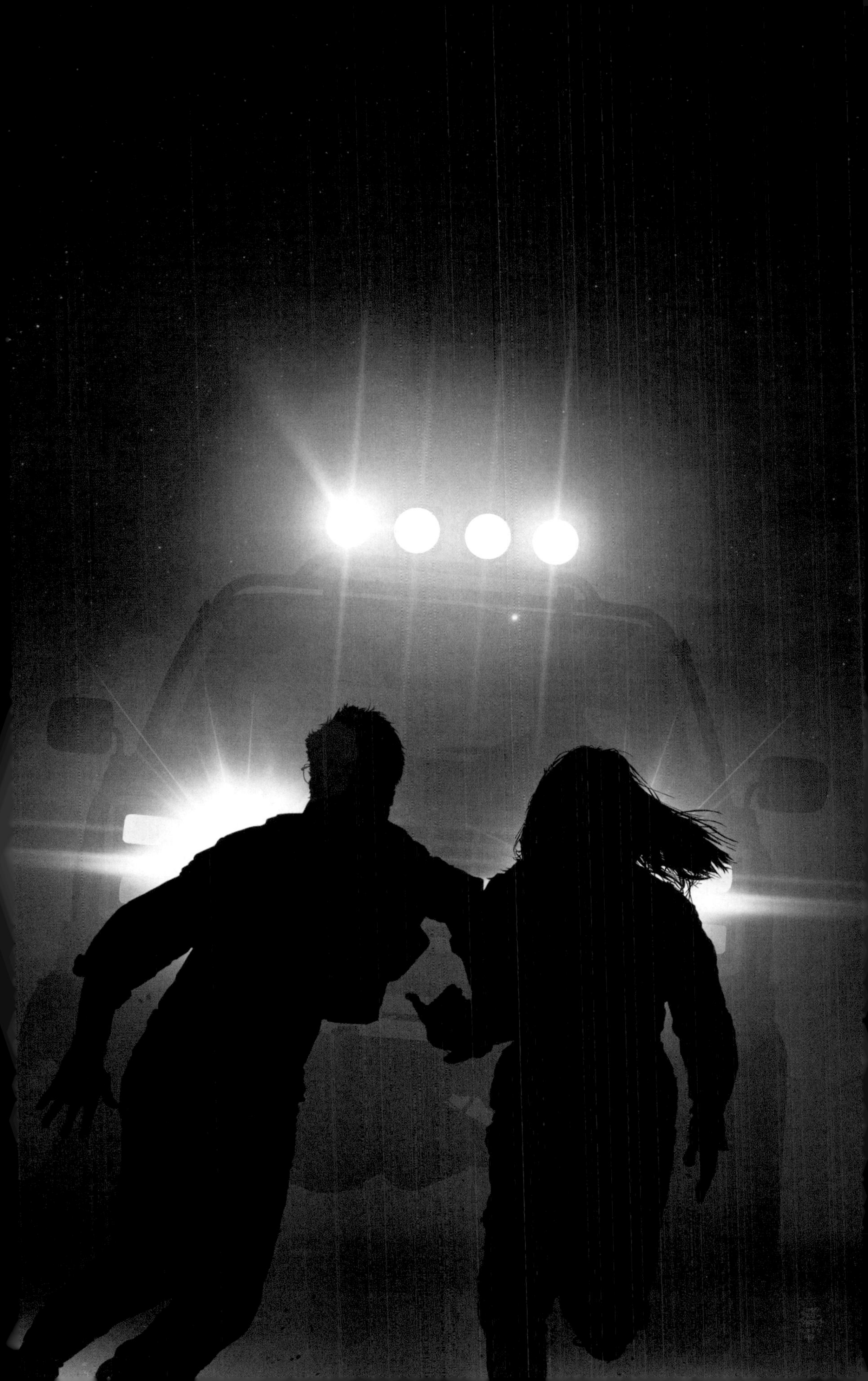

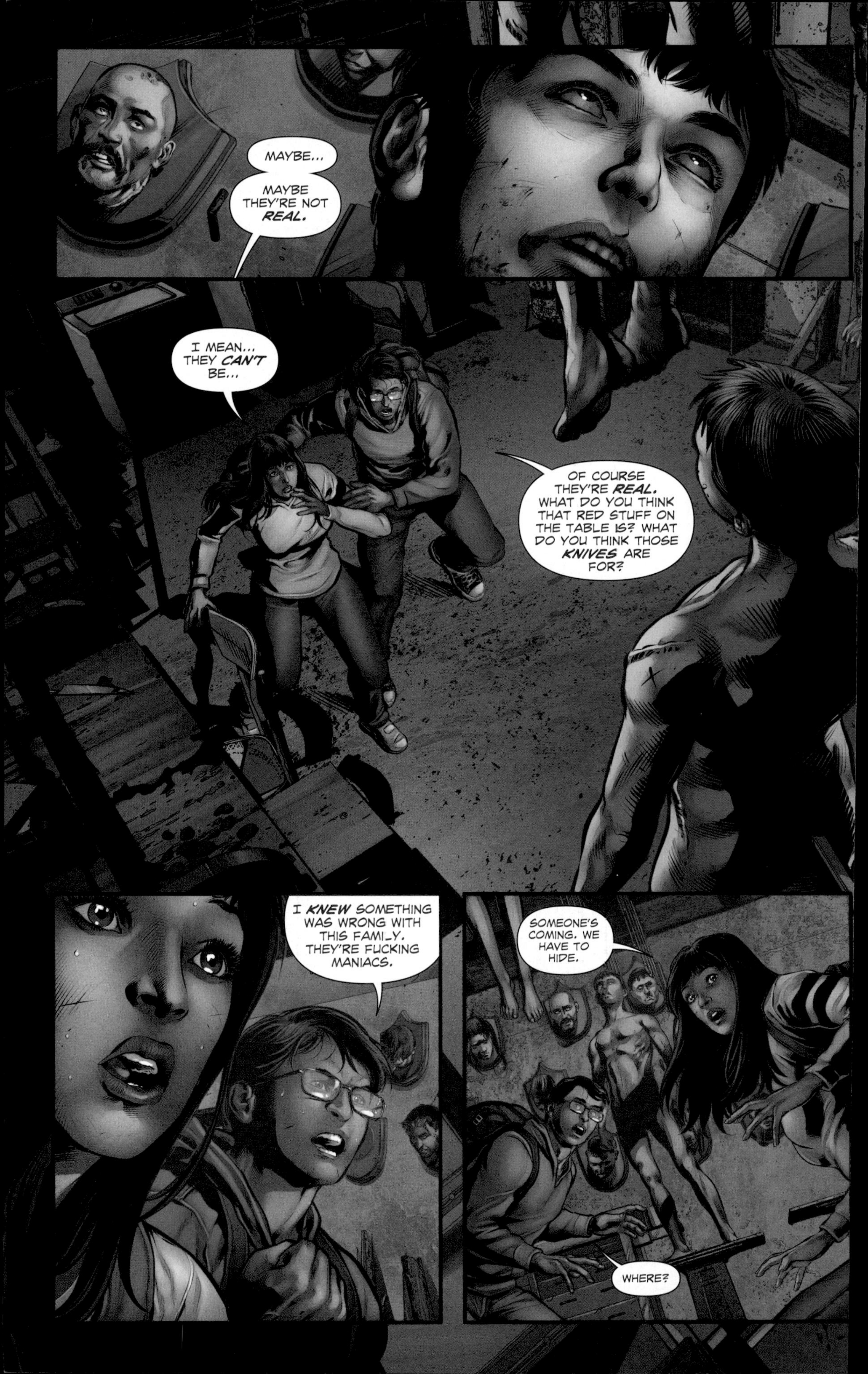
MAYBE...
MAYBE THEY'RE NOT *REAL.*
I MEAN... THEY *CAN'T* BE...
OF COURSE THEY'RE *REAL.* WHAT DO YOU THINK THAT RED STUFF ON THE TABLE IS? WHAT DO YOU THINK THOSE *KNIVES* ARE FOR?
I *KNEW* SOMETHING WAS WRONG WITH THIS FAMILY. THEY'RE FUCKING MANIACS.
SOMEONE'S COMING. WE HAVE TO HIDE.
WHERE?

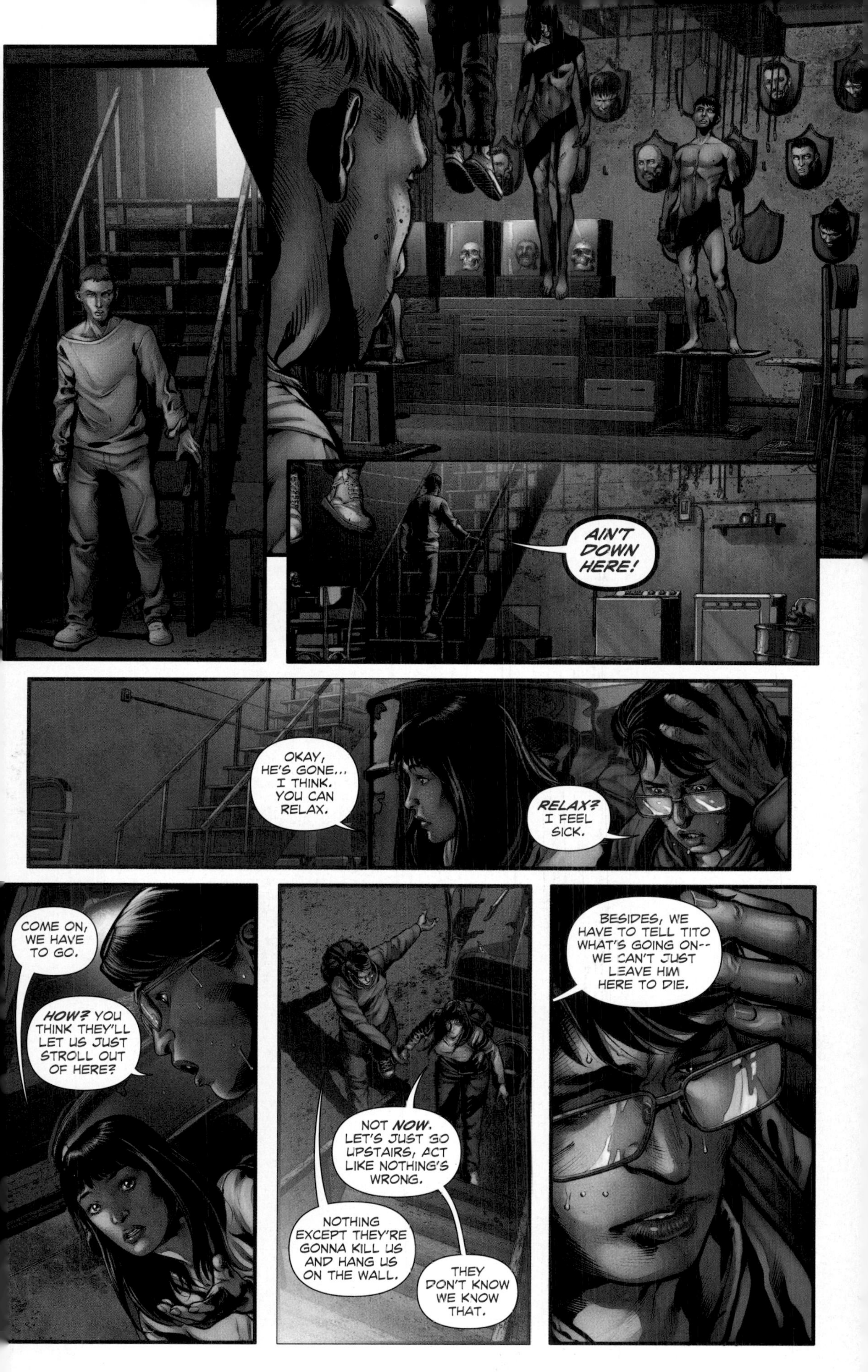
AIN'T DOWN HERE!
OKAY, HE'S GONE... I THINK. YOU CAN RELAX.
RELAX? I FEEL SICK.
COME ON, WE HAVE TO GO.
HOW? YOU THINK THEY'LL LET US JUST STROLL OUT OF HERE?
NOT NOW. LET'S JUST GO UPSTAIRS, ACT LIKE NOTHING'S WRONG.
NOTHING EXCEPT THEY'RE GONNA KILL US AND HANG US ON THE WALL.
THEY DON'T KNOW WE KNOW THAT.
BESIDES, WE HAVE TO TELL TITO WHAT'S GOING ON-- WE CAN'T JUST LEAVE HIM HERE TO DIE.

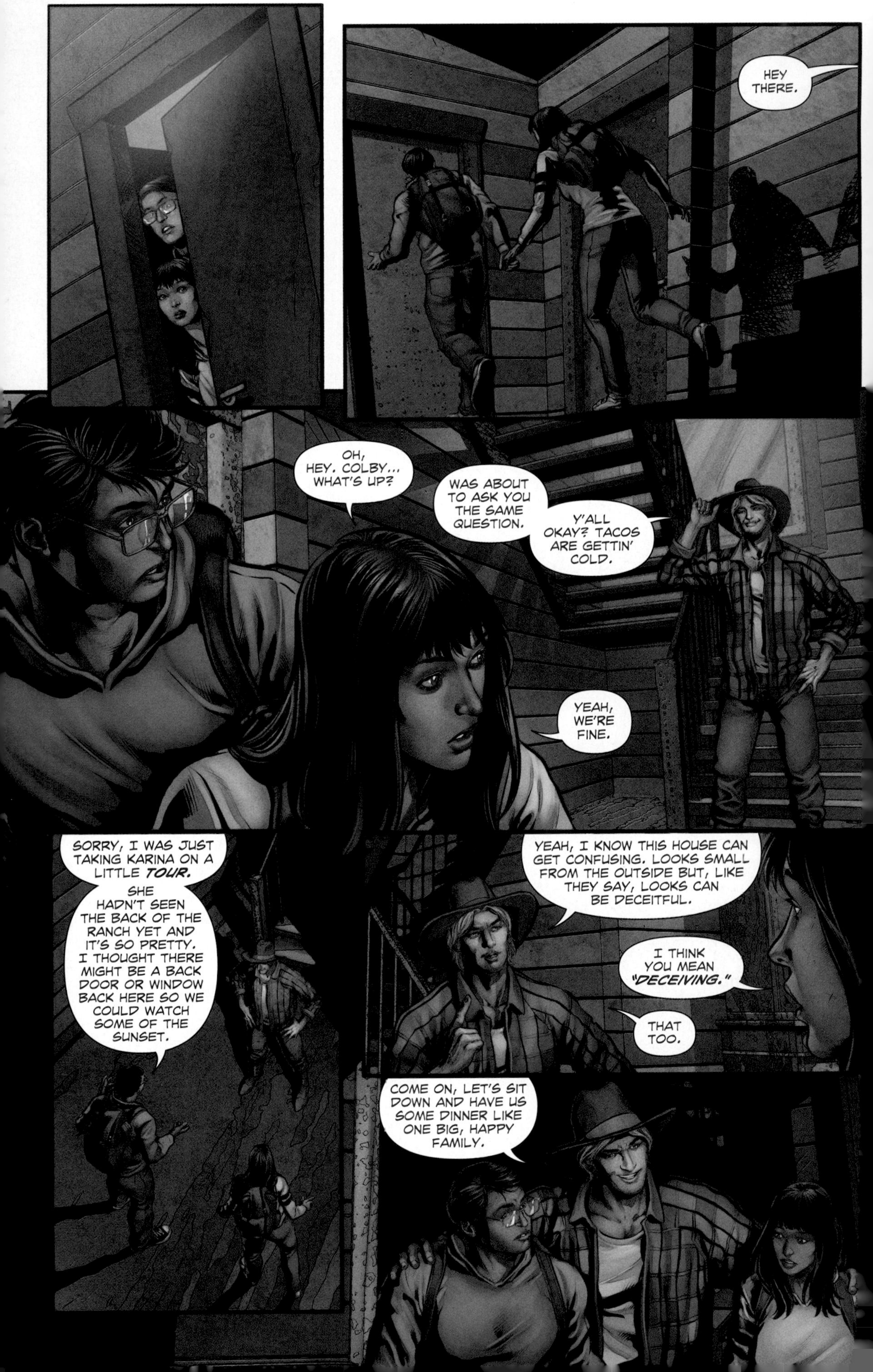
HEY THERE.
OH, HEY. COLBY... WHAT'S UP?
WAS ABOUT TO ASK YOU THE SAME QUESTION.
Y'ALL OKAY? TACOS ARE GETTIN' COLD.
YEAH, WE'RE FINE.
SORRY, I WAS JUST TAKING KARINA ON A LITTLE ***TOUR.***
SHE HADN'T SEEN THE BACK OF THE RANCH YET AND IT'S SO PRETTY. I THOUGHT THERE MIGHT BE A BACK DOOR OR WINDOW BACK HERE SO WE COULD WATCH SOME OF THE SUNSET.
YEAH, I KNOW THIS HOUSE CAN GET CONFUSING. LOOKS SMALL FROM THE OUTSIDE BUT, LIKE THEY SAY, LOOKS CAN BE DECEITFUL.
I THINK YOU MEAN ***"DECEIVING."***
THAT TOO.
COME ON, LET'S SIT DOWN AND HAVE US SOME DINNER LIKE ONE BIG, HAPPY FAMILY.

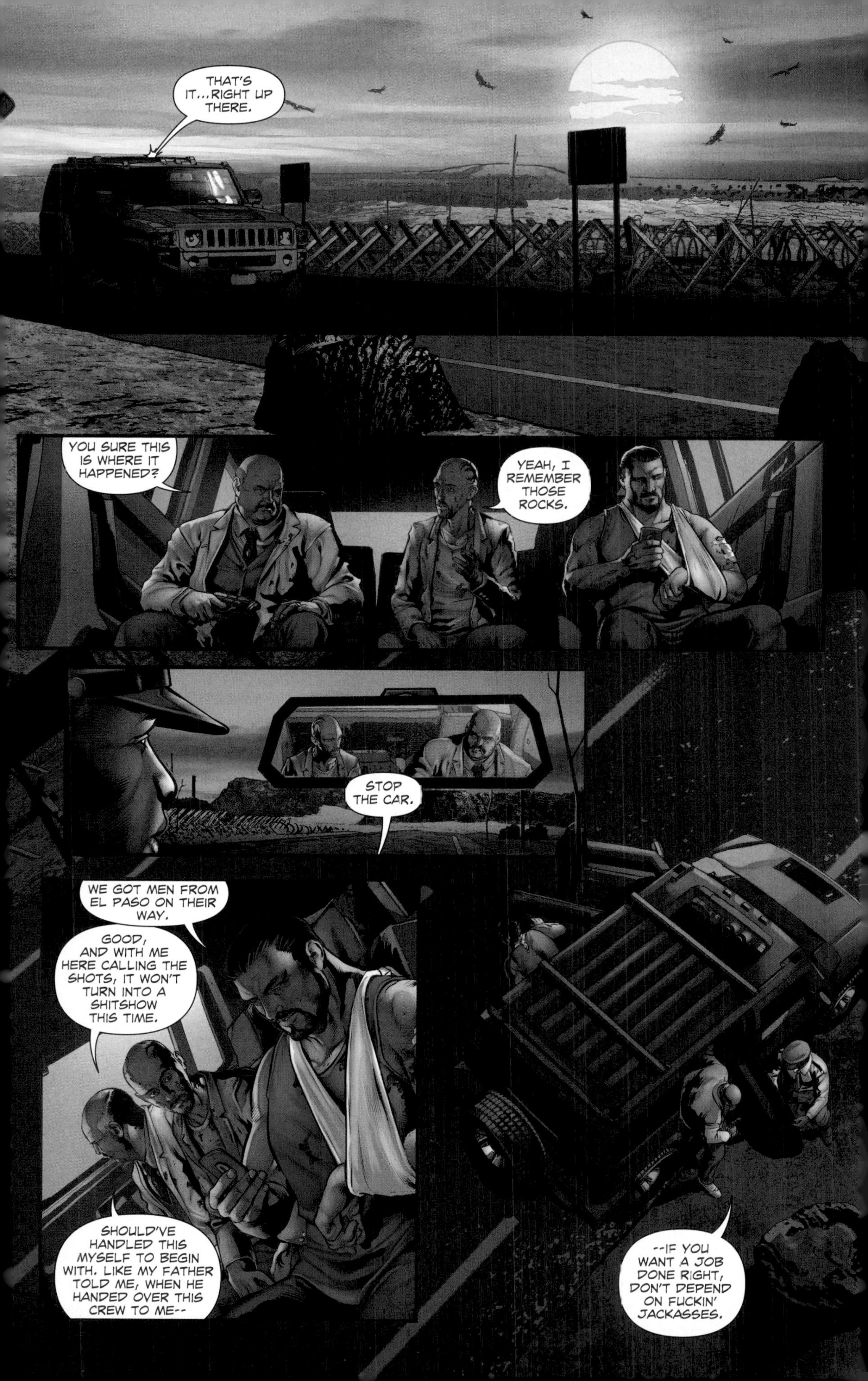
THAT'S IT...RIGHT UP THERE.
YOU SURE THIS IS WHERE IT HAPPENED?
YEAH, I REMEMBER THOSE ROCKS.
STOP THE CAR.
WE GOT MEN FROM EL PASO ON THEIR WAY.
GOOD, AND WITH ME HERE CALLING THE SHOTS, IT WON'T TURN INTO A SHITSHOW THIS TIME.
SHOULD'VE HANDLED THIS MYSELF TO BEGIN WITH. LIKE MY FATHER TOLD ME, WHEN HE HANDED OVER THIS CREW TO ME--
--IF YOU WANT A JOB DONE RIGHT, DON'T DEPEND ON FUCKIN' JACKASSES.

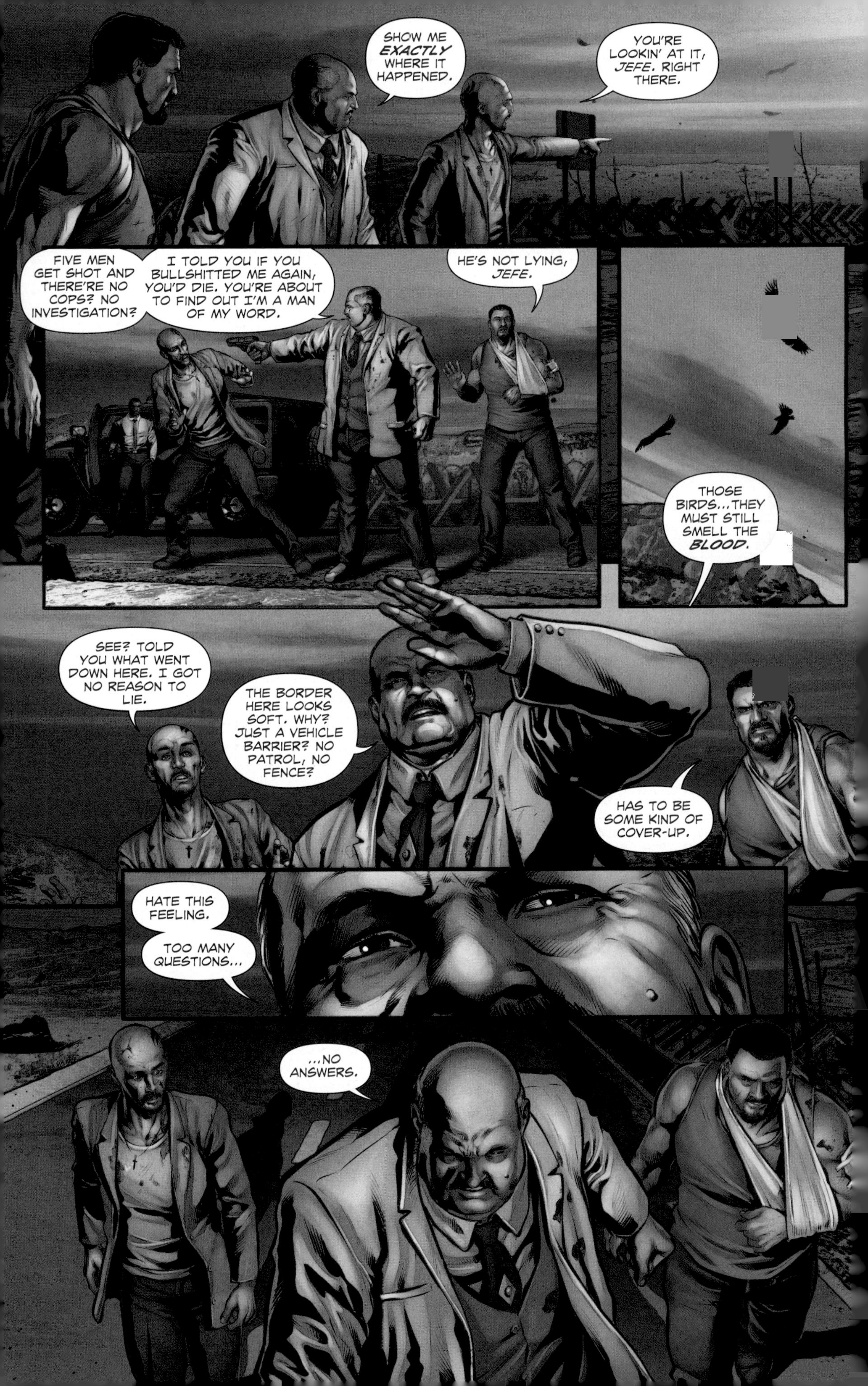
SHOW ME *EXACTLY* WHERE IT HAPPENED.
YOU'RE LOOKIN' AT IT, *JEFE*. RIGHT THERE.
FIVE MEN GET SHOT AND THERE'RE NO COPS? NO INVESTIGATION?
I TOLD YOU IF YOU BULLSHITTED ME AGAIN, YOU'D DIE. YOU'RE ABOUT TO FIND OUT I'M A MAN OF MY WORD.
HE'S NOT LYING, *JEFE*.
THOSE BIRDS...THEY MUST STILL SMELL THE *BLOOD*.
SEE? TOLD YOU WHAT WENT DOWN HERE. I GOT NO REASON TO LIE.
THE BORDER HERE LOOKS SOFT. WHY? JUST A VEHICLE BARRIER? NO PATROL, NO FENCE?
HAS TO BE SOME KIND OF COVER-UP.
HATE THIS FEELING.
TOO MANY QUESTIONS...
...NO ANSWERS.

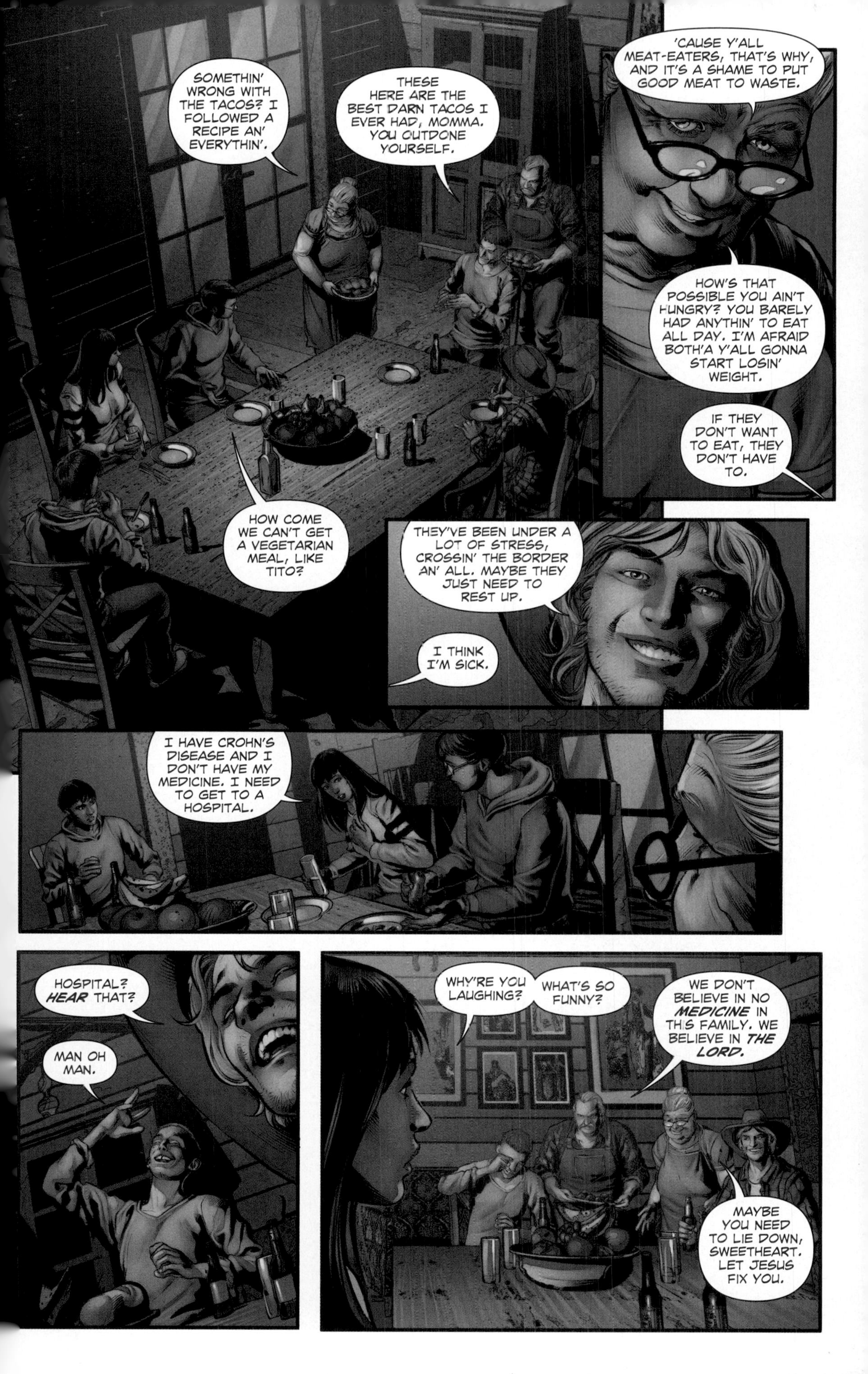

SOMETHIN' WRONG WITH THE TACOS? I FOLLOWED A RECIPE AN' EVERYTHIN'.
THESE HERE ARE THE BEST DARN TACOS I EVER HAD, MOMMA. YOU OUTDONE YOURSELF.
HOW COME WE CAN'T GET A VEGETARIAN MEAL, LIKE TITO?
'CAUSE Y'ALL MEAT-EATERS, THAT'S WHY, AND IT'S A SHAME TO PUT GOOD MEAT TO WASTE.
HOW'S THAT POSSIBLE YOU AIN'T HUNGRY? YOU BARELY HAD ANYTHIN' TO EAT ALL DAY. I'M AFRAID BOTH'A Y'ALL GONNA START LOSIN' WEIGHT.
IF THEY DON'T WANT TO EAT, THEY DON'T HAVE TO.
THEY'VE BEEN UNDER A LOT OF STRESS, CROSSIN' THE BORDER AN' ALL. MAYBE THEY JUST NEED TO REST UP.
I THINK I'M SICK.
I HAVE CROHN'S DISEASE AND I DON'T HAVE MY MEDICINE. I NEED TO GET TO A HOSPITAL.
HOSPITAL? ***HEAR*** THAT?
MAN OH MAN.
WHY'RE YOU LAUGHING?
WHAT'S SO FUNNY?
WE DON'T BELIEVE IN NO ***MEDICINE*** IN THIS FAMILY. WE BELIEVE IN ***THE LORD.***
MAYBE YOU NEED TO LIE DOWN, SWEETHEART. LET JESUS FIX YOU.

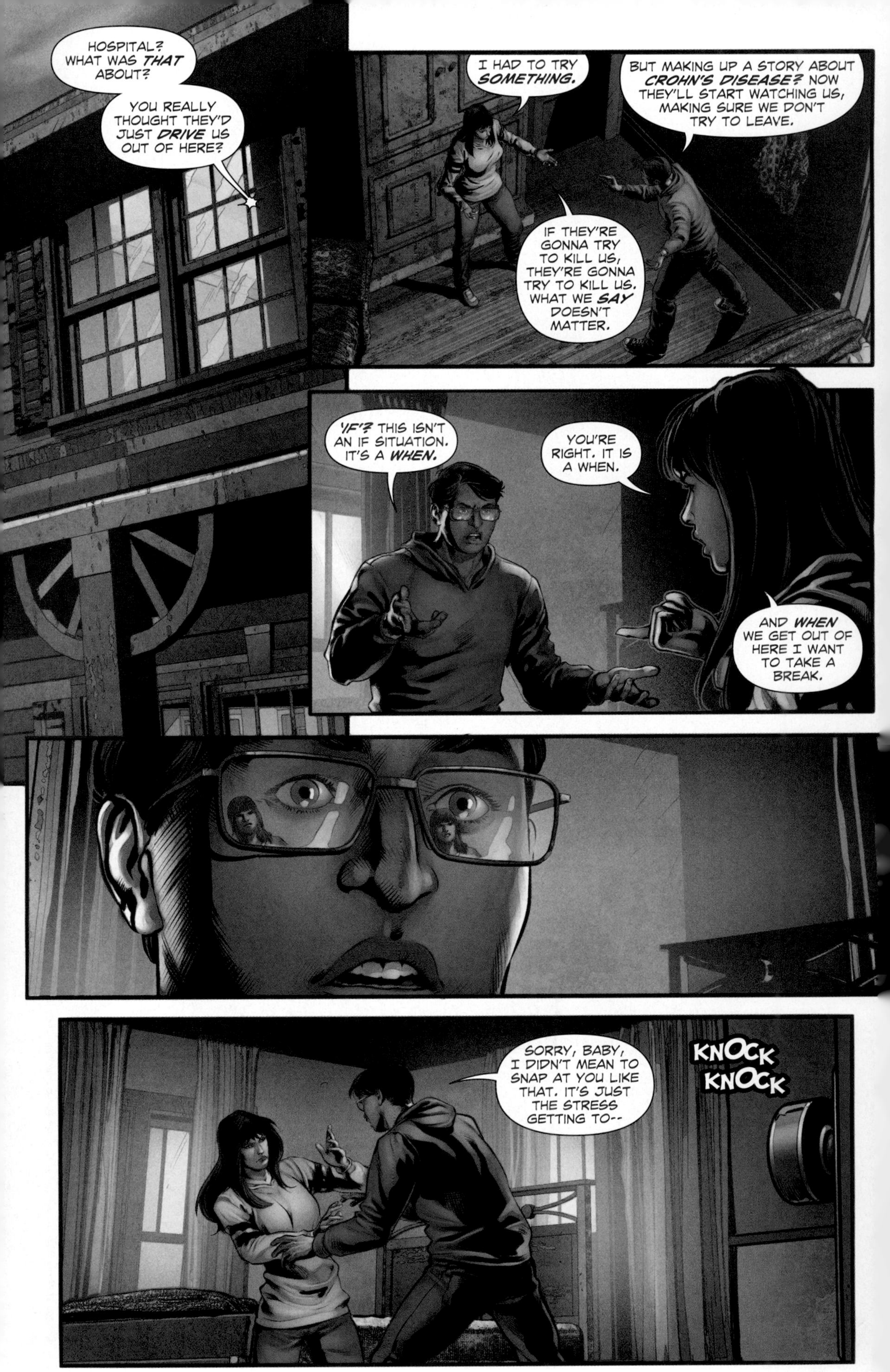
HOSPITAL? WHAT WAS THAT ABOUT?
YOU REALLY THOUGHT THEY'D JUST DRIVE US OUT OF HERE?
I HAD TO TRY SOMETHING.
BUT MAKING UP A STORY ABOUT CROHN'S DISEASE? NOW THEY'LL START WATCHING US, MAKING SURE WE DON'T TRY TO LEAVE.
IF THEY'RE GONNA TRY TO KILL US, THEY'RE GONNA TRY TO KILL US. WHAT WE SAY DOESN'T MATTER.
'IF'? THIS ISN'T AN IF SITUATION. IT'S A WHEN.
YOU'RE RIGHT. IT IS A WHEN.
AND WHEN WE GET OUT OF HERE I WANT TO TAKE A BREAK.
SORRY, BABY, I DIDN'T MEAN TO SNAP AT YOU LIKE THAT. IT'S JUST THE STRESS GETTING TO--
KNOCK KNOCK

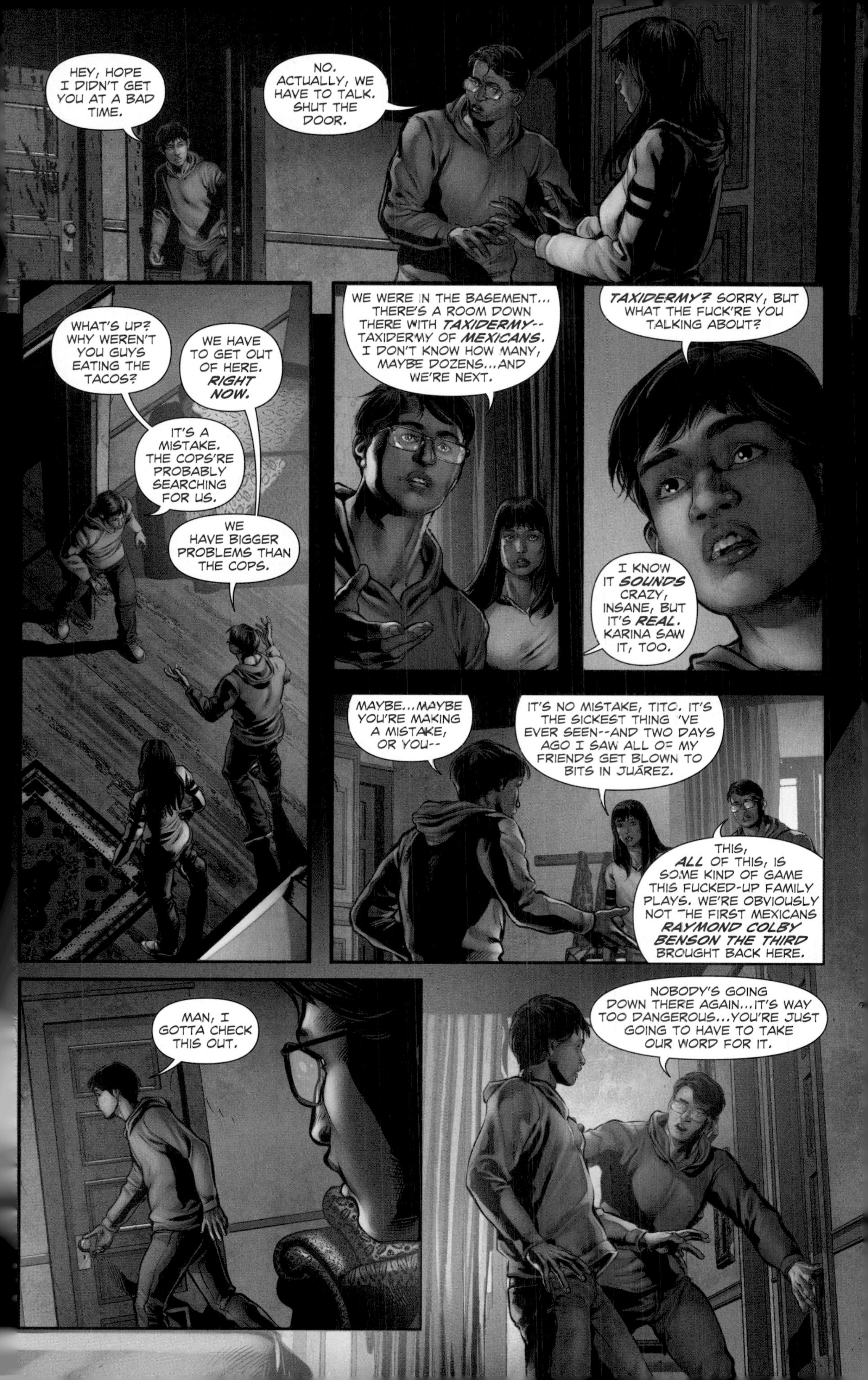
HEY, HOPE I DIDN'T GET YOU AT A BAD TIME.
NO. ACTUALLY, WE HAVE TO TALK. SHUT THE DOOR.
WHAT'S UP? WHY WEREN'T YOU GUYS EATING THE TACOS?
WE HAVE TO GET OUT OF HERE. RIGHT NOW.
IT'S A MISTAKE. THE COPS'RE PROBABLY SEARCHING FOR US.
WE HAVE BIGGER PROBLEMS THAN THE COPS.
WE WERE IN THE BASEMENT... THERE'S A ROOM DOWN THERE WITH TAXIDERMY-- TAXIDERMY OF MEXICANS. I DON'T KNOW HOW MANY, MAYBE DOZENS...AND WE'RE NEXT.
TAXIDERMY? SORRY, BUT WHAT THE FUCK'RE YOU TALKING ABOUT?
I KNOW IT SOUNDS CRAZY, INSANE, BUT IT'S REAL. KARINA SAW IT, TOO.
MAYBE...MAYBE YOU'RE MAKING A MISTAKE, OR YOU--
IT'S NO MISTAKE, TITO. IT'S THE SICKEST THING I'VE EVER SEEN--AND TWO DAYS AGO I SAW ALL OF MY FRIENDS GET BLOWN TO BITS IN JUÁREZ.
THIS, ALL OF THIS, IS SOME KIND OF GAME THIS FUCKED-UP FAMILY PLAYS. WE'RE OBVIOUSLY NOT THE FIRST MEXICANS RAYMOND COLBY BENSON THE THIRD BROUGHT BACK HERE.
MAN, I GOTTA CHECK THIS OUT.
NOBODY'S GOING DOWN THERE AGAIN...IT'S WAY TOO DANGEROUS...YOU'RE JUST GOING TO HAVE TO TAKE OUR WORD FOR IT.

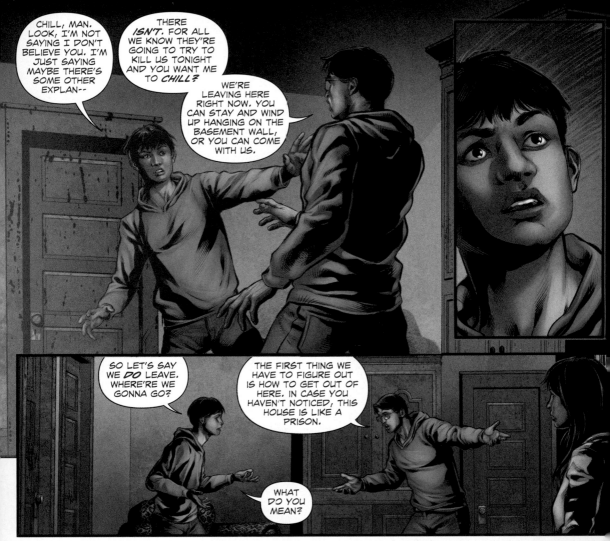

CHILL, MAN. LOOK, I'M NOT SAYING I DON'T BELIEVE YOU. I'M JUST SAYING MAYBE THERE'S SOME OTHER EXPLAN--

THERE *ISN'T*. FOR ALL WE KNOW THEY'RE GOING TO TRY TO KILL US TONIGHT AND YOU WANT ME TO *CHILL*?

WE'RE LEAVING HERE RIGHT NOW. YOU CAN STAY AND WIND UP HANGING ON THE BASEMENT WALL, OR YOU CAN COME WITH US.

SO LET'S SAY WE *DO* LEAVE. WHERE'RE WE GONNA GO?

THE FIRST THING WE HAVE TO FIGURE OUT IS HOW TO GET OUT OF HERE. IN CASE YOU HAVEN'T NOTICED, THIS HOUSE IS LIKE A PRISON.

WHAT DO YOU MEAN?

HAVE YOU TRIED TO OPEN YOUR WINDOW?

YEAH, I TRIED TO OPEN IT LAST NIGHT. THOUGHT IT WAS STUCK.

IT'S NOT STUCK, IT'S *LOCKED*. THEY'RE KEEPING US HERE, LIKE ANIMALS THEY'RE GETTING READY TO SLAUGHTER.

I SAY WE TAKE OUR CHANCES AND MAKE A RUN FOR IT TONIGHT.

NOT TONIGHT. *NOW.*

YOU HAVE YOUR LIGHTER?

WHY? YOU WANNA SMOKE A JOINT TO CALM DOWN?

JUST GIVE IT TO ME.

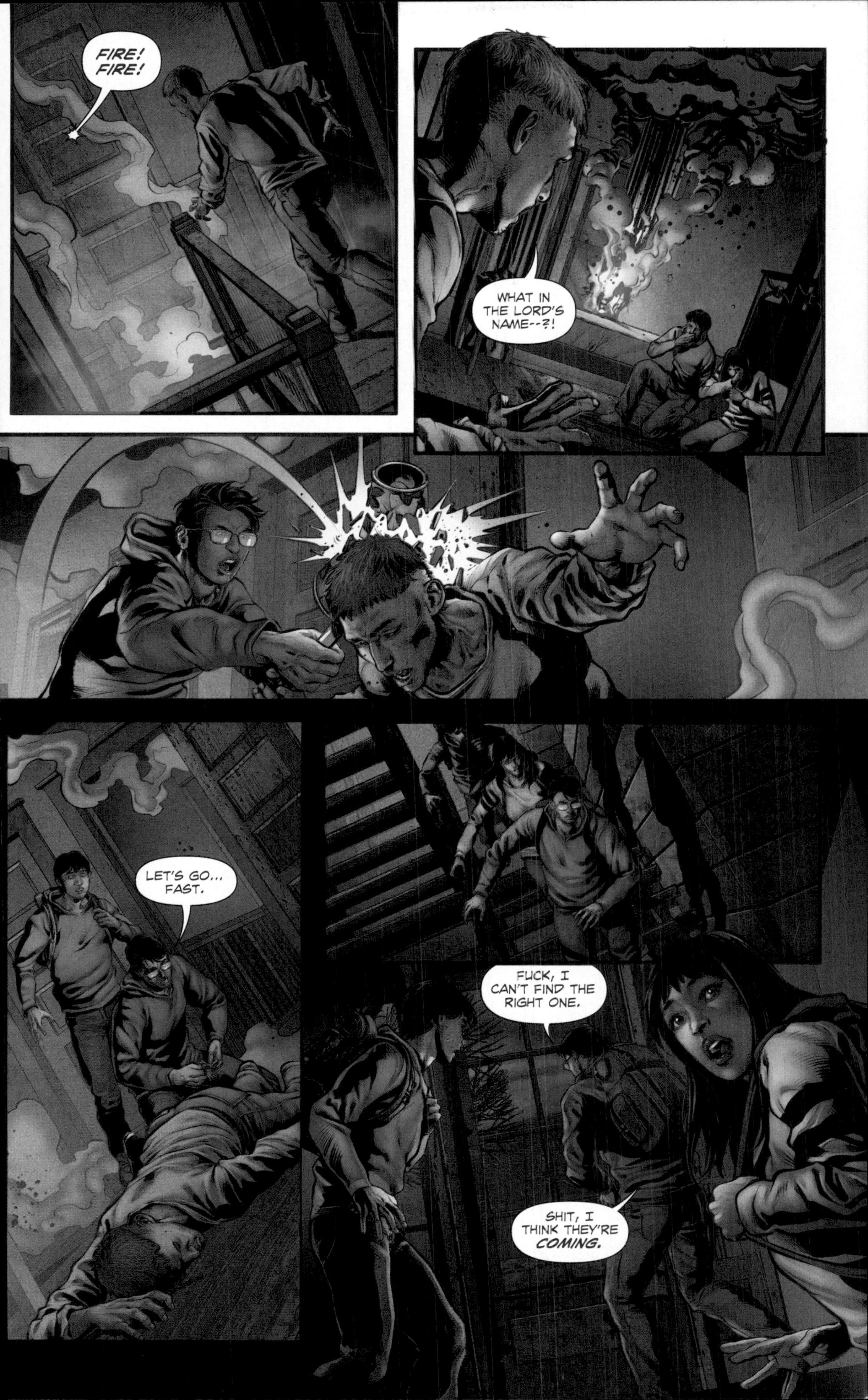
FIRE! FIRE!
WHAT IN THE LORD'S NAME--?!
LET'S GO... FAST.
FUCK, I CAN'T FIND THE RIGHT ONE.
SHIT, I THINK THEY'RE *COMING.*

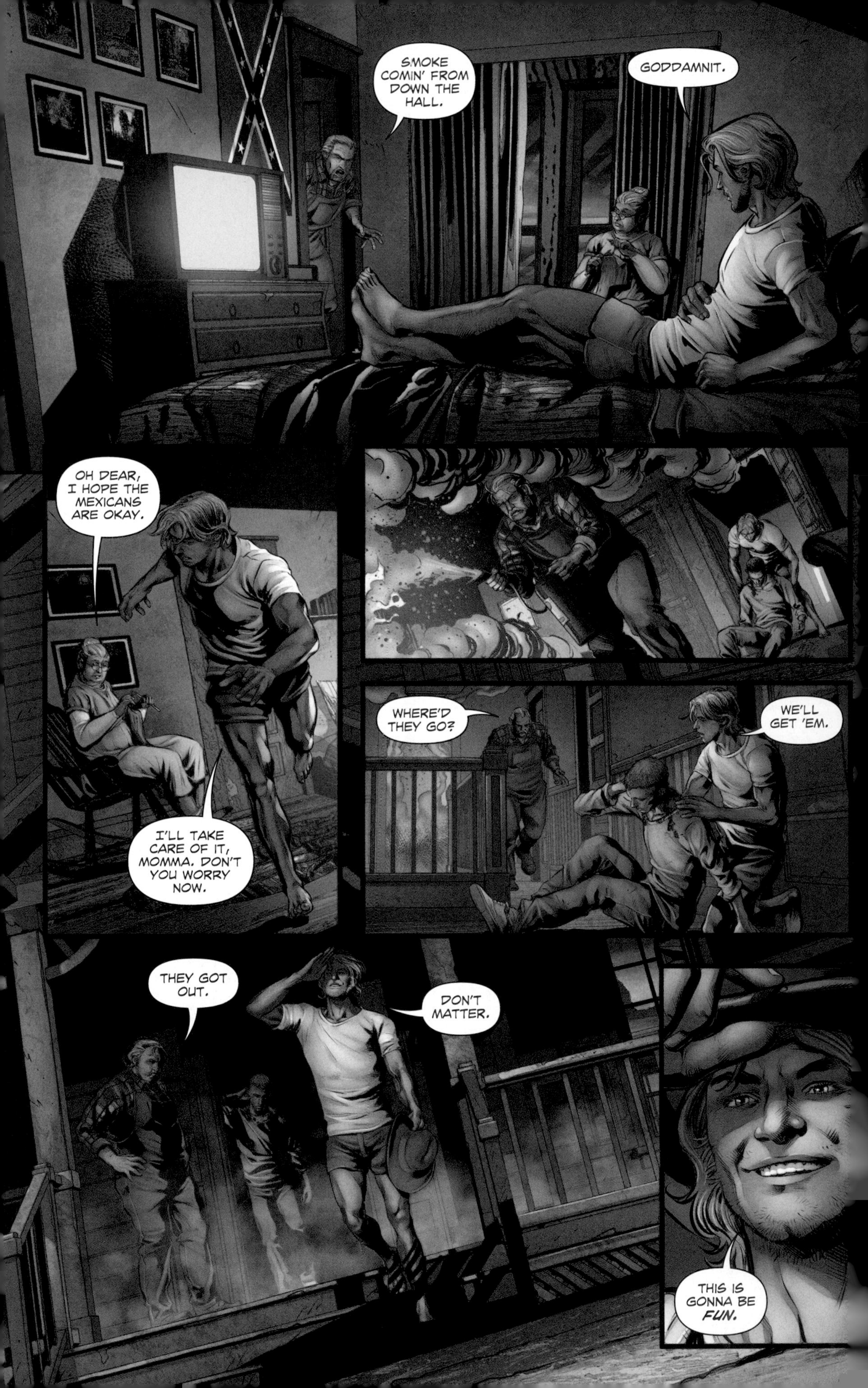
SMOKE COMIN' FROM DOWN THE HALL.
GODDAMNIT.
OH DEAR, I HOPE THE MEXICANS ARE OKAY.
I'LL TAKE CARE OF IT, MOMMA. DON'T YOU WORRY NOW.
WHERE'D THEY GO?
WE'LL GET 'EM.
THEY GOT OUT.
DON'T MATTER.
THIS IS GONNA BE *FUN.*

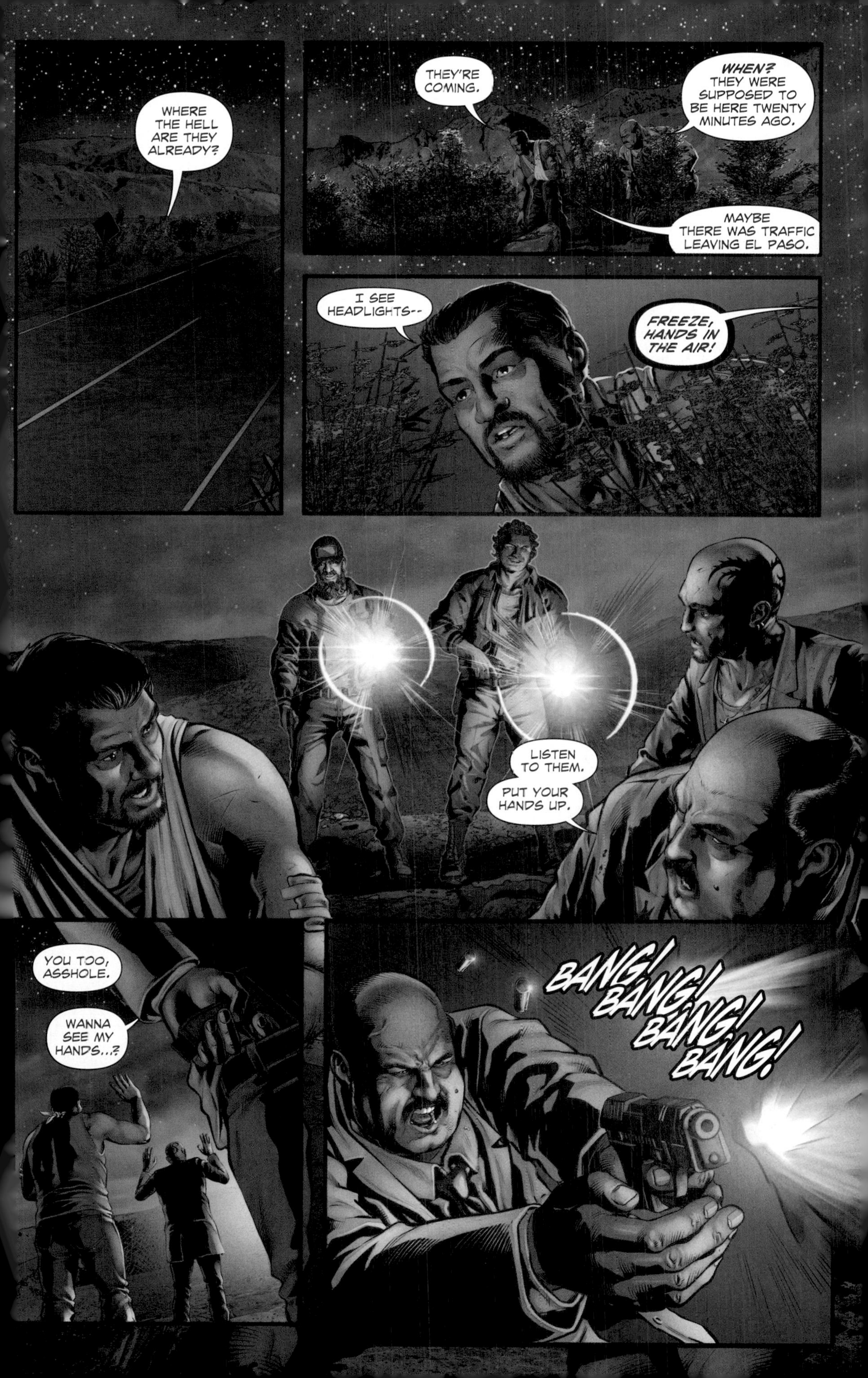
WHERE THE HELL ARE THEY ALREADY?
THEY'RE COMING.
WHEN? THEY WERE SUPPOSED TO BE HERE TWENTY MINUTES AGO.
MAYBE THERE WAS TRAFFIC LEAVING EL PASO.
I SEE HEADLIGHTS--
FREEZE, HANDS IN THE AIR!
LISTEN TO THEM.
PUT YOUR HANDS UP.
YOU TOO, ASSHOLE.
WANNA SEE MY HANDS...?
BANG! BANG! BANG! BANG!

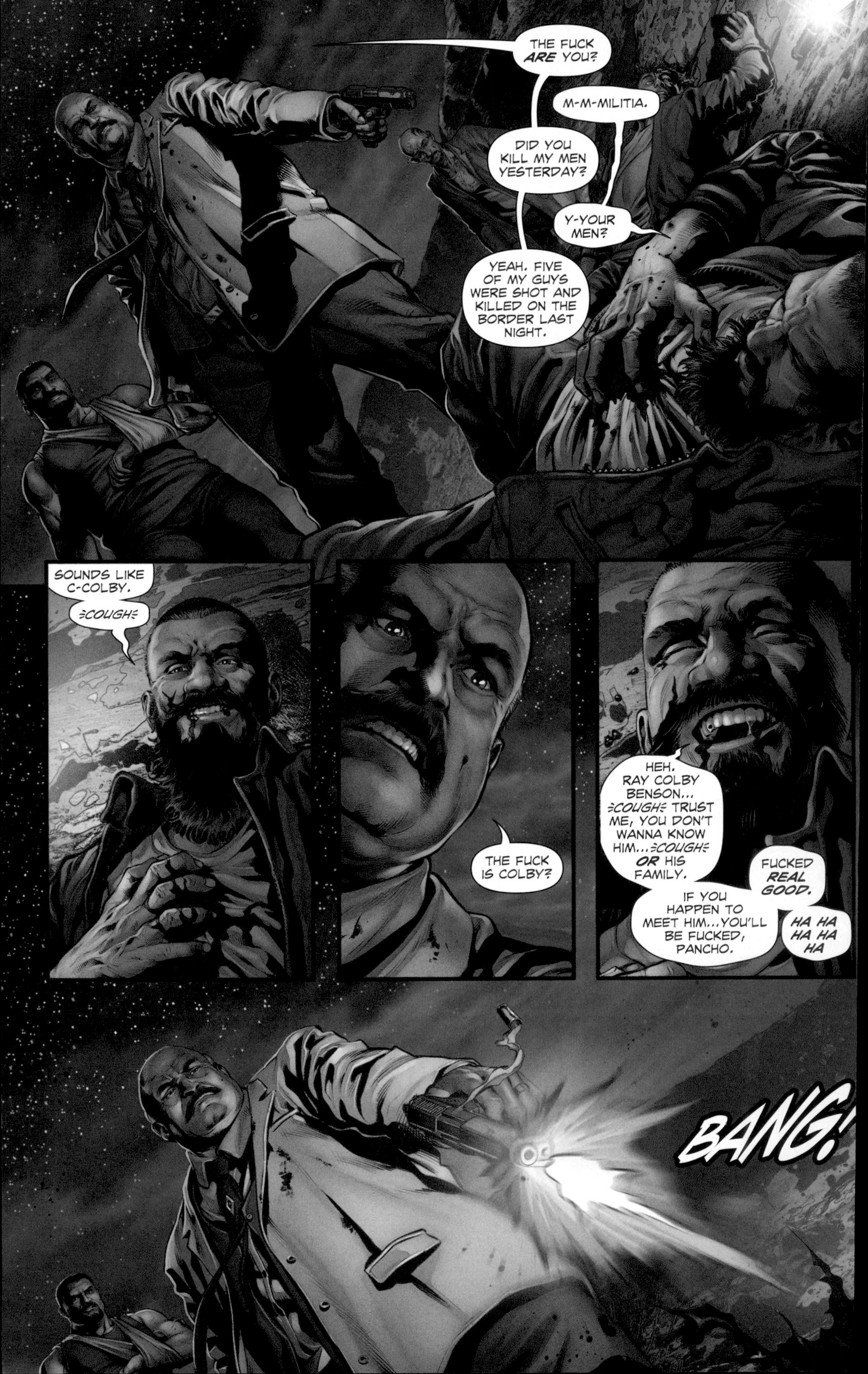
THE FUCK *ARE* YOU?
M-M-MILITIA.
DID YOU KILL MY MEN YESTERDAY?
Y-YOUR MEN?
YEAH. FIVE OF MY GUYS WERE SHOT AND KILLED ON THE BORDER LAST NIGHT.
SOUNDS LIKE C-COLBY.
COUGH
THE FUCK IS COLBY?
HEH. RAY COLBY BENSON... *COUGH* TRUST ME, YOU DON'T WANNA KNOW HIM... *COUGH* *OR* HIS FAMILY.
IF YOU HAPPEN TO MEET HIM... YOU'LL BE FUCKED, PANCHO.
FUCKED *REAL GOOD.*
HA HA HA HA HA
BANG!

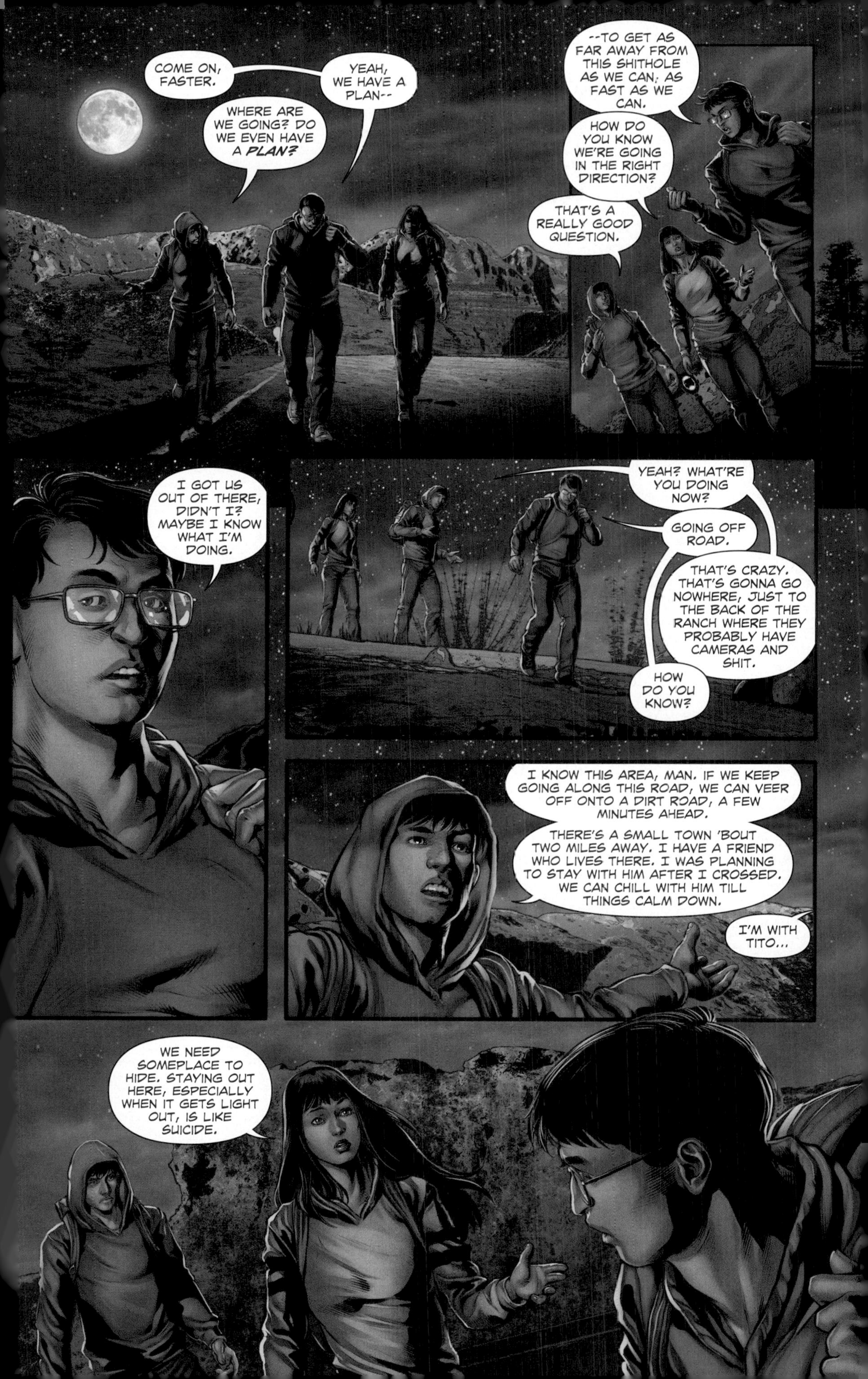
COME ON, FASTER.
WHERE ARE WE GOING? DO WE EVEN HAVE A PLAN?
YEAH, WE HAVE A PLAN--
--TO GET AS FAR AWAY FROM THIS SHITHOLE AS WE CAN; AS FAST AS WE CAN.
HOW DO YOU KNOW WE'RE GOING IN THE RIGHT DIRECTION?
THAT'S A REALLY GOOD QUESTION.
I GOT US OUT OF THERE, DIDN'T I? MAYBE I KNOW WHAT I'M DOING.
YEAH? WHAT'RE YOU DOING NOW?
GOING OFF ROAD.
THAT'S CRAZY. THAT'S GONNA GO NOWHERE, JUST TO THE BACK OF THE RANCH WHERE THEY PROBABLY HAVE CAMERAS AND SHIT.
HOW DO YOU KNOW?
I KNOW THIS AREA, MAN. IF WE KEEP GOING ALONG THIS ROAD, WE CAN VEER OFF ONTO A DIRT ROAD, A FEW MINUTES AHEAD.
THERE'S A SMALL TOWN 'BOUT TWO MILES AWAY. I HAVE A FRIEND WHO LIVES THERE. I WAS PLANNING TO STAY WITH HIM AFTER I CROSSED. WE CAN CHILL WITH HIM TILL THINGS CALM DOWN.
I'M WITH TITO...
WE NEED SOMEPLACE TO HIDE. STAYING OUT HERE, ESPECIALLY WHEN IT GETS LIGHT OUT, IS LIKE SUICIDE.

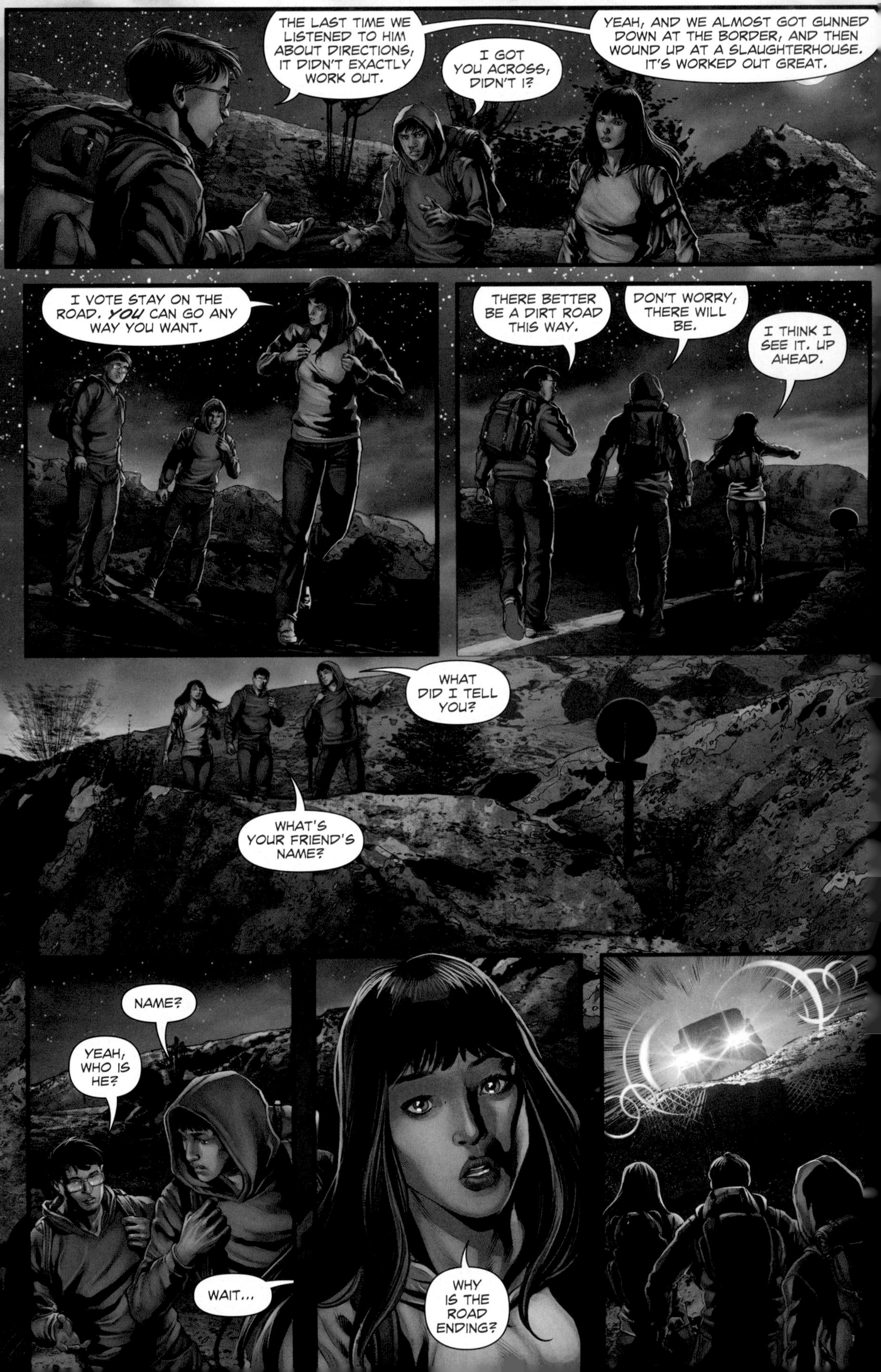
THE LAST TIME WE LISTENED TO HIM ABOUT DIRECTIONS, IT DIDN'T EXACTLY WORK OUT.
I GOT YOU ACROSS, DIDN'T I?
YEAH, AND WE ALMOST GOT GUNNED DOWN AT THE BORDER, AND THEN WOUND UP AT A SLAUGHTERHOUSE. IT'S WORKED OUT GREAT.
I VOTE STAY ON THE ROAD. YOU CAN GO ANY WAY YOU WANT.
THERE BETTER BE A DIRT ROAD THIS WAY.
DON'T WORRY, THERE WILL BE.
I THINK I SEE IT. UP AHEAD.
WHAT DID I TELL YOU?
WHAT'S YOUR FRIEND'S NAME?
NAME?
YEAH, WHO IS HE?
WAIT...
WHY IS THE ROAD ENDING?

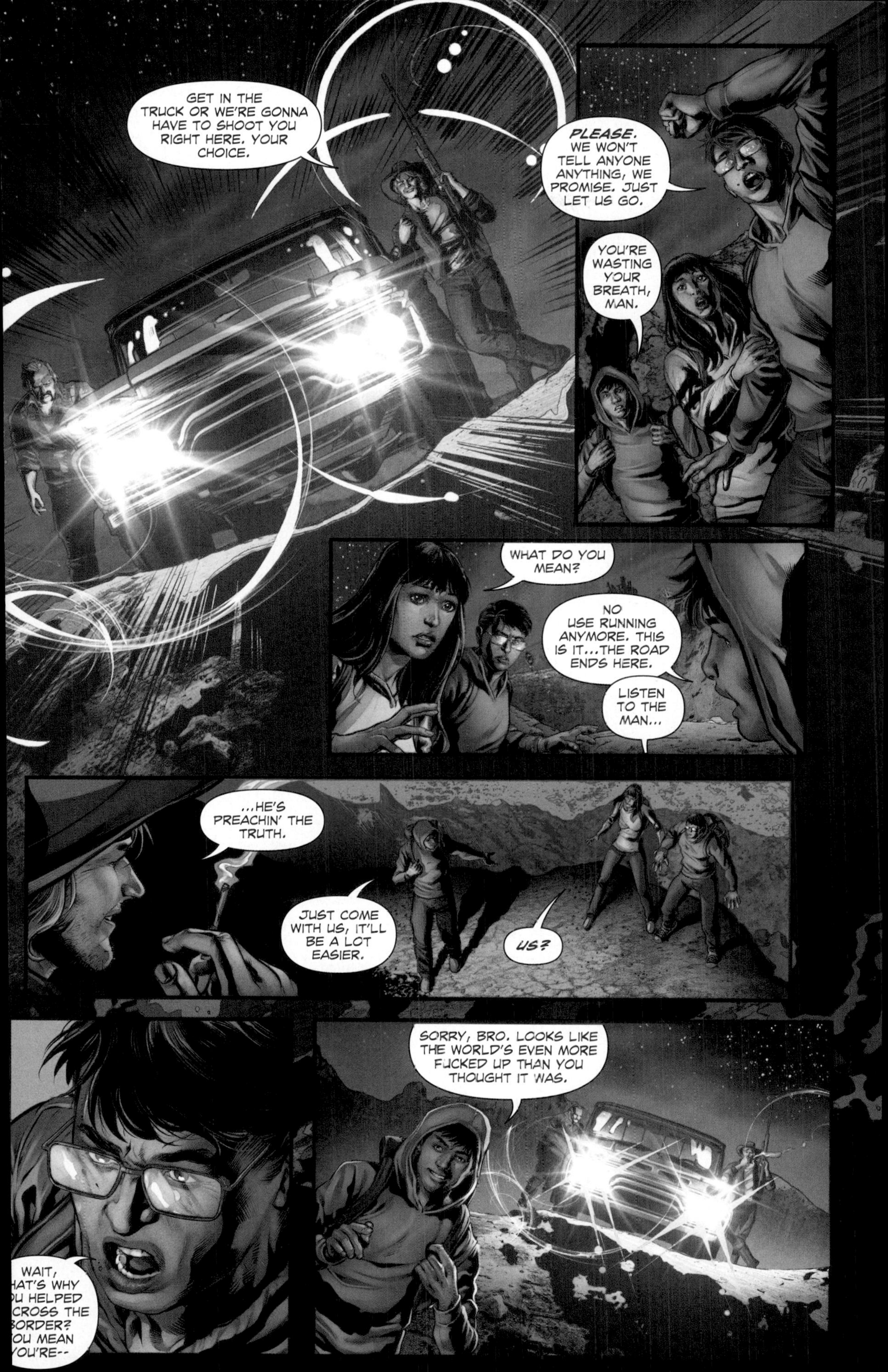
GET IN THE TRUCK OR WE'RE GONNA HAVE TO SHOOT YOU RIGHT HERE. YOUR CHOICE.
PLEASE. WE WON'T TELL ANYONE ANYTHING, WE PROMISE. JUST LET US GO.
YOU'RE WASTING YOUR BREATH, MAN.
WHAT DO YOU MEAN?
NO USE RUNNING ANYMORE. THIS IS IT...THE ROAD ENDS HERE.
LISTEN TO THE MAN...
...HE'S PREACHIN' THE TRUTH.
JUST COME WITH US, IT'LL BE A LOT EASIER.
US?
WAIT, HAT'S WHY OU HELPED CROSS THE BORDER? OU MEAN YOU'RE--
SORRY, BRO. LOOKS LIKE THE WORLD'S EVEN MORE FUCKED UP THAN YOU THOUGHT IT WAS.

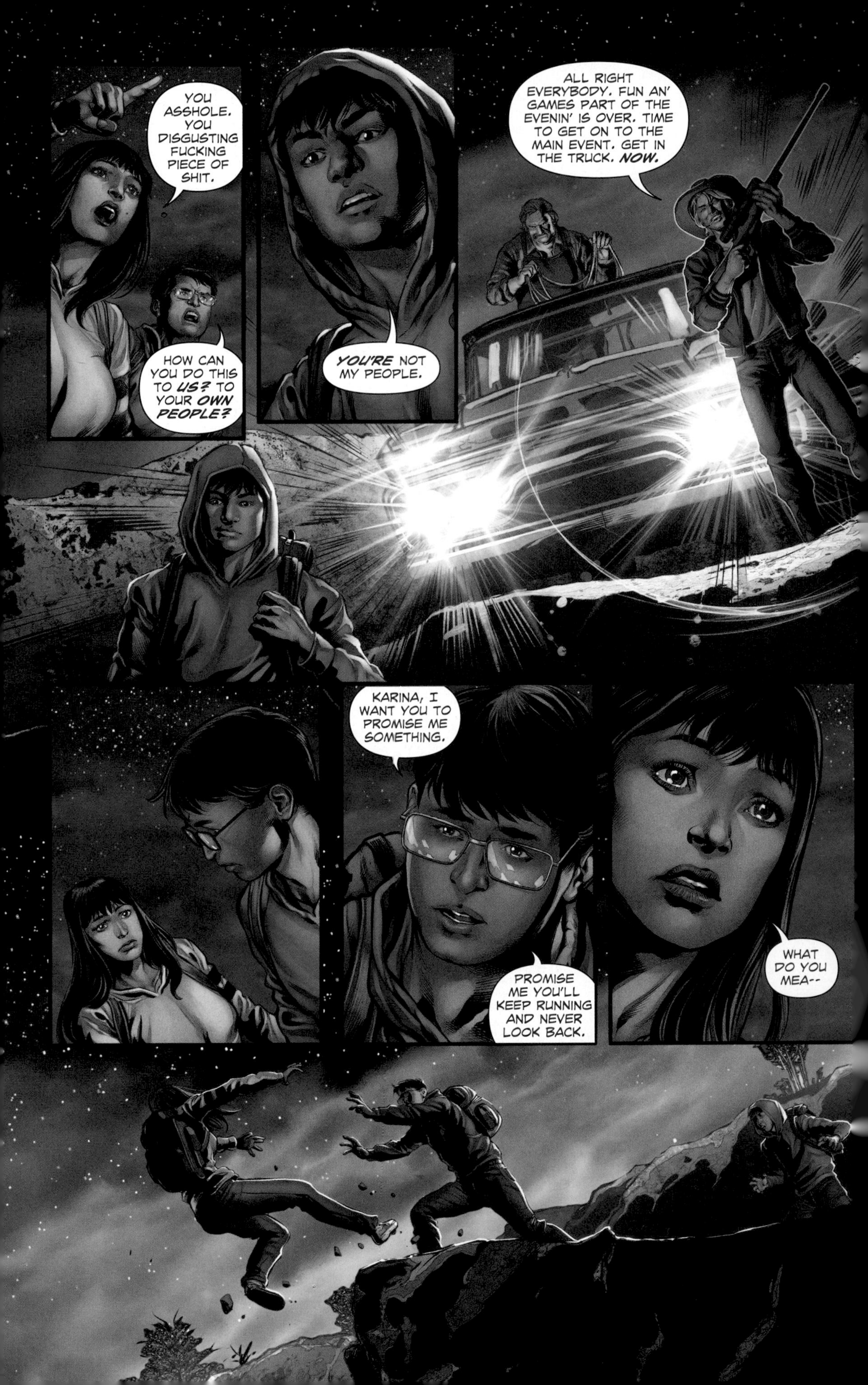
YOU ASSHOLE. YOU DISGUSTING FUCKING PIECE OF SHIT.
HOW CAN YOU DO THIS TO US? TO YOUR OWN PEOPLE?
YOU'RE NOT MY PEOPLE.
ALL RIGHT EVERYBODY. FUN AN' GAMES PART OF THE EVENIN' IS OVER. TIME TO GET ON TO THE MAIN EVENT. GET IN THE TRUCK. NOW.
KARINA, I WANT YOU TO PROMISE ME SOMETHING.
PROMISE ME YOU'LL KEEP RUNNING AND NEVER LOOK BACK.
WHAT DO YOU MEA--

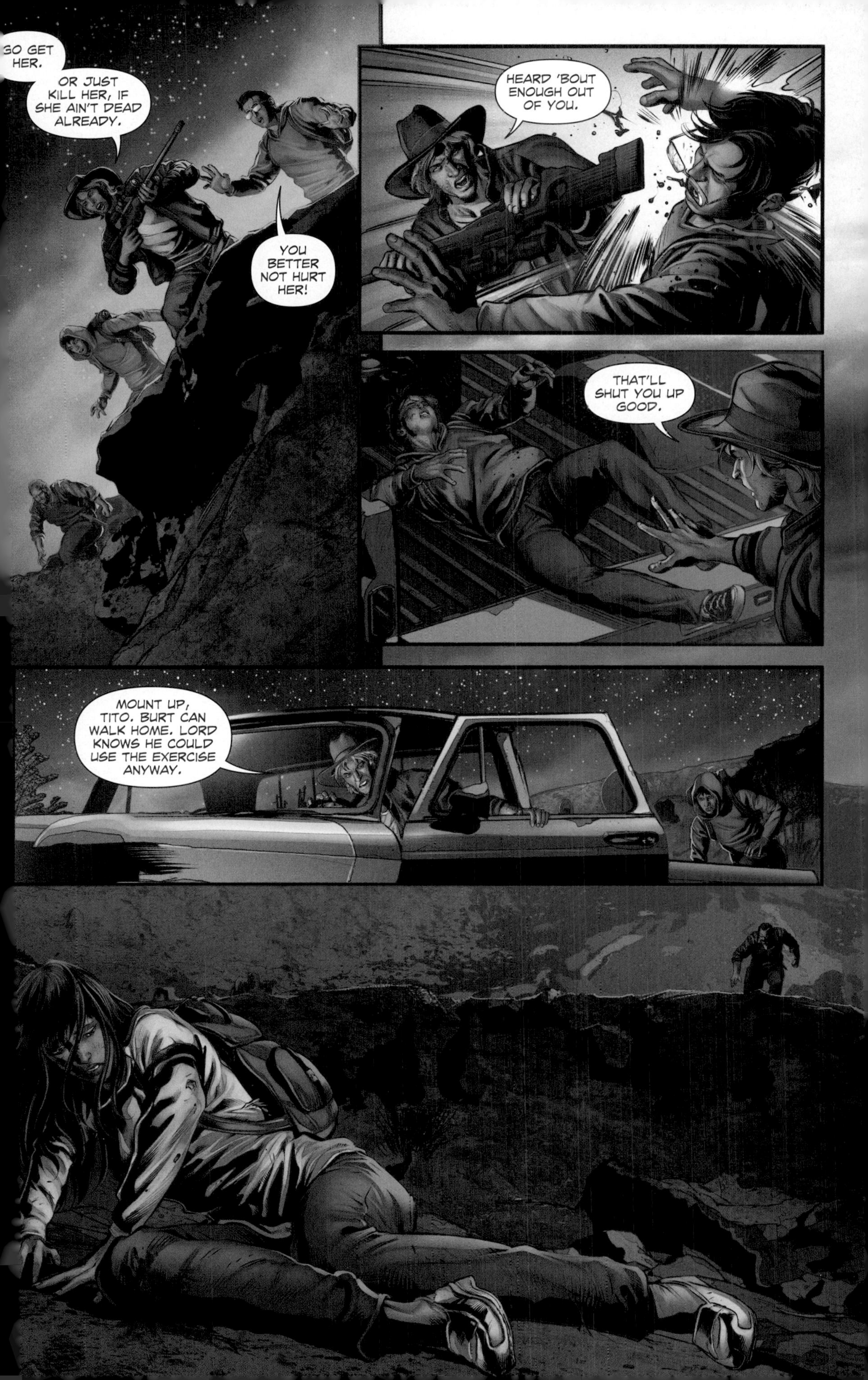
GO GET HER.
OR JUST KILL HER, IF SHE AIN'T DEAD ALREADY.
YOU BETTER NOT HURT HER!
HEARD 'BOUT ENOUGH OUT OF YOU.
THAT'LL SHUT YOU UP GOOD.
MOUNT UP, TITO. BURT CAN WALK HOME. LORD KNOWS HE COULD USE THE EXERCISE ANYWAY.

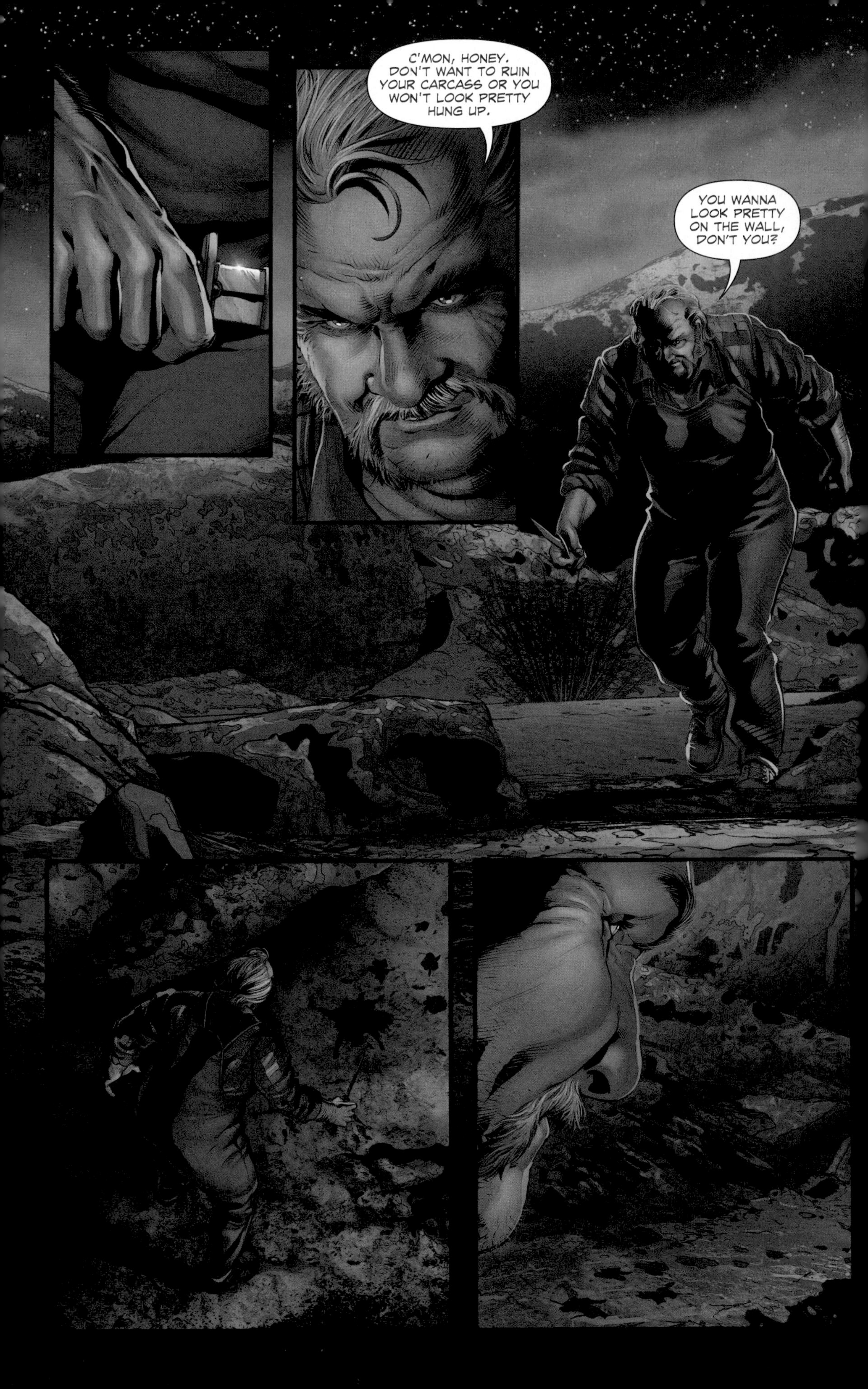
C'MON, HONEY. DON'T WANT TO RUIN YOUR CARCASS OR YOU WON'T LOOK PRETTY HUNG UP.
YOU WANNA LOOK PRETTY ON THE WALL, DON'T YOU?

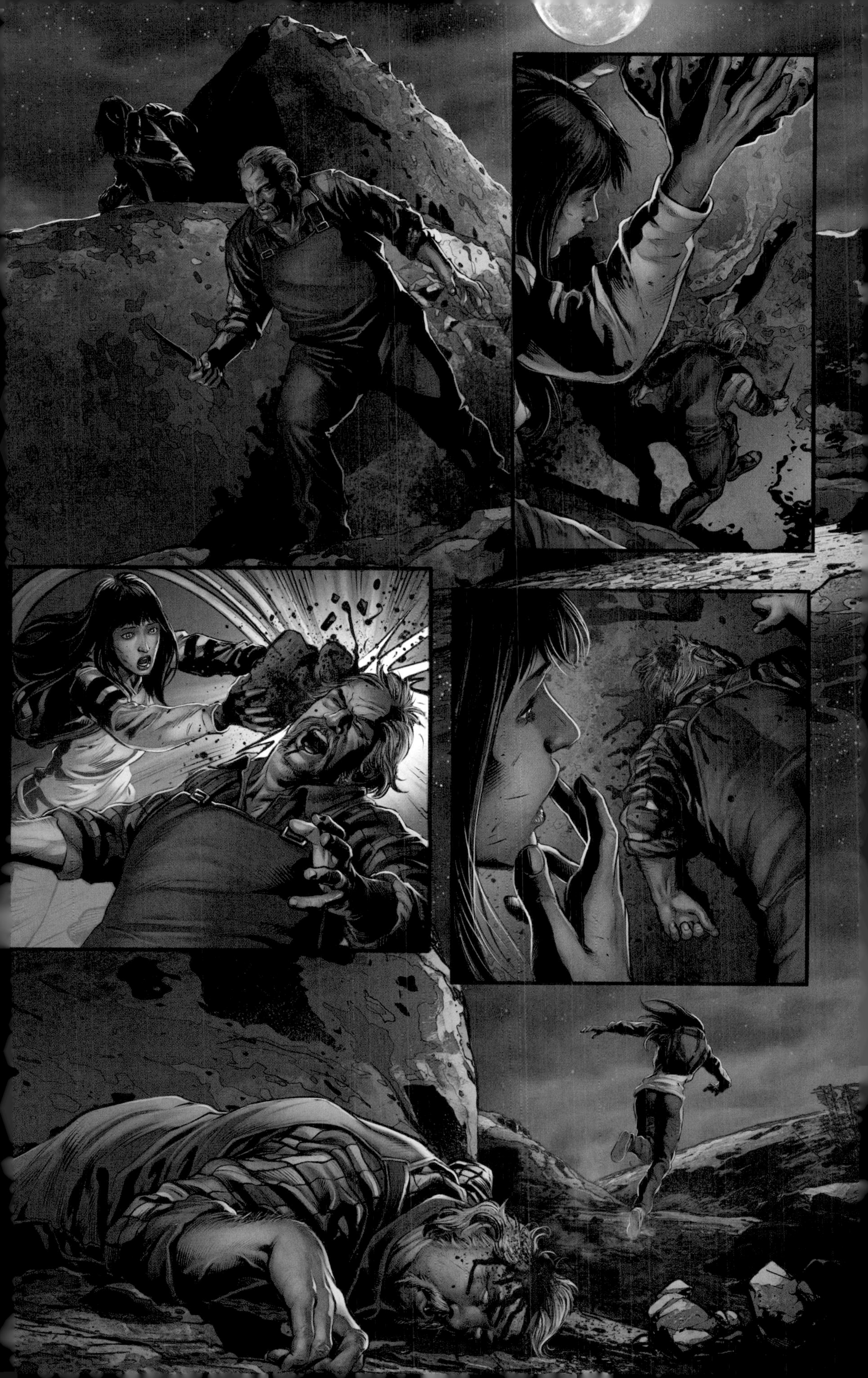

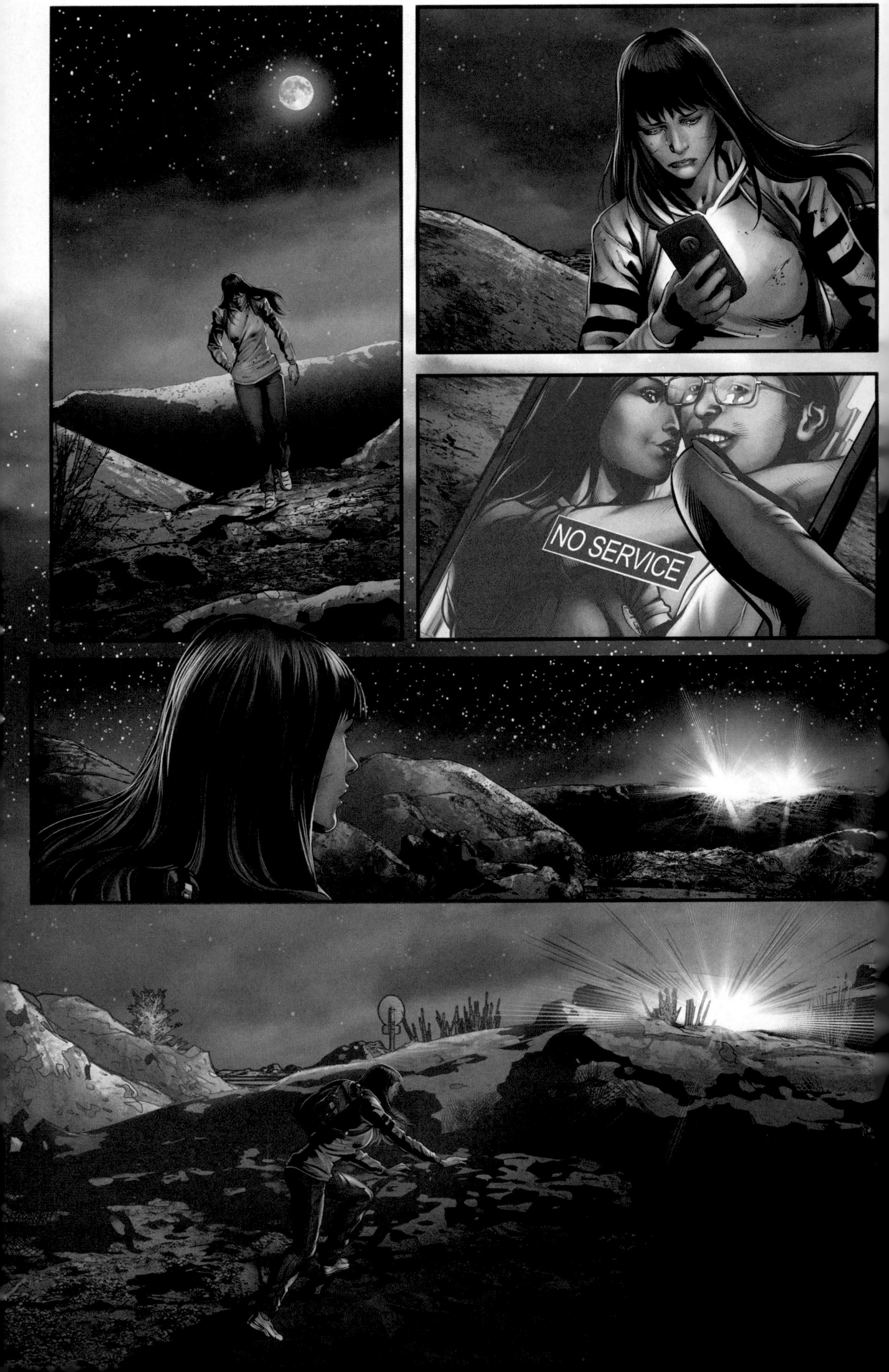
NO SERVICE

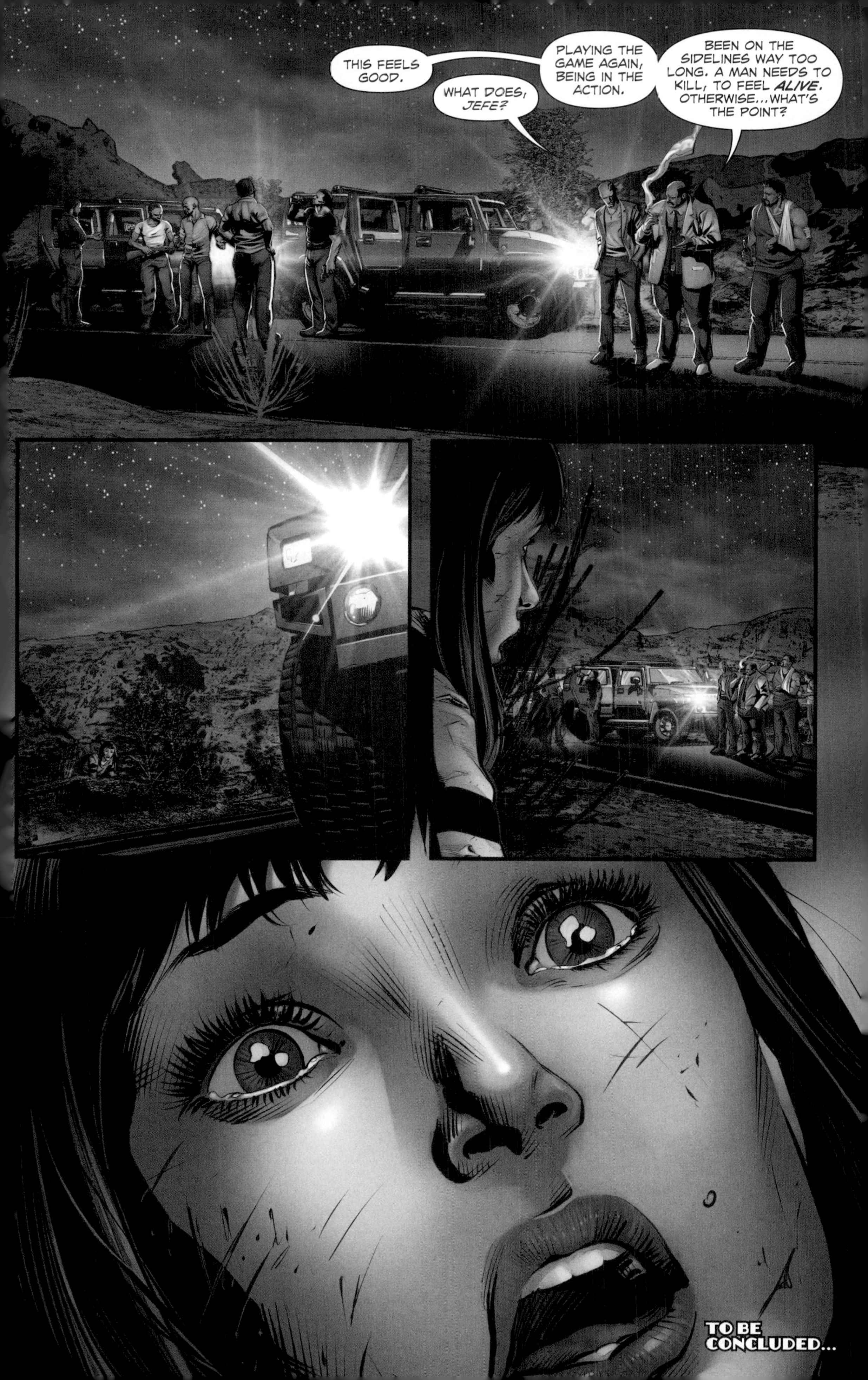
THIS FEELS GOOD.
WHAT DOES, JEFE?
PLAYING THE GAME AGAIN, BEING IN THE ACTION.
BEEN ON THE SIDELINES WAY TOO LONG. A MAN NEEDS TO KILL, TO FEEL ALIVE. OTHERWISE...WHAT'S THE POINT?
TO BE CONCLUDED...

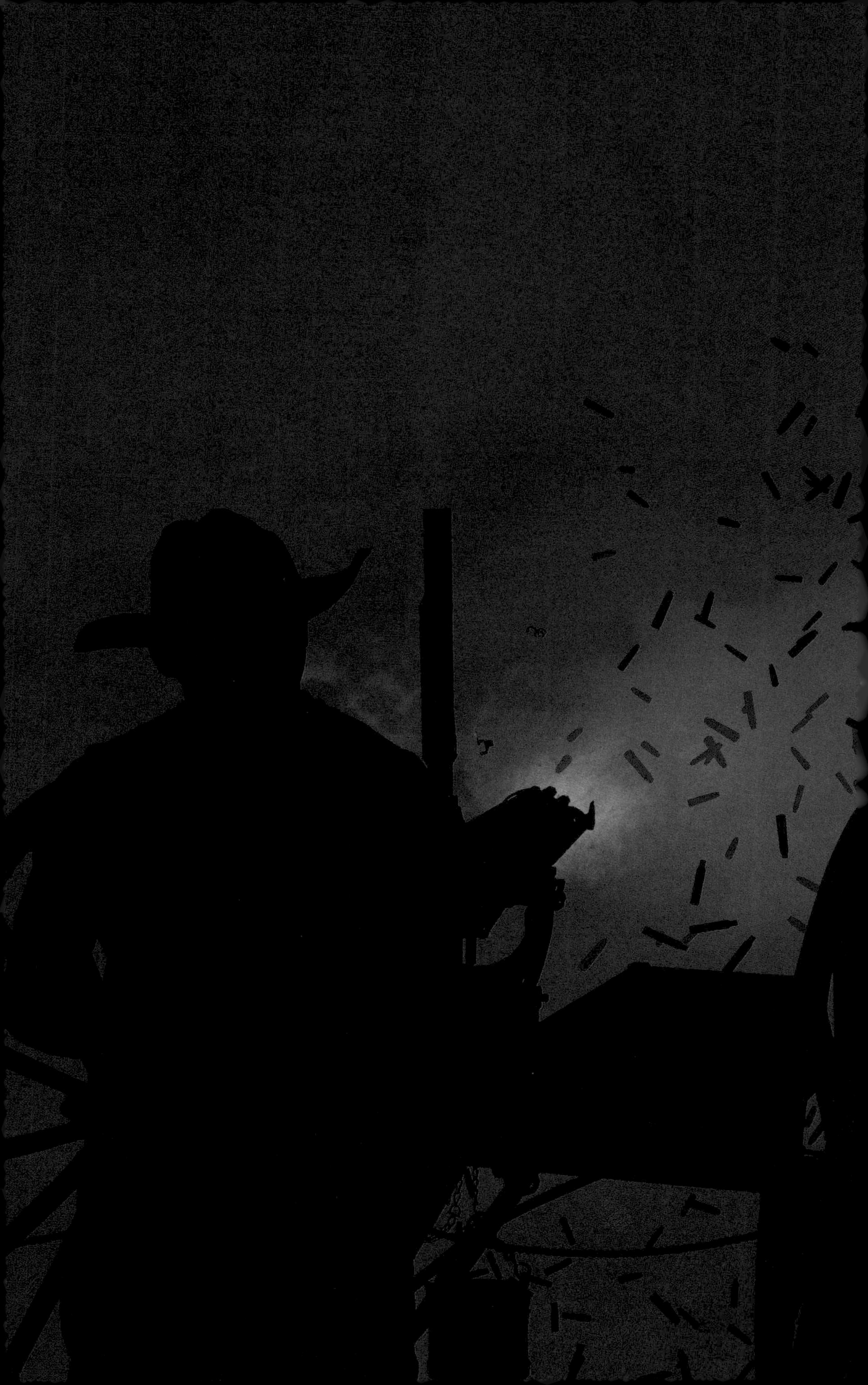

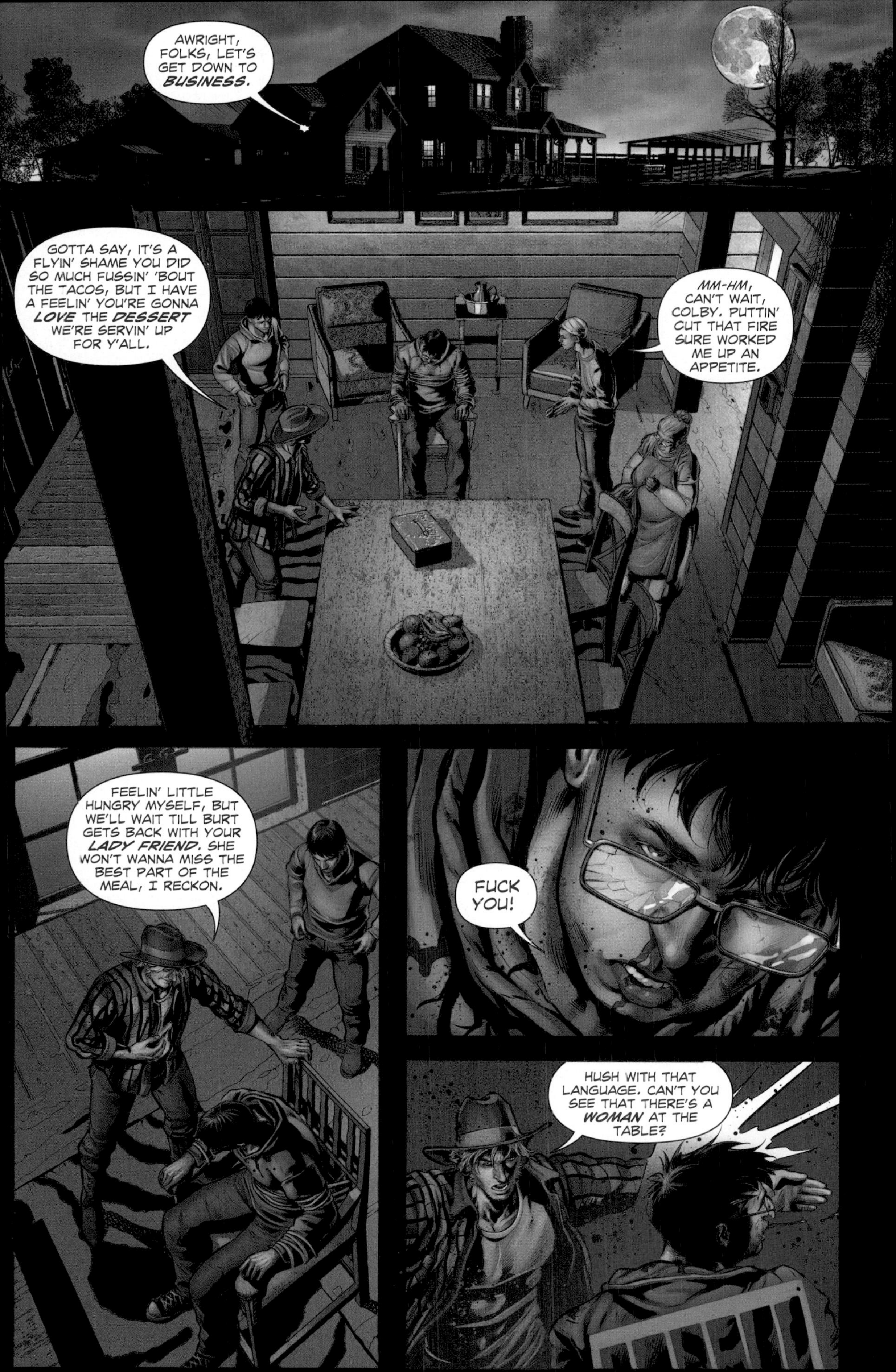
AWRIGHT, FOLKS, LET'S GET DOWN TO BUSINESS.
GOTTA SAY, IT'S A FLYIN' SHAME YOU DID SO MUCH FUSSIN' 'BOUT THE TACOS, BUT I HAVE A FEELIN' YOU'RE GONNA LOVE THE DESSERT WE'RE SERVIN' UP FOR Y'ALL.
MM-HM, CAN'T WAIT, COLBY. PUTTIN' OUT THAT FIRE SURE WORKED ME UP AN APPETITE.
FEELIN' LITTLE HUNGRY MYSELF, BUT WE'LL WAIT TILL BURT GETS BACK WITH YOUR LADY FRIEND. SHE WON'T WANNA MISS THE BEST PART OF THE MEAL, I RECKON.
FUCK YOU!
HUSH WITH THAT LANGUAGE. CAN'T YOU SEE THAT THERE'S A WOMAN AT THE TABLE?

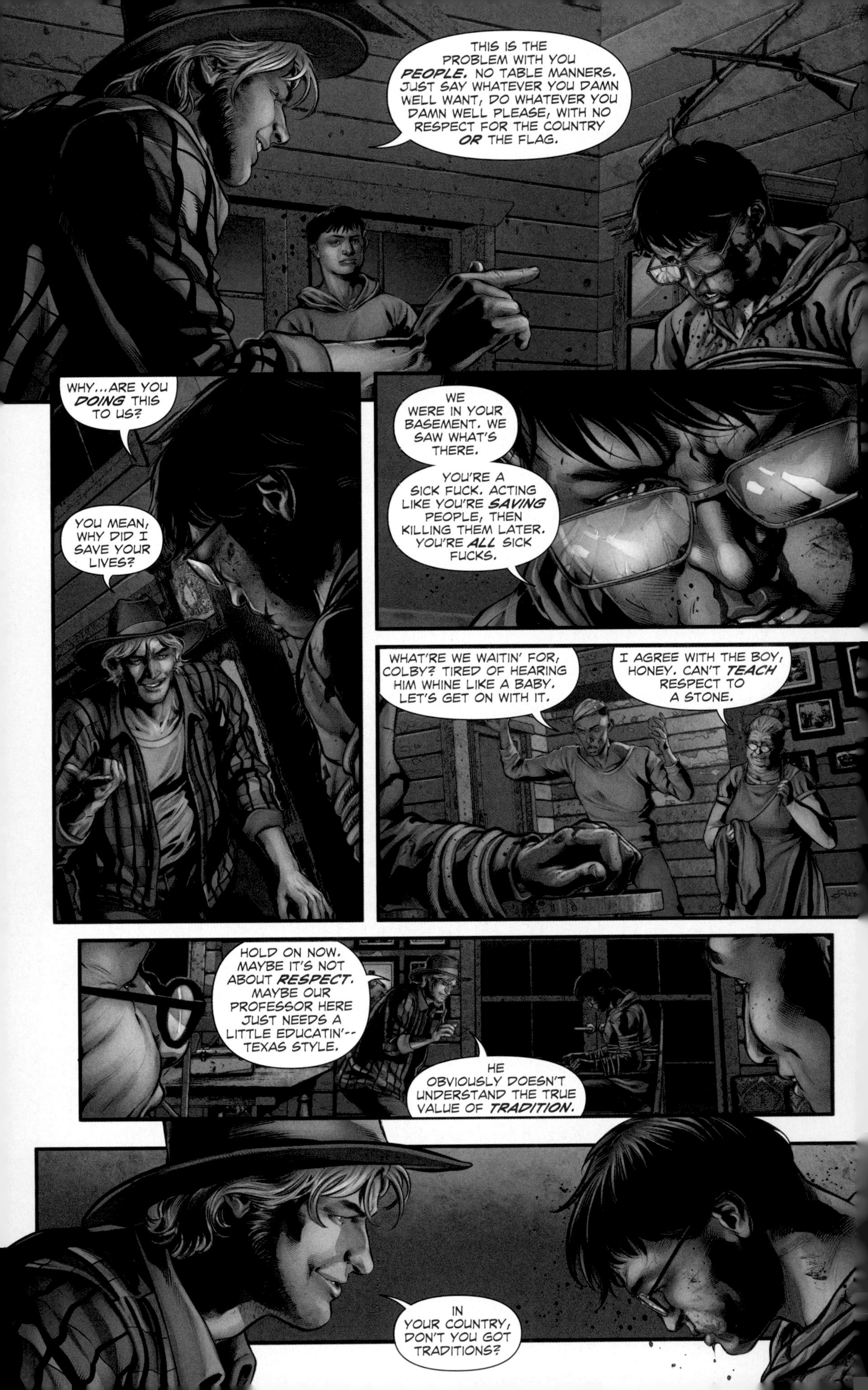
THIS IS THE PROBLEM WITH YOU PEOPLE. NO TABLE MANNERS. JUST SAY WHATEVER YOU DAMN WELL WANT, DO WHATEVER YOU DAMN WELL PLEASE, WITH NO RESPECT FOR THE COUNTRY OR THE FLAG.
WHY...ARE YOU DOING THIS TO US?
YOU MEAN, WHY DID I SAVE YOUR LIVES?
WE WERE IN YOUR BASEMENT. WE SAW WHAT'S THERE.
YOU'RE A SICK FUCK. ACTING LIKE YOU'RE SAVING PEOPLE, THEN KILLING THEM LATER. YOU'RE ALL SICK FUCKS.
WHAT'RE WE WAITIN' FOR, COLBY? TIRED OF HEARING HIM WHINE LIKE A BABY. LET'S GET ON WITH IT.
I AGREE WITH THE BOY, HONEY. CAN'T TEACH RESPECT TO A STONE.
HOLD ON NOW. MAYBE IT'S NOT ABOUT RESPECT. MAYBE OUR PROFESSOR HERE JUST NEEDS A LITTLE EDUCATIN'--TEXAS STYLE.
HE OBVIOUSLY DOESN'T UNDERSTAND THE TRUE VALUE OF TRADITION.
IN YOUR COUNTRY, DON'T YOU GOT TRADITIONS?

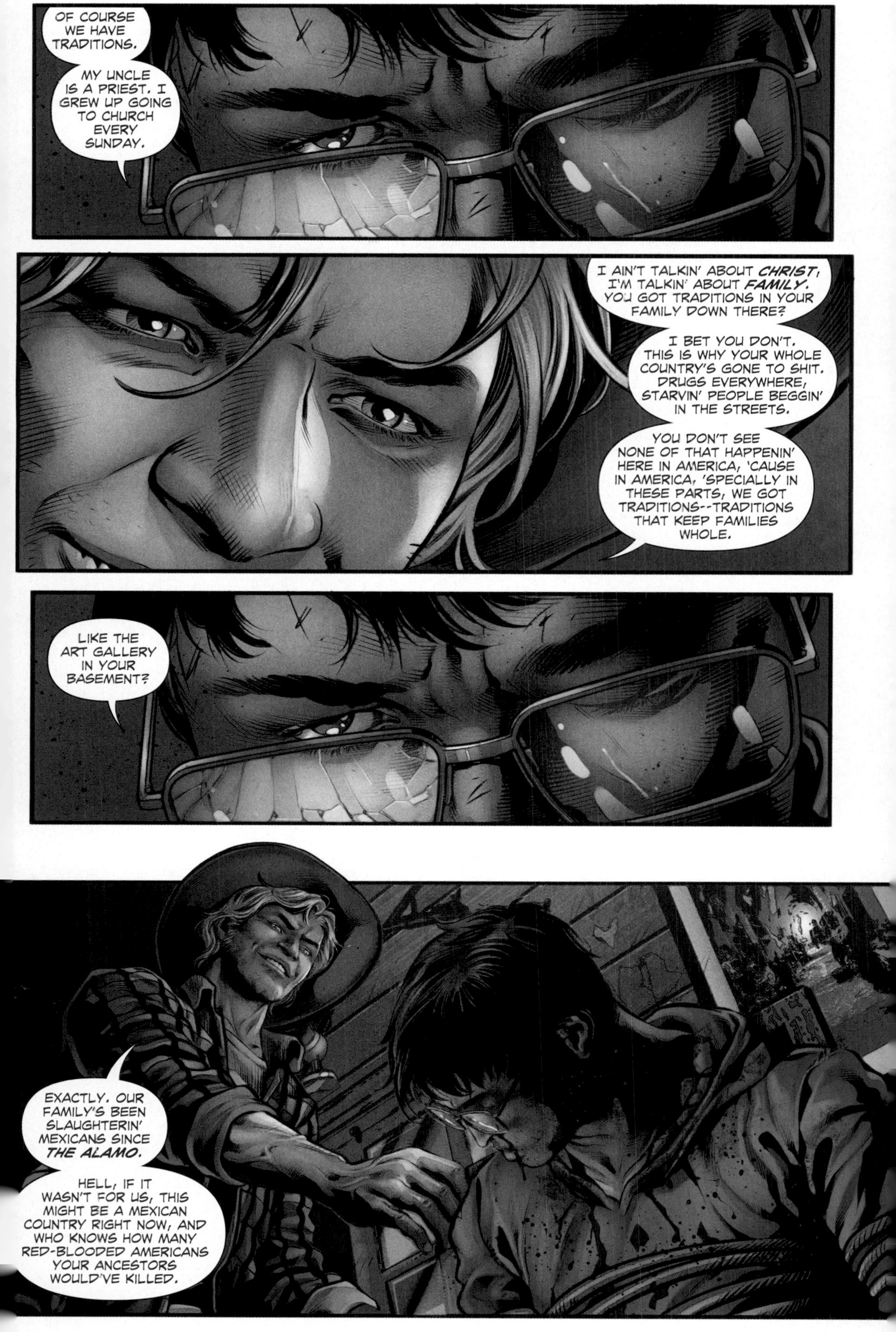
OF COURSE WE HAVE TRADITIONS.
MY UNCLE IS A PRIEST. I GREW UP GOING TO CHURCH EVERY SUNDAY.
I AIN'T TALKIN' ABOUT *CHRIST*, I'M TALKIN' ABOUT *FAMILY*. YOU GOT TRADITIONS IN YOUR FAMILY DOWN THERE?
I BET YOU DON'T. THIS IS WHY YOUR WHOLE COUNTRY'S GONE TO SHIT. DRUGS EVERYWHERE, STARVIN' PEOPLE BEGGIN' IN THE STREETS.
YOU DON'T SEE NONE OF THAT HAPPENIN' HERE IN AMERICA, 'CAUSE IN AMERICA, 'SPECIALLY IN THESE PARTS, WE GOT TRADITIONS--TRADITIONS THAT KEEP FAMILIES WHOLE.
LIKE THE ART GALLERY IN YOUR BASEMENT?
EXACTLY. OUR FAMILY'S BEEN SLAUGHTERIN' MEXICANS SINCE ***THE ALAMO***.
HELL, IF IT WASN'T FOR US, THIS MIGHT BE A MEXICAN COUNTRY RIGHT NOW, AND WHO KNOWS HOW MANY RED-BLOODED AMERICANS YOUR ANCESTORS WOULD'VE KILLED.

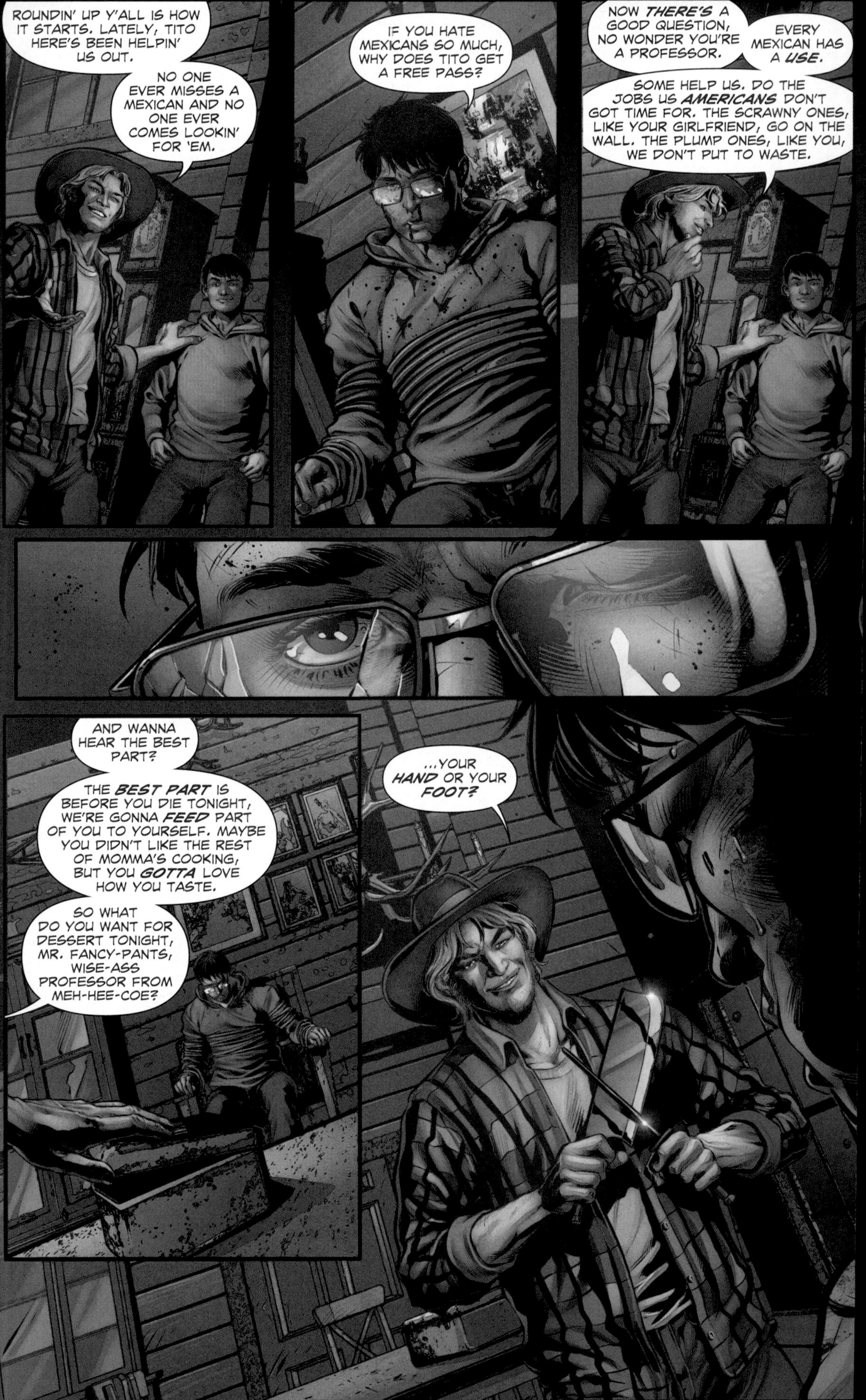
ROUNDIN' UP Y'ALL IS HOW IT STARTS. LATELY, TITO HERE'S BEEN HELPIN' US OUT.
NO ONE EVER MISSES A MEXICAN AND NO ONE EVER COMES LOOKIN' FOR 'EM.
IF YOU HATE MEXICANS SO MUCH, WHY DOES TITO GET A FREE PASS?
NOW THERE'S A GOOD QUESTION, NO WONDER YOU'RE A PROFESSOR.
EVERY MEXICAN HAS A USE.
SOME HELP US. DO THE JOBS US AMERICANS DON'T GOT TIME FOR. THE SCRAWNY ONES, LIKE YOUR GIRLFRIEND, GO ON THE WALL. THE PLUMP ONES, LIKE YOU, WE DON'T PUT TO WASTE.
AND WANNA HEAR THE BEST PART?
THE BEST PART IS BEFORE YOU DIE TONIGHT, WE'RE GONNA FEED PART OF YOU TO YOURSELF. MAYBE YOU DIDN'T LIKE THE REST OF MOMMA'S COOKING, BUT YOU GOTTA LOVE HOW YOU TASTE.
SO WHAT DO YOU WANT FOR DESSERT TONIGHT, MR. FANCY-PANTS, WISE-ASS PROFESSOR FROM MEH-HEE-COE?
...YOUR HAND OR YOUR FOOT?

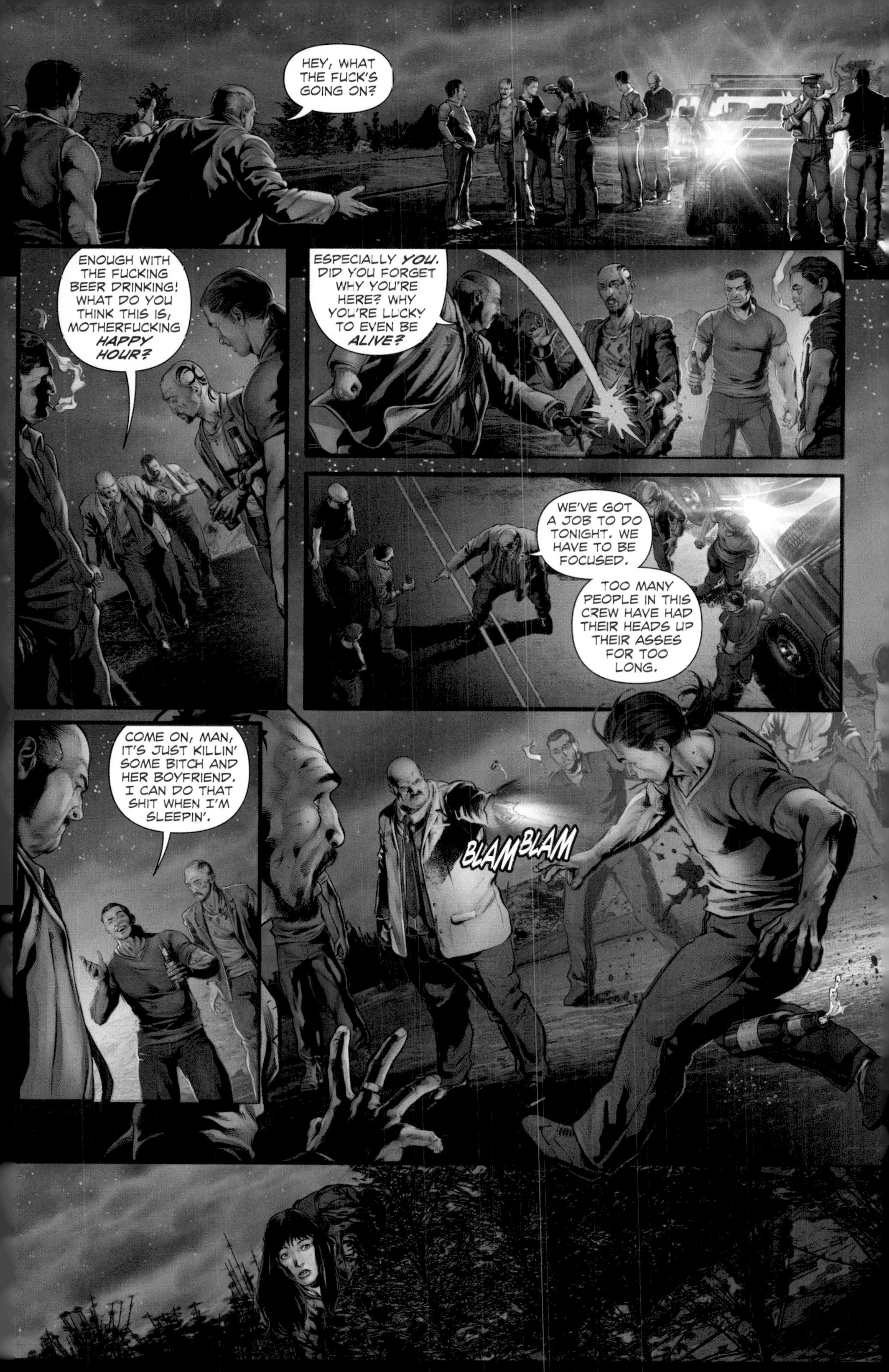
HEY, WHAT THE FUCK'S GOING ON?
ENOUGH WITH THE FUCKING BEER DRINKING! WHAT DO YOU THINK THIS IS, MOTHERFUCKING *HAPPY HOUR?*
ESPECIALLY *YOU.* DID YOU FORGET WHY YOU'RE HERE? WHY YOU'RE LUCKY TO EVEN BE *ALIVE?*
WE'VE GOT A JOB TO DO TONIGHT. WE HAVE TO BE FOCUSED.
TOO MANY PEOPLE IN THIS CREW HAVE HAD THEIR HEADS UP THEIR ASSES FOR TOO LONG.
COME ON, MAN, IT'S JUST KILLIN' SOME BITCH AND HER BOYFRIEND. I CAN DO THAT SHIT WHEN I'M SLEEPIN'.
BLAM BLAM

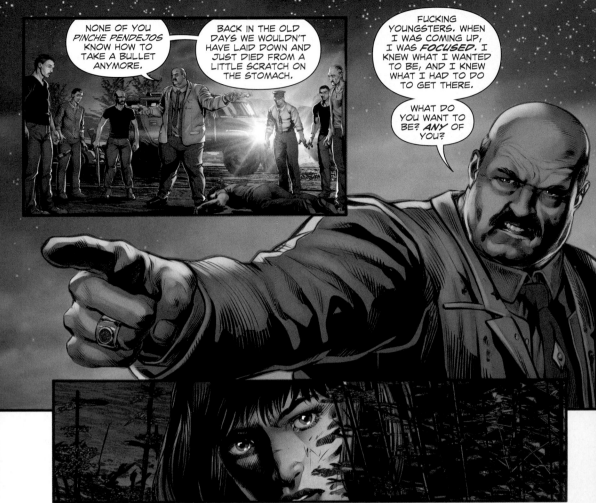

NONE OF YOU *PINCHE PENDEJOS* KNOW HOW TO TAKE A BULLET ANYMORE.

BACK IN THE OLD DAYS WE WOULDN'T HAVE LAID DOWN AND JUST DIED FROM A LITTLE SCRATCH ON THE STOMACH.

FUCKING YOUNGSTERS. WHEN I WAS COMING UP, I WAS *FOCUSED*. I KNEW WHAT I WANTED TO BE, AND I KNEW WHAT I HAD TO DO TO GET THERE.

WHAT DO YOU WANT TO BE? *ANY* OF YOU?

THESE DAYS YOU'RE ALL DISTRACTED, LOOKING AT YOUR FUCKING PHONES, WHILE LIFE PASSES YOU BY.

YOU'RE GONNA WAKE UP ONE DAY AND BE MY AGE--IF ANY OF YOU LIVE THAT LONG-- AND YOU'RE GONNA WONDER WHERE YOUR LIFE WENT.

I GOT A WIFE, A SISTER, A MOTHER BREATHING DOWN MY ASS TO GET PAYBACK, AND YOU KNOW WHAT? THEY GOT MORE *COJONES* THAN ALL OF YOU.

JEFE... I THINK SOMEONE'S THERE.

THE FUCK YOU WAITING FOR? GO CHECK IT OUT.

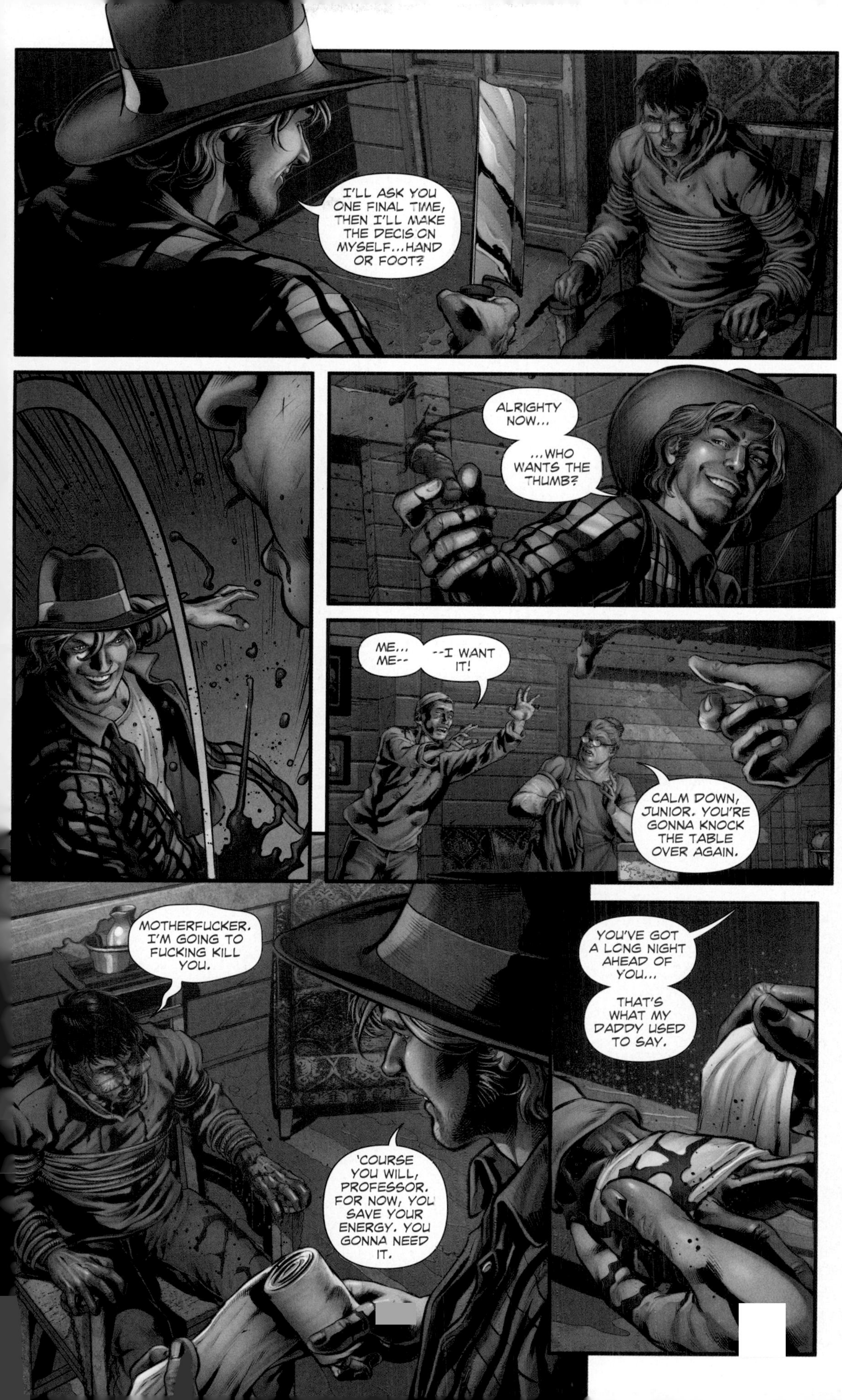
I'LL ASK YOU ONE FINAL TIME, THEN I'LL MAKE THE DECIS ON MYSELF...HAND OR FOOT?
ALRIGHTY NOW...
...WHO WANTS THE THUMB?
ME... ME--
--I WANT IT!
CALM DOWN, JUNIOR. YOU'RE GONNA KNOCK THE TABLE OVER AGAIN.
MOTHERFUCKER. I'M GOING TO FUCKING KILL YOU.
'COURSE YOU WILL, PROFESSOR. FOR NOW, YOU SAVE YOUR ENERGY. YOU GONNA NEED IT.
YOU'VE GOT A LONG NIGHT AHEAD OF YOU...
THAT'S WHAT MY DADDY USED TO SAY.

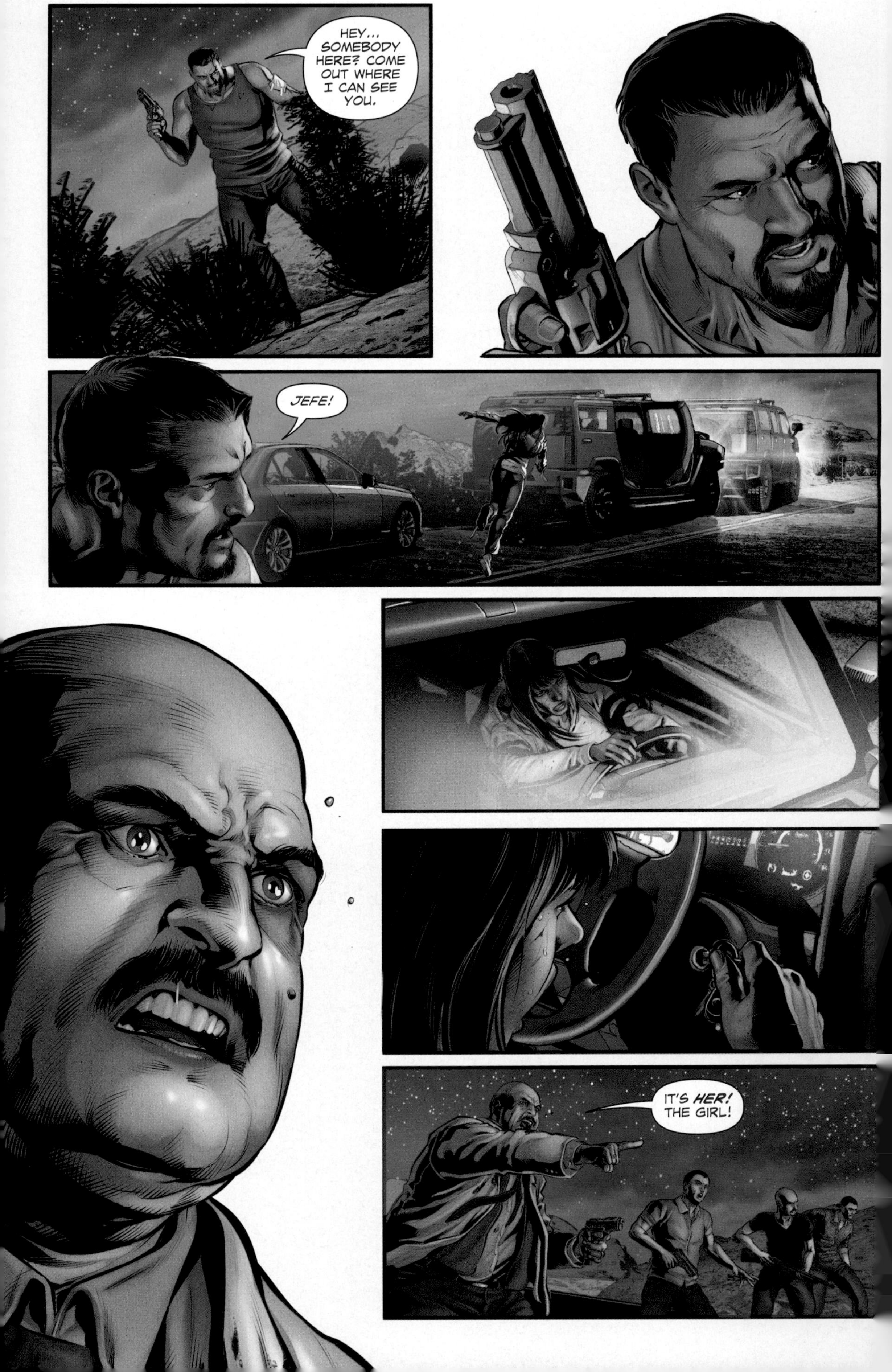
HEY... SOMEBODY HERE? COME OUT WHERE I CAN SEE YOU.
JEFE!
IT'S HER! THE GIRL!

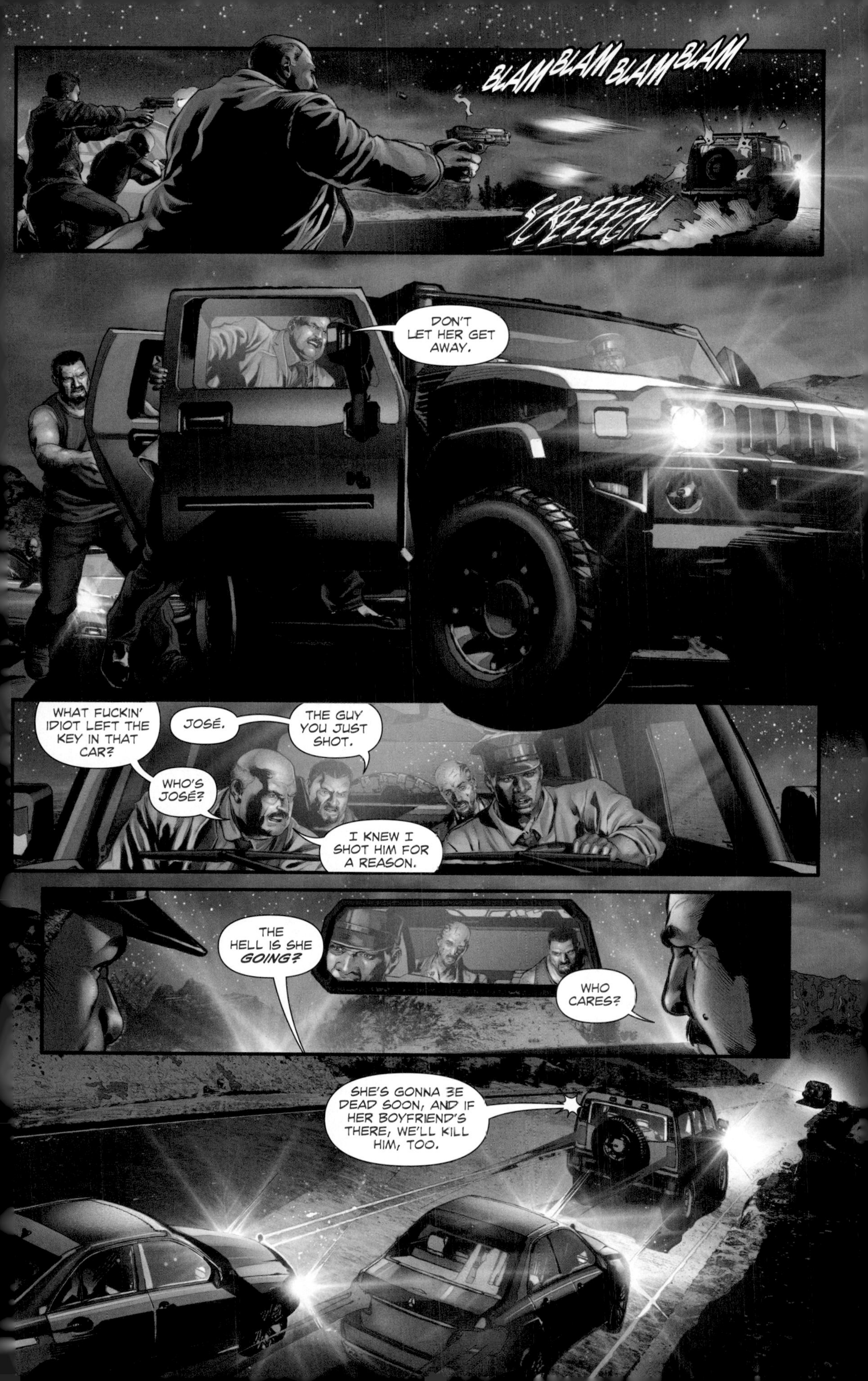
BLAM BLAM BLAM BLAM
SCREEEECH
DON'T LET HER GET AWAY.
WHAT FUCKIN' IDIOT LEFT THE KEY IN THAT CAR?
JOSÉ.
THE GUY YOU JUST SHOT.
WHO'S JOSÉ?
I KNEW I SHOT HIM FOR A REASON.
THE HELL IS SHE GOING?
WHO CARES?
SHE'S GONNA BE DEAD SOON, AND IF HER BOYFRIEND'S THERE, WE'LL KILL HIM, TOO.

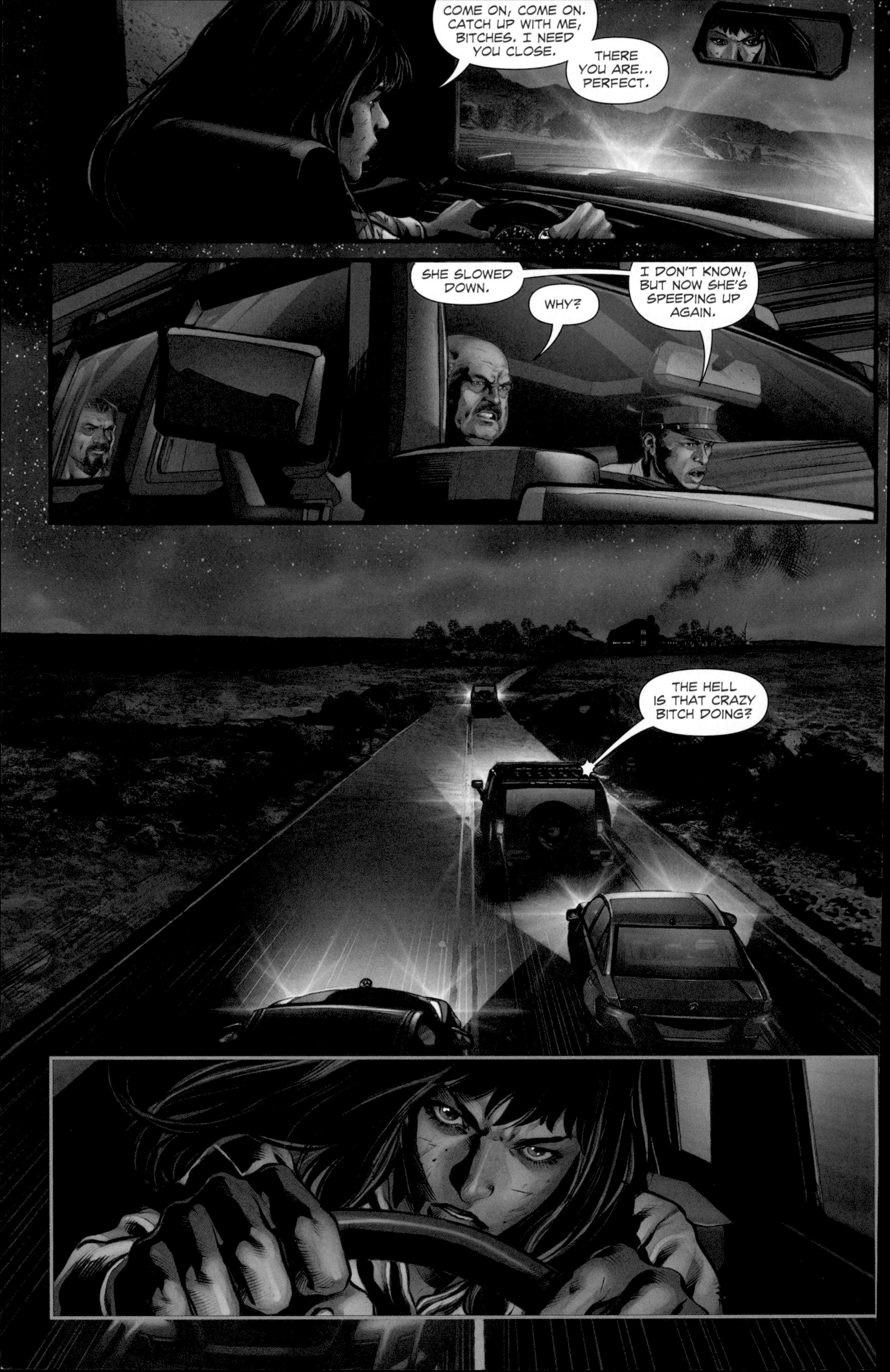
COME ON, COME ON. CATCH UP WITH ME, BITCHES. I NEED YOU CLOSE.
THERE YOU ARE... PERFECT.
SHE SLOWED DOWN.
WHY?
I DON'T KNOW, BUT NOW SHE'S SPEEDING UP AGAIN.
THE HELL IS THAT CRAZY BITCH DOING?

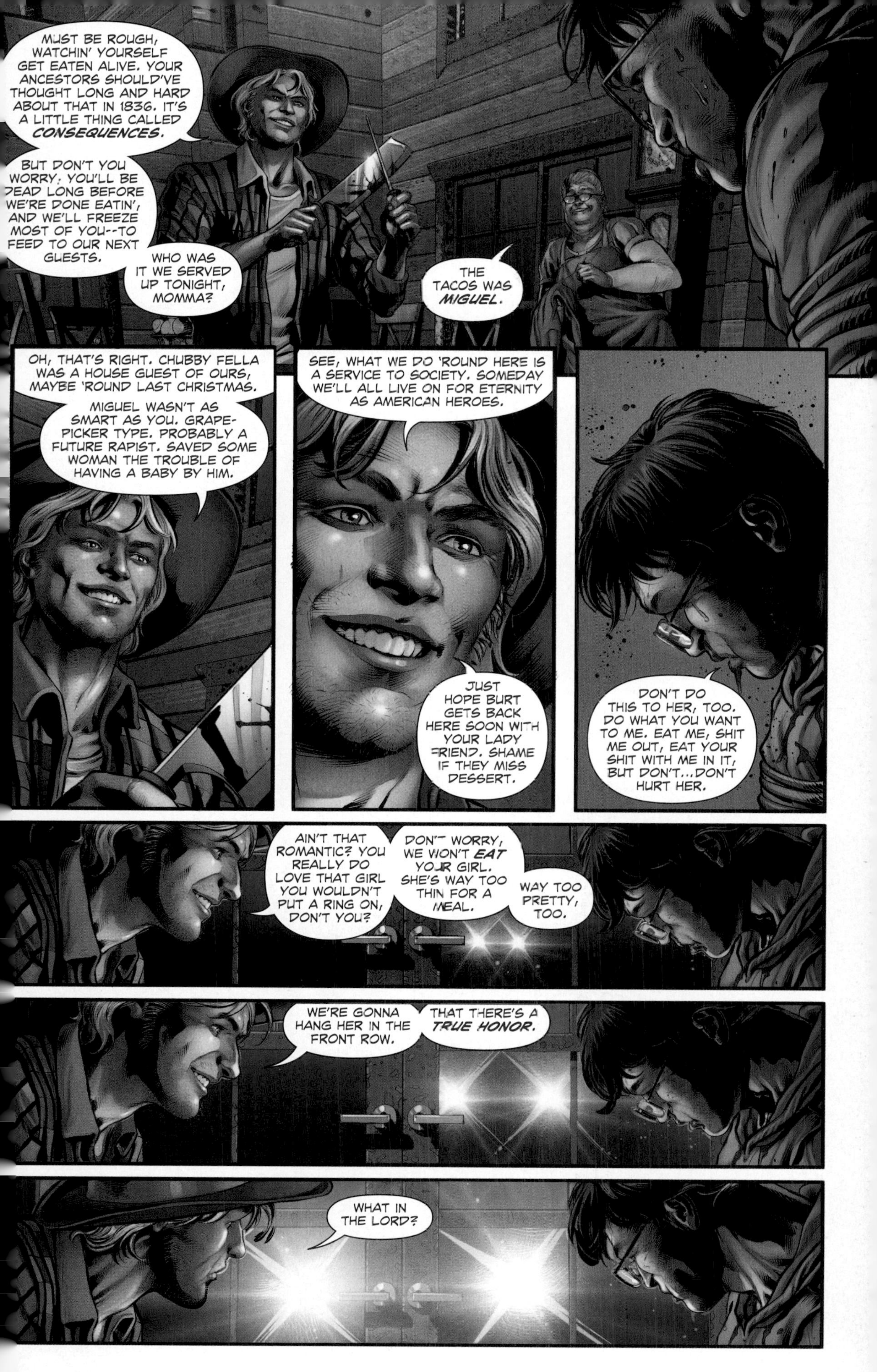
MUST BE ROUGH, WATCHIN' YOURSELF GET EATEN ALIVE. YOUR ANCESTORS SHOULD'VE THOUGHT LONG AND HARD ABOUT THAT IN 1836. IT'S A LITTLE THING CALLED CONSEQUENCES.
BUT DON'T YOU WORRY: YOU'LL BE DEAD LONG BEFORE WE'RE DONE EATIN', AND WE'LL FREEZE MOST OF YOU--TO FEED TO OUR NEXT GUESTS.
WHO WAS IT WE SERVED UP TONIGHT, MOMMA?
THE TACOS WAS MIGUEL.
OH, THAT'S RIGHT. CHUBBY FELLA WAS A HOUSE GUEST OF OURS, MAYBE 'ROUND LAST CHRISTMAS.
MIGUEL WASN'T AS SMART AS YOU. GRAPE-PICKER TYPE. PROBABLY A FUTURE RAPIST. SAVED SOME WOMAN THE TROUBLE OF HAVING A BABY BY HIM.
SEE, WHAT WE DO 'ROUND HERE IS A SERVICE TO SOCIETY. SOMEDAY WE'LL ALL LIVE ON FOR ETERNITY AS AMERICAN HEROES.
JUST HOPE BURT GETS BACK HERE SOON WITH YOUR LADY FRIEND. SHAME IF THEY MISS DESSERT.
DON'T DO THIS TO HER, TOO. DO WHAT YOU WANT TO ME. EAT ME, SHIT ME OUT, EAT YOUR SHIT WITH ME IN IT, BUT DON'T...DON'T HURT HER.
AIN'T THAT ROMANTIC? YOU REALLY DO LOVE THAT GIRL YOU WOULDN'T PUT A RING ON, DON'T YOU?
DON'T WORRY, WE WON'T EAT YOUR GIRL. SHE'S WAY TOO THIN FOR A MEAL.
WAY TOO PRETTY, TOO.
WE'RE GONNA HANG HER IN THE FRONT ROW.
THAT THERE'S A TRUE HONOR.
WHAT IN THE LORD?

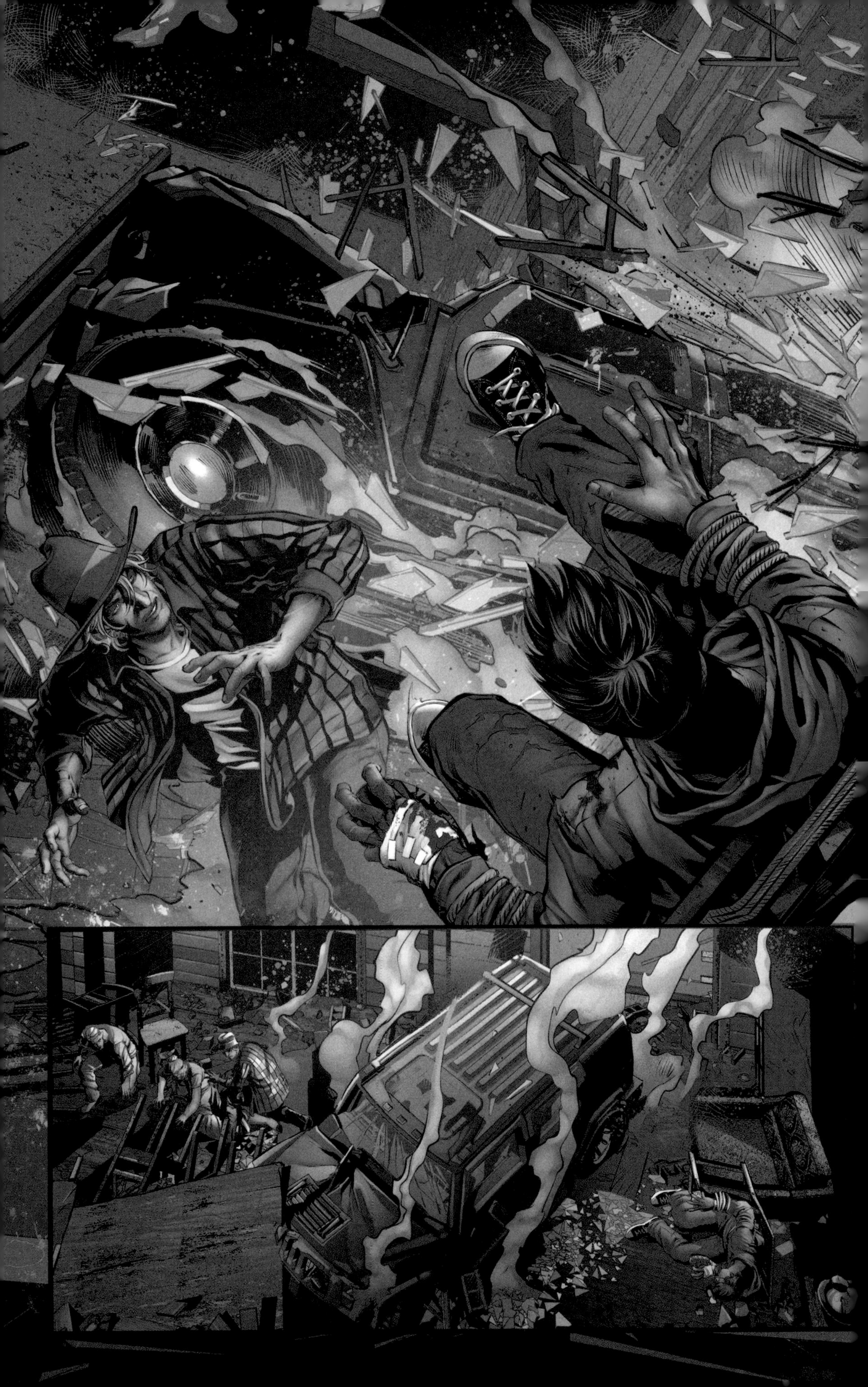

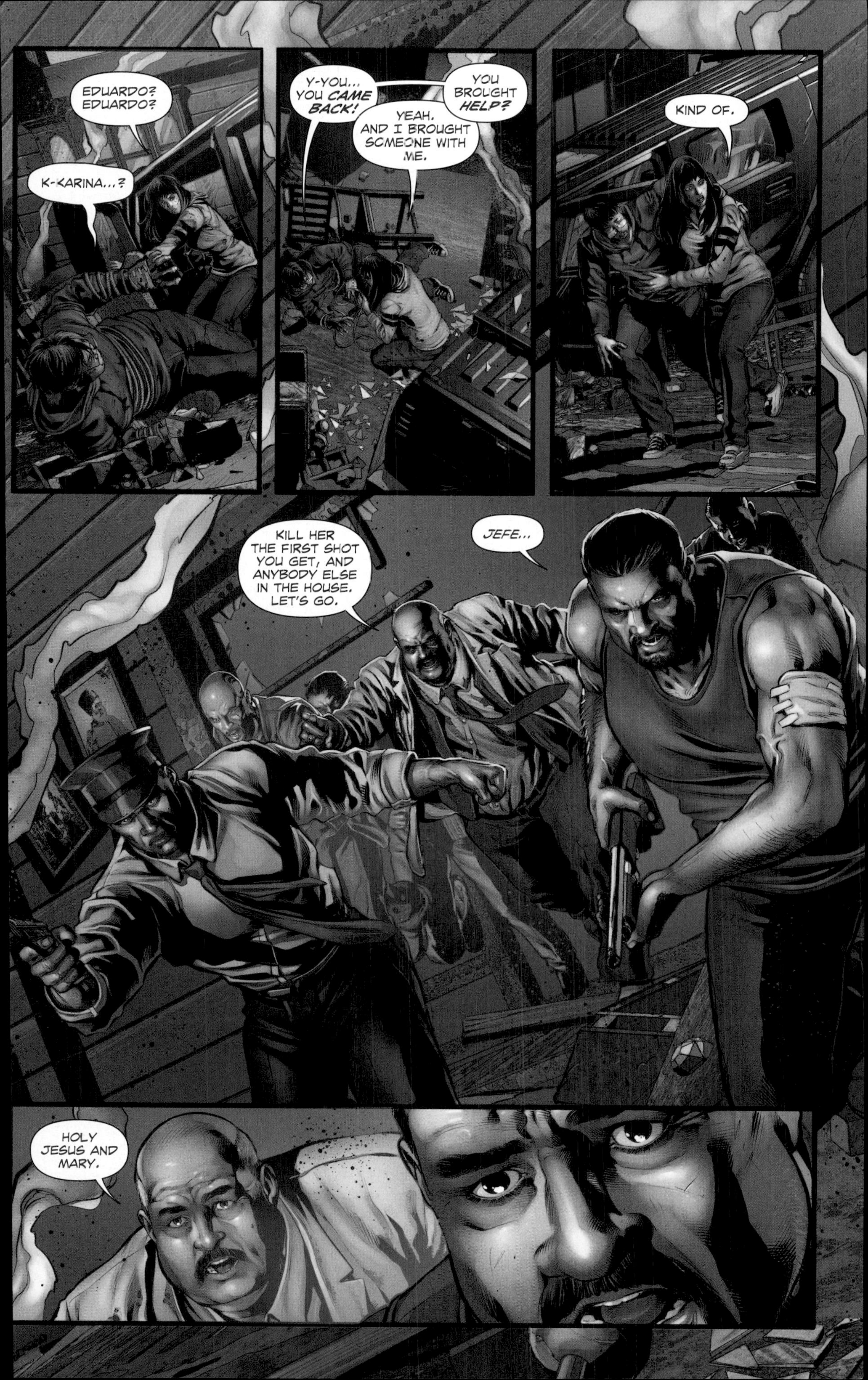
EDUARDO? EDUARDO?
K-KARINA...?
Y-YOU... YOU CAME BACK!
YEAH. AND I BROUGHT SOMEONE WITH ME.
YOU BROUGHT HELP?
KIND OF.
KILL HER THE FIRST SHOT YOU GET, AND ANYBODY ELSE IN THE HOUSE. LET'S GO.
JEFE...
HOLY JESUS AND MARY.

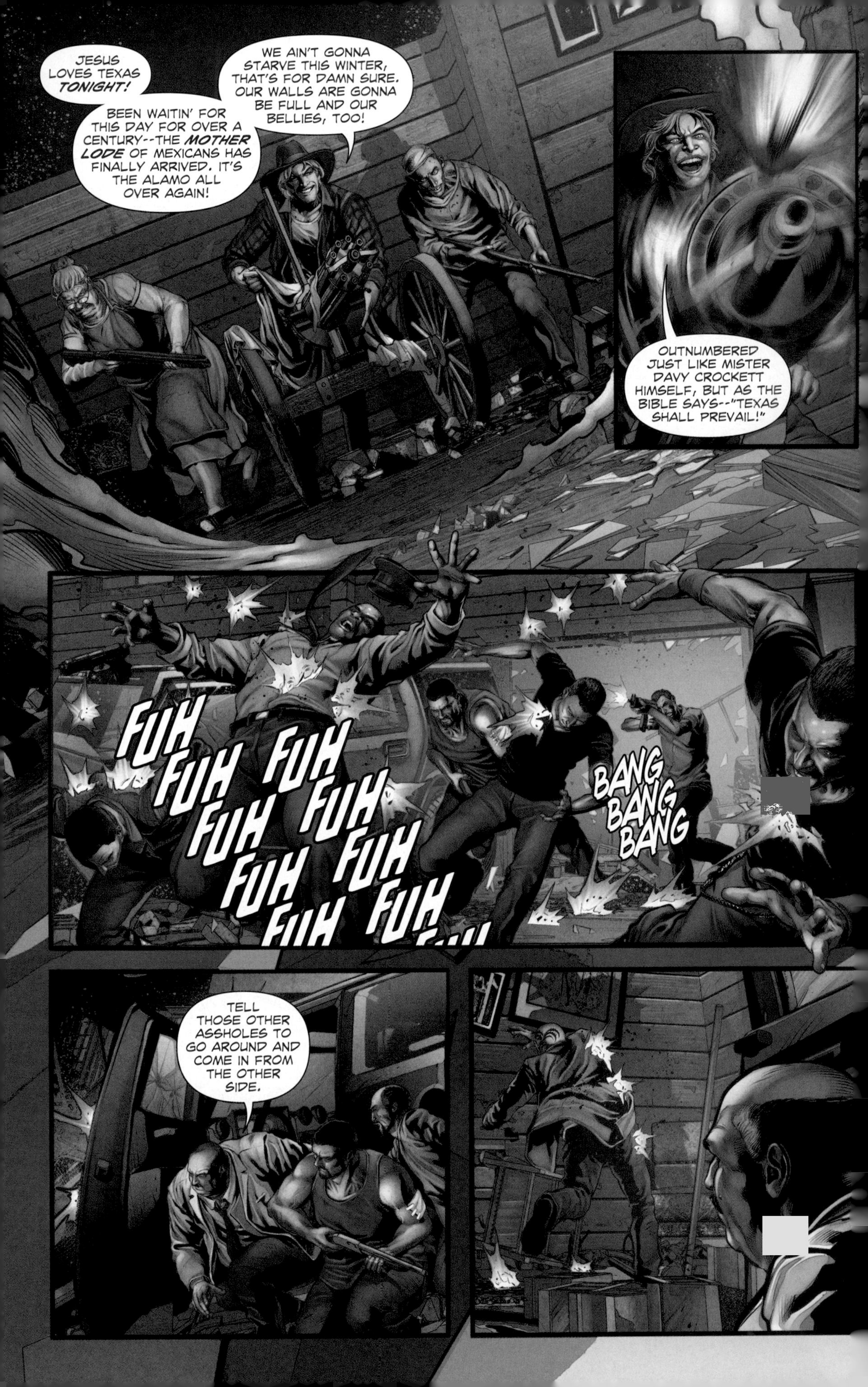
JESUS LOVES TEXAS *TONIGHT!*
BEEN WAITIN' FOR THIS DAY FOR OVER A CENTURY--THE ***MOTHER LODE*** OF MEXICANS HAS FINALLY ARRIVED. IT'S THE ALAMO ALL OVER AGAIN!
WE AIN'T GONNA STARVE THIS WINTER, THAT'S FOR DAMN SURE. OUR WALLS ARE GONNA BE FULL AND OUR BELLIES, TOO!
OUTNUMBERED JUST LIKE MISTER DAVY CROCKETT HIMSELF, BUT AS THE BIBLE SAYS--"TEXAS SHALL PREVAIL!"
FUH FUH FUH FUH FUH FUH FUH FUH
BANG BANG BANG
TELL THOSE OTHER ASSHOLES TO GO AROUND AND COME IN FROM THE OTHER SIDE.

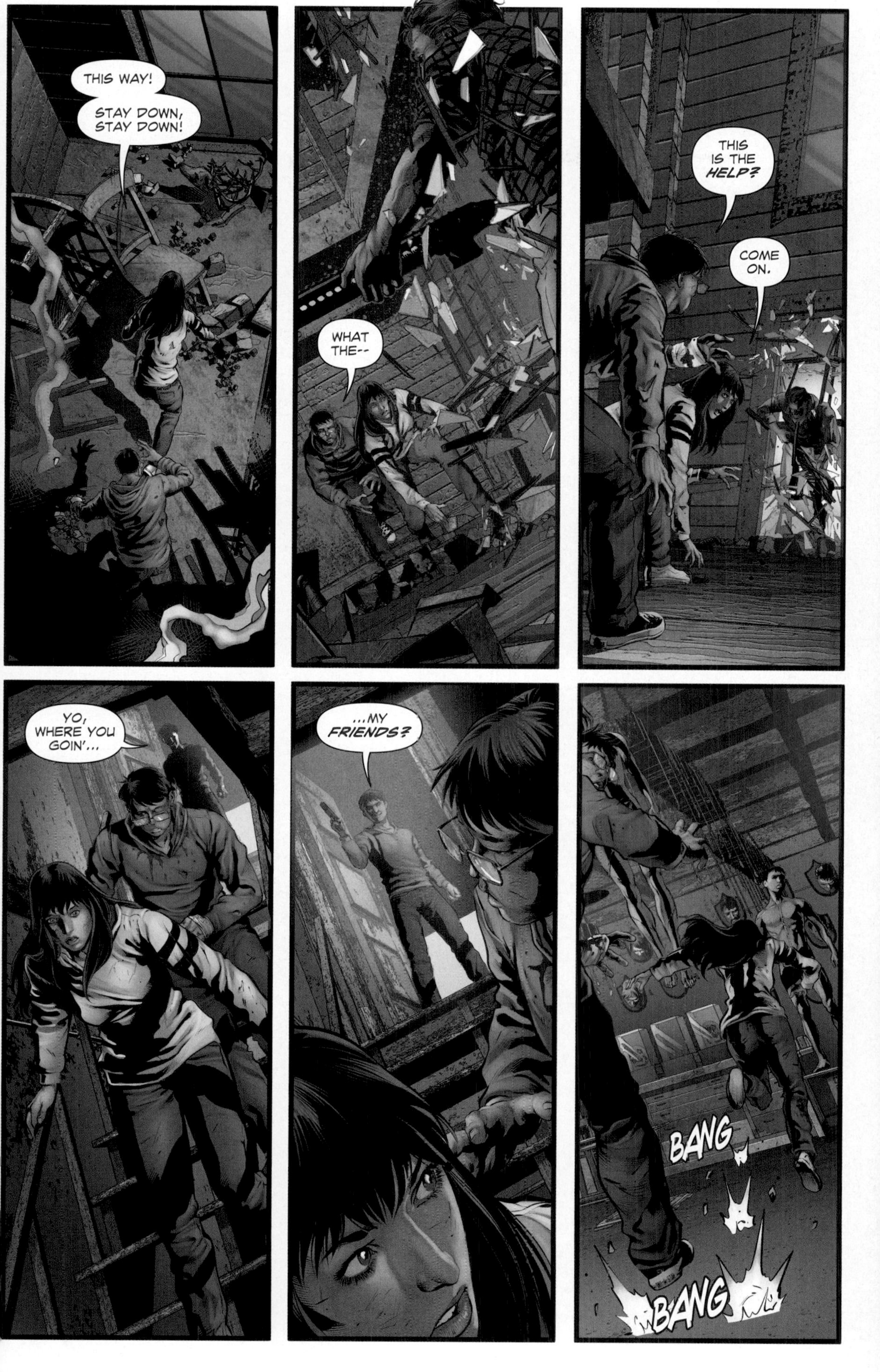
THIS WAY!
STAY DOWN, STAY DOWN!
WHAT THE--
THIS IS THE HELP?
COME ON.
YO, WHERE YOU GOIN'...
...MY FRIENDS?
BANG
BANG

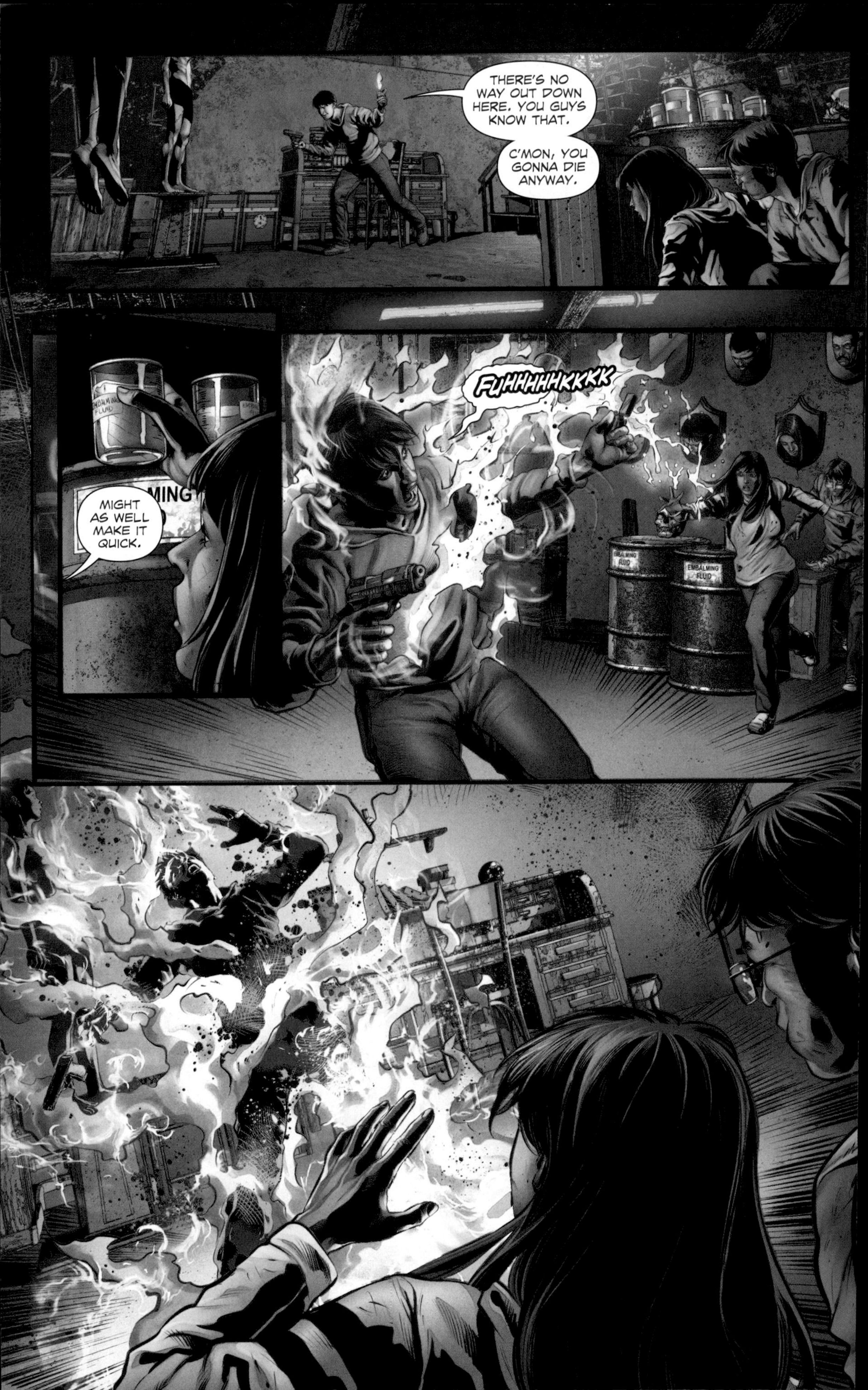

THERE'S NO WAY OUT DOWN HERE. YOU GUYS KNOW THAT.
C'MON, YOU GONNA DIE ANYWAY.
EMBALMING FLUID
MING
MIGHT AS WELL MAKE IT QUICK.
FUHHHHHKKKK
EMBALMING FLUID
EMBALMING FLUID

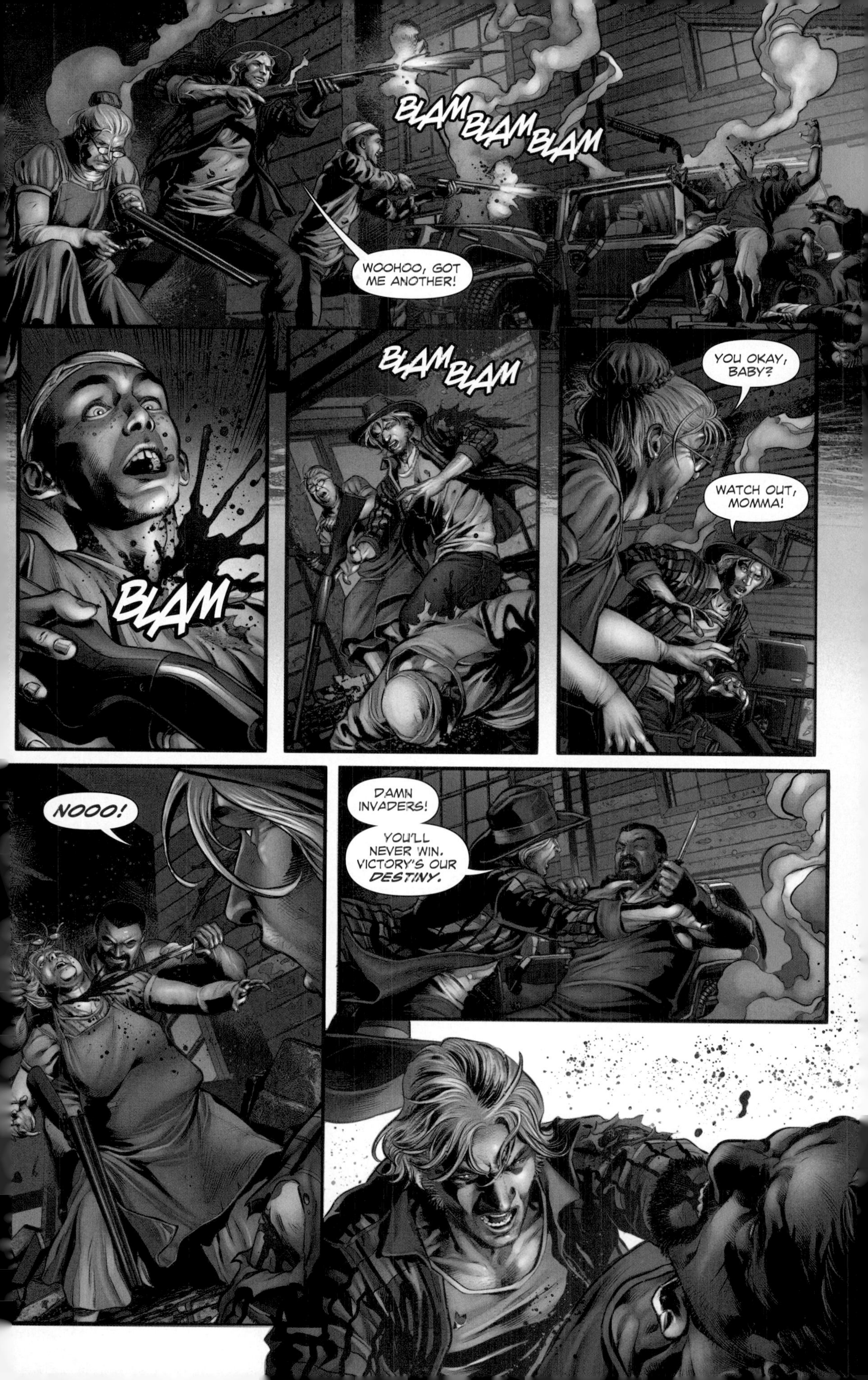

BLAM BLAM BLAM
WOOHOO, GOT ME ANOTHER!
BLAM
BLAM BLAM
YOU OKAY, BABY?
WATCH OUT, MOMMA!
NOOO!
DAMN INVADERS!
YOU'LL NEVER WIN. VICTORY'S OUR *DESTINY*.

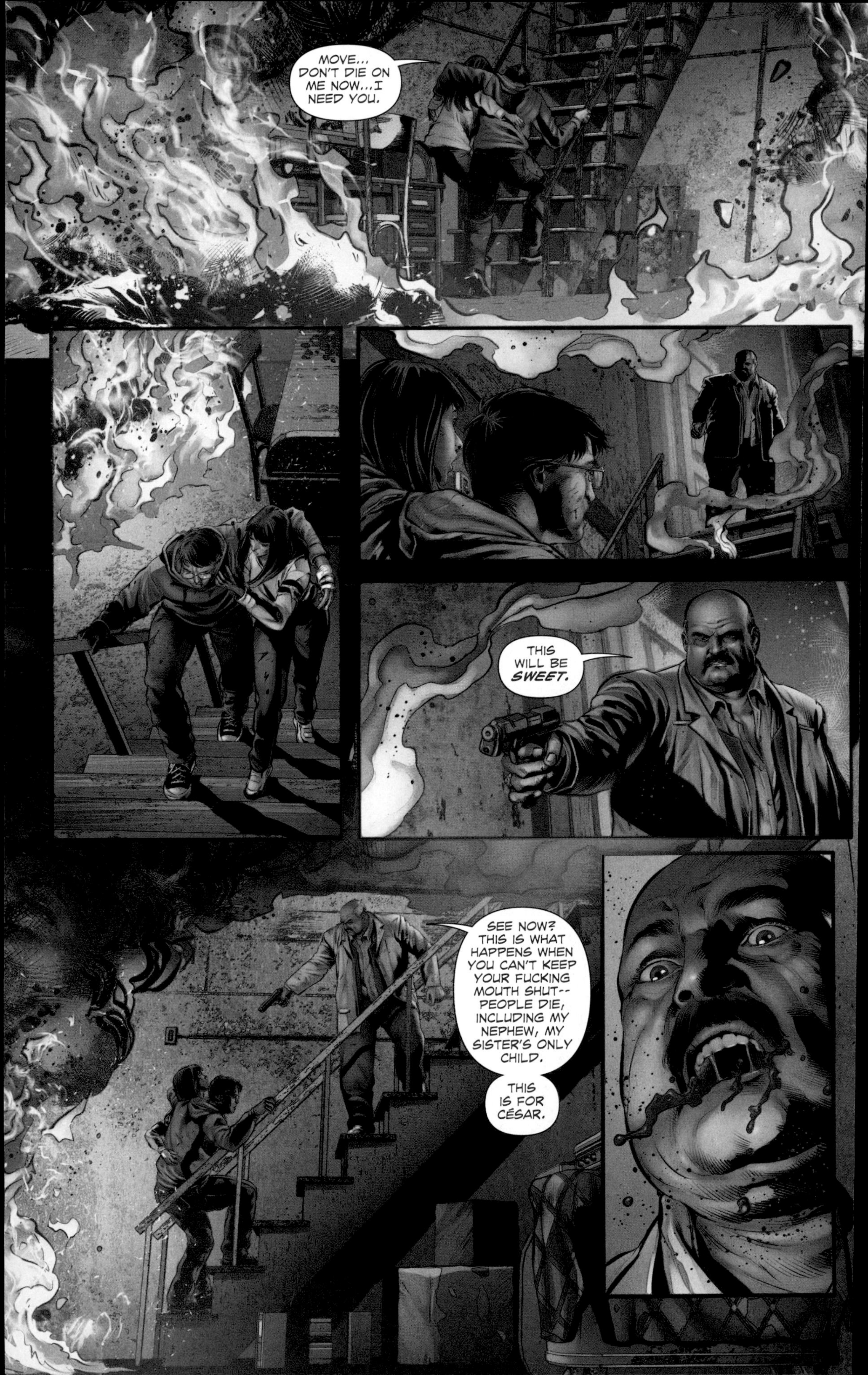
MOVE... DON'T DIE ON ME NOW...I NEED YOU.
THIS WILL BE SWEET.
SEE NOW? THIS IS WHAT HAPPENS WHEN YOU CAN'T KEEP YOUR FUCKING MOUTH SHUT-- PEOPLE DIE, INCLUDING MY NEPHEW, MY SISTER'S ONLY CHILD.
THIS IS FOR CÉSAR.

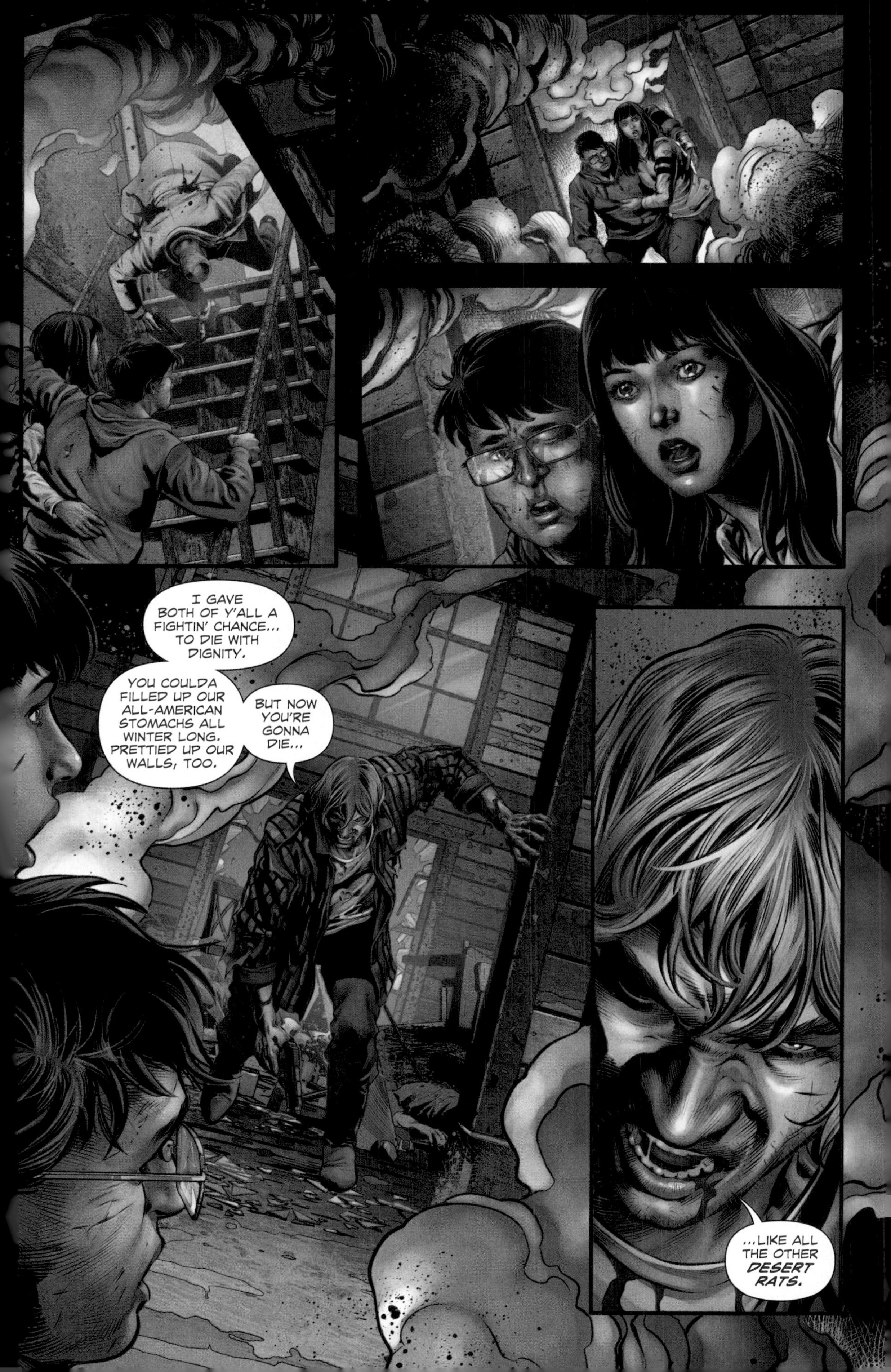
I GAVE BOTH OF Y'ALL A FIGHTIN' CHANCE... TO DIE WITH DIGNITY.
YOU COULDA FILLED UP OUR ALL-AMERICAN STOMACHS ALL WINTER LONG. PRETTIED UP OUR WALLS, TOO.
BUT NOW YOU'RE GONNA DIE...
...LIKE ALL THE OTHER *DESERT RATS.*

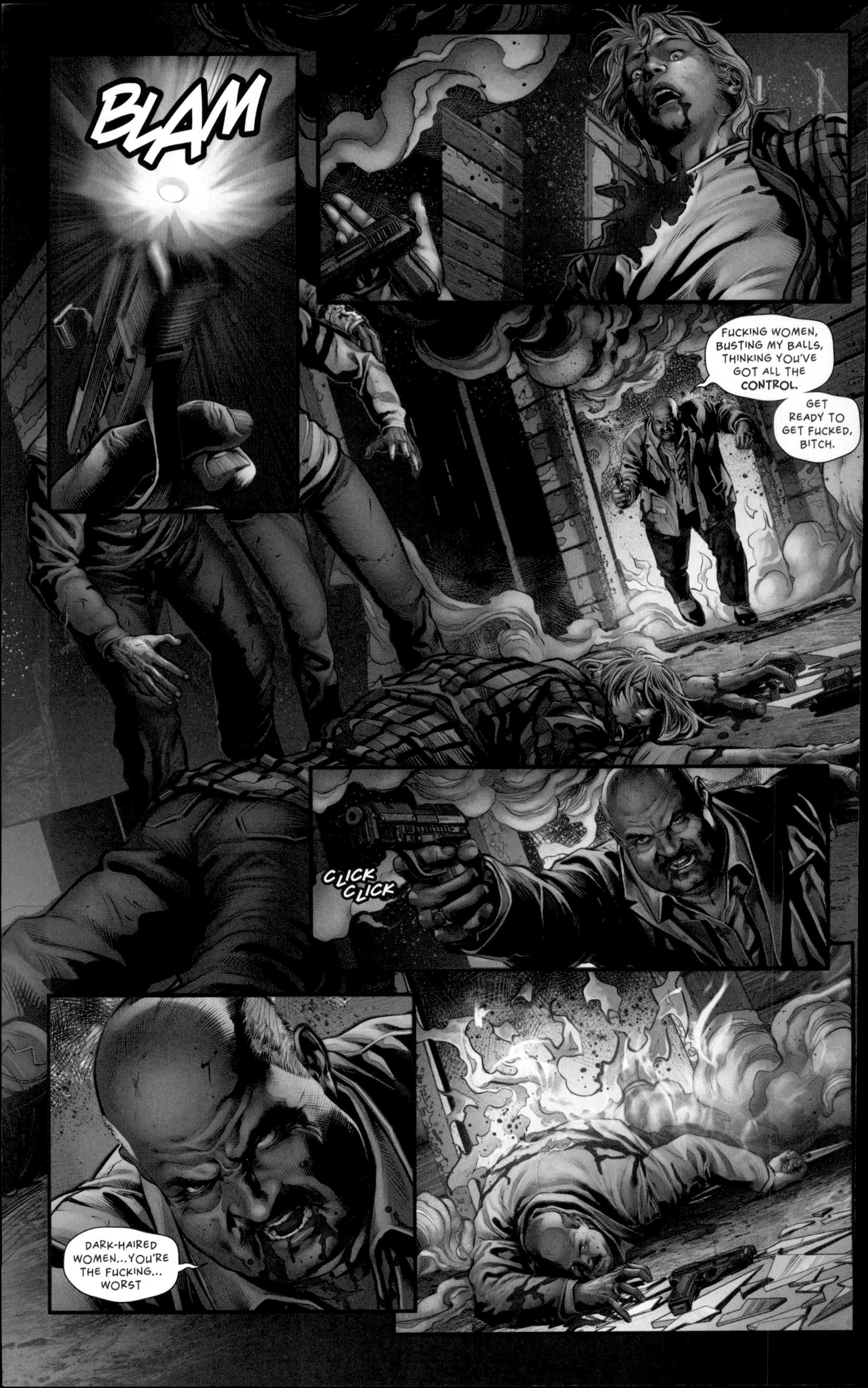
BLAM
FUCKING WOMEN, BUSTING MY BALLS, THINKING YOU'VE GOT ALL THE **CONTROL.**
GET READY TO GET FUCKED, BITCH.
CLICK CLICK
DARK-HAIRED WOMEN... YOU'RE THE FUCKING... WORST

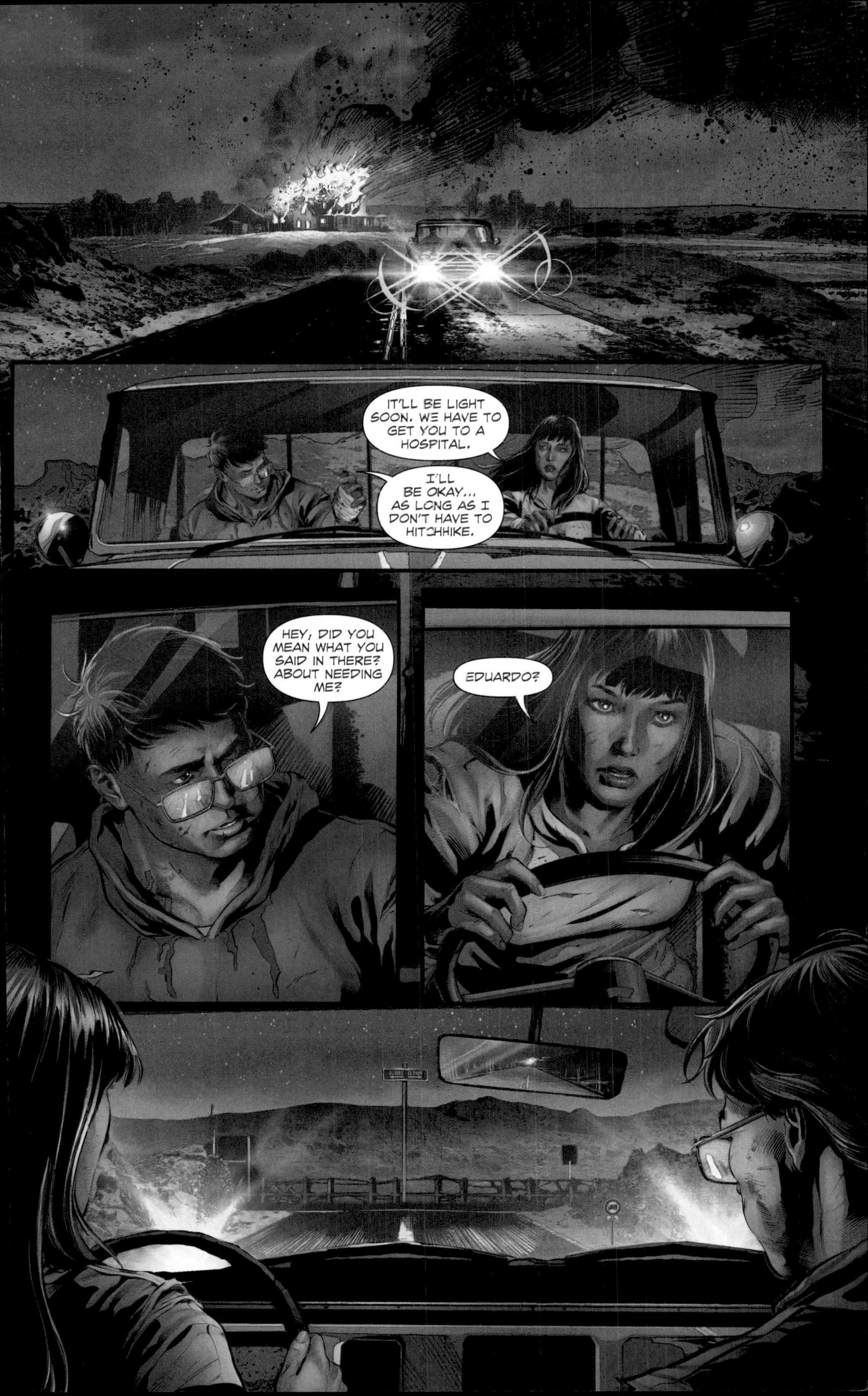
IT'LL BE LIGHT SOON. WE HAVE TO GET YOU TO A HOSPITAL.
I'LL BE OKAY... AS LONG AS I DON'T HAVE TO HITCHHIKE.
HEY, DID YOU MEAN WHAT YOU SAID IN THERE? ABOUT NEEDING ME?
EDUARDO?

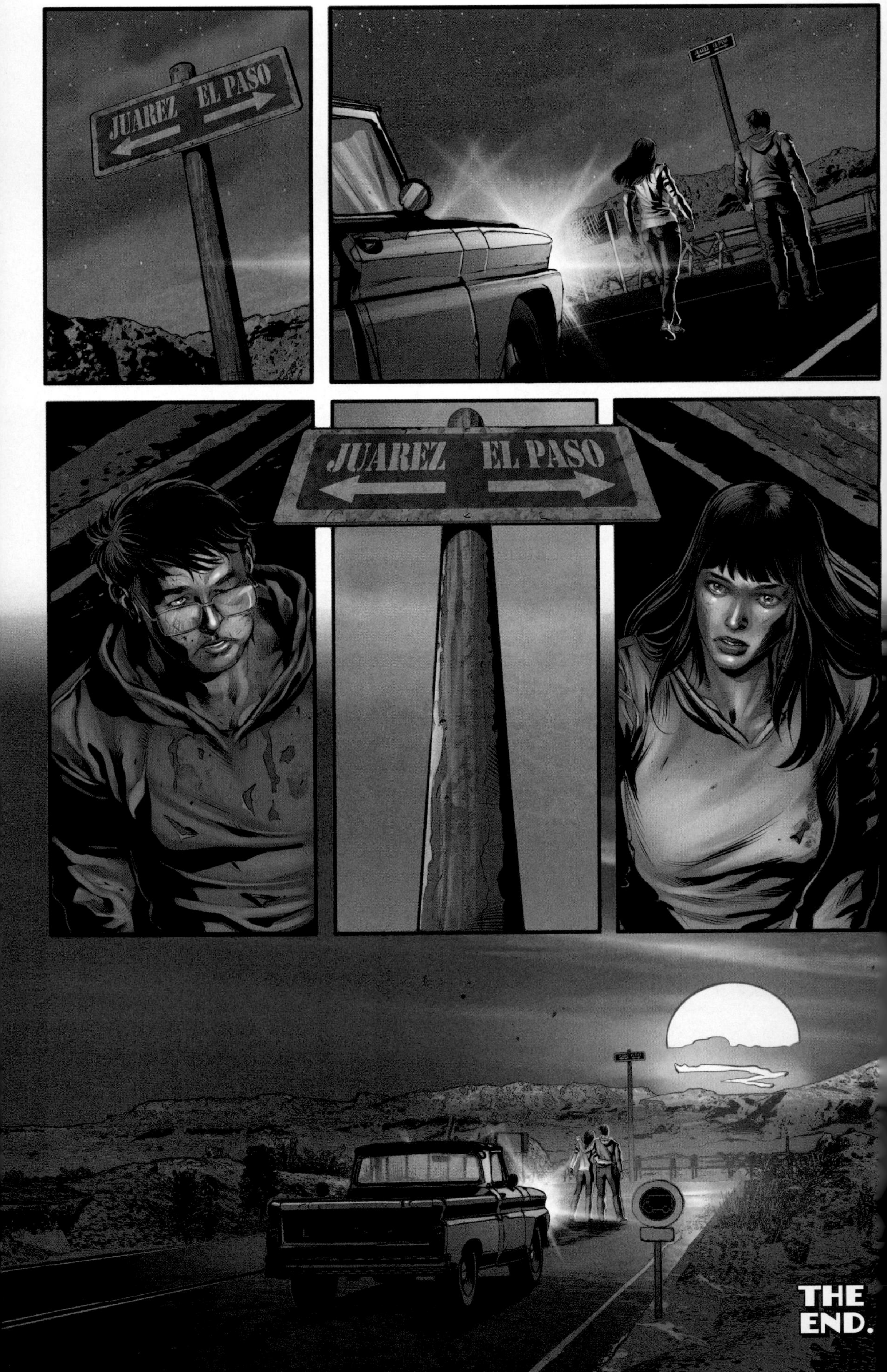
JUAREZ
EL PASO
JUAREZ
EL PASO
THE END.

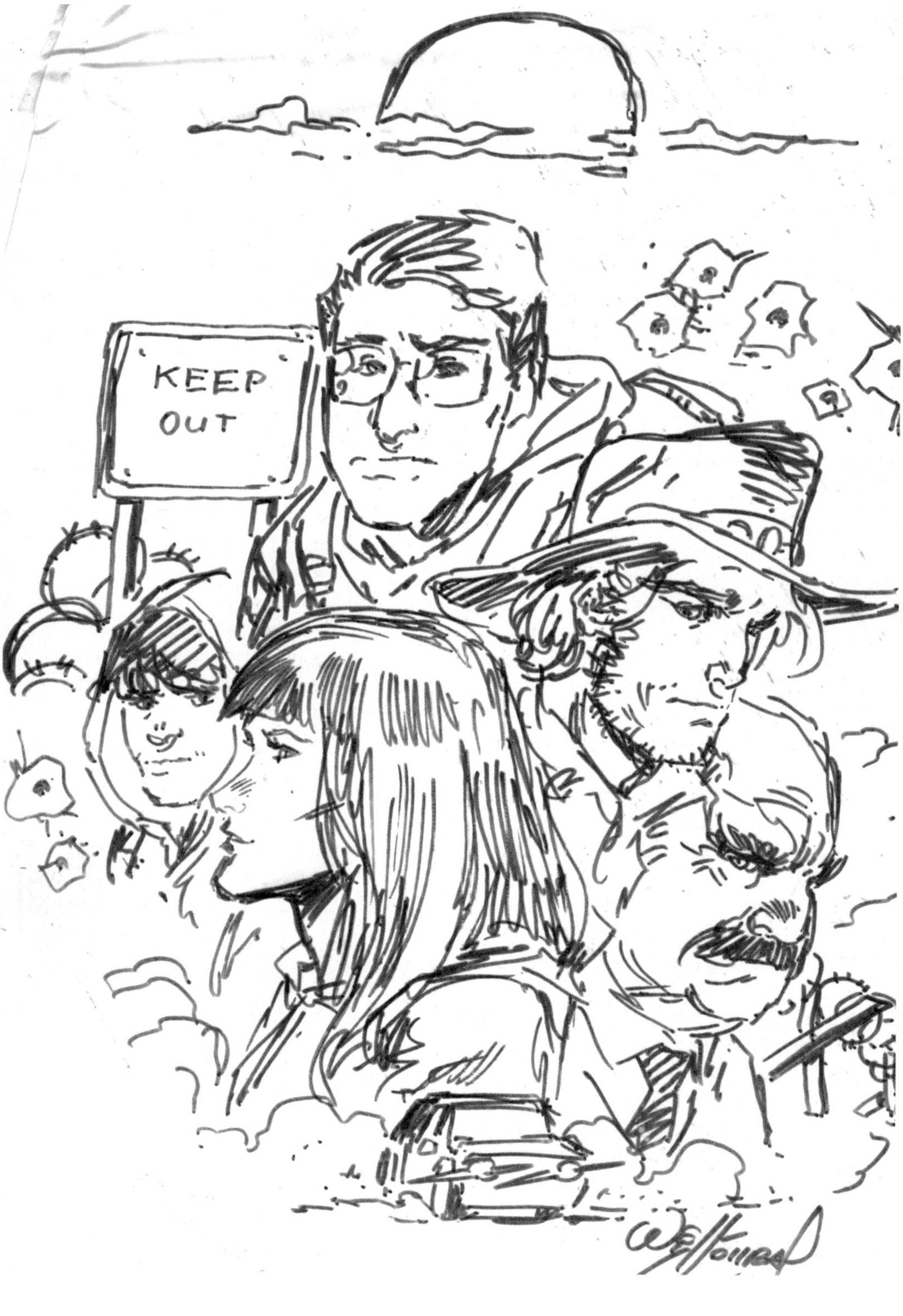
KEEP OUT

Tablecloth Sketch by Will Conrad from 2019 New York Comic Con Signing

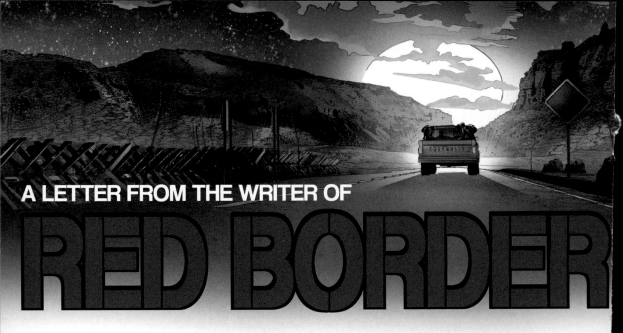

A LETTER FROM THE WRITER OF
RED BORDER

Welcome to RED BORDER.

When Axel Alonso asked me to pitch some ideas for AWA/Upshot, the new comics company he was co-founding with fellow Marvel alum Bill Jemas and Jonathan Miller, of course I said yes. I was eager to do new creator-owned projects and this sounded like the perfect opportunity. AWA had already assembled some amazing talent, including legends such as Garth Ennis, J. Michael Straczynski, and Frank Cho, and working with AWA felt like getting involved during the early days of Marvel or DC.

I'd worked with Axel on several other projects. When he was Editor-in-Chief at Marvel, he offered me and fellow crime fiction novelists Victor Gischler, Duane Swierczynski, and Gregg Hurwitz some of our first opportunities in comics. Under Axel's editorship, I wrote the entire *Wolverine Max* series, *Punisher Max*, and an original Ant-Man prose novel, *Ant-Man: Natural Enemy*.

I loved Axel's vision for AWA Studios—building a new universe from scratch, beginning with Straczynski's *The Resistance*, but also producing dark, edgy comics reminiscent of the stuff that Marvel Max and Vertigo have done. This seemed to fit squarely into my wheelhouse. Most of my novels, such as *Cold Caller*, *Panic Attack*, and *Twisted City*, lean toward the dark, edgy, noir side of the crime thriller genre, and some of my original graphic novels, like *The Returning* (Boom) and *The Chill* (Vertigo), are full-blown horror. I knew I wanted to write a dark, fun horror thriller for AWA Studios, but on a bigger scale

than my previous comics, with more action, bigger set pieces, and with provocative social and political undertones.

Some writers start with characters; for me, it's all about the plot. I need to know where the story is going, and then I can envision the characters.

I pitched several ideas to Axel by email, and the one we liked most was set on the U.S.-Mexico border; he suggested I flesh it out. I was excited in particular about the subject matter. I lived in Mexico for a while in my twenties, with a family in Guadalajara, and had always wanted to write in some way about my experiences.

A common question that all writers get is Where did you get your ideas? I never know how to answer that. I have no idea where I get mine, but I know what I'm doing when I get them—I'm usually either running or in a hot shower. Maybe it has to do with feeling hot or relaxed,

> If you're easily offended by anything that happens in this book, blame [the characters], not me.

laxed, but whenever I need some inspiration, or feel stuck with a plot, I go for a run or take a long shower and somehow the ideas break through.

So I went for a run in the park and the basic plot for *Red Border* came to me: a young Mexican couple escape a cartel in Mexico and wind up in a worse situation after they cross the border, trapped in a house of horrors in Texas. Worse, the cartel is still after them.

I emailed the pitch to Axel and I knew I was on to something because he called me immediately to discuss it. Within a few days, we had a mock cover for *Red Border*, and it was chosen as one of AWA Studios's launch titles. Now all I had to do was actually *write* it.

Axel and I agreed this story would be more complex and have more impact if the heroes were *mestizo* Mexicans, who never expected to find themselves in this situation—on the run from a cartel and desperately having to cross the border and enter the United States. It would be a metaphor for what's going on at the border right now—how people can't return to their country out of fear of violence, and yet America isn't exactly a safe haven either. As we continue develop-

> It would be a metaphor for what's going on at the border right now—how people can't return to their country out of fear of violence, and yet America isn't exactly a safe haven either.

ing the plot, the characters of the young couple, Eduardo and Karina, came to life. The same occurred with the other main characters: including Javier, the cartel boss who's going through a midlife crisis, and Colby, a charming yet crazed Texan who I knew would be a memorable villain and a blast to write.

While writing issue one, I was mainly concerned with creating a fun, exciting story. That's always my main objective when I'm writing—to entertain. But I knew this subject matter would hit on many hot button issues, and the twisted motives of the characters would stir controversy. While some political and cultural debate takes place in this comic, I was always careful not to take sides. I didn't write any of this from a liberal or conservative, or American or Mexican, point of view. Once I started writing, I purposely let the characters take over. So if you're easily offended

by anything that happens in this book—blame them, not me.

The best news for *Red Border* came when editor Dulce Montoya at AWA Studios told me that comics artist Will Conrad loves the project and wants to come on board as co-creator. I knew Will mainly from his superhero work at Marvel and DC, and his cinematic approach and ability to capture deep emotions in his characters seemed like a dream match for this material. When I saw his first pencils and inks, I was blown away—he took the project to a whole other level, adding new dimensions to the story. Will is a true artist, always creating. At a signing of an advance edition of *Red Border* at New York Comic-Con, he was sketching the characters from our comic on a scrap of paper *during* our signing. I think his passion for this material is evident on every page of this book.

Later we added colorist Ivan Nunes, expert letterer Sal Cipriano, and master cover artist Tim Bradstreet to the team. Nunes's stark yet vibrant colors enhanced Will's inks and took the book to another level.

So here it is, over a year since its inception: issue 1 of *Red Border* is finally in your hands. Co-creating this comic has been a wild ride, and we're thrilled to have you on board with us.

Perhaps Will Conrad put it best while working on his elaborate doodle at our signing:

"Get ready."

- Jason Starr

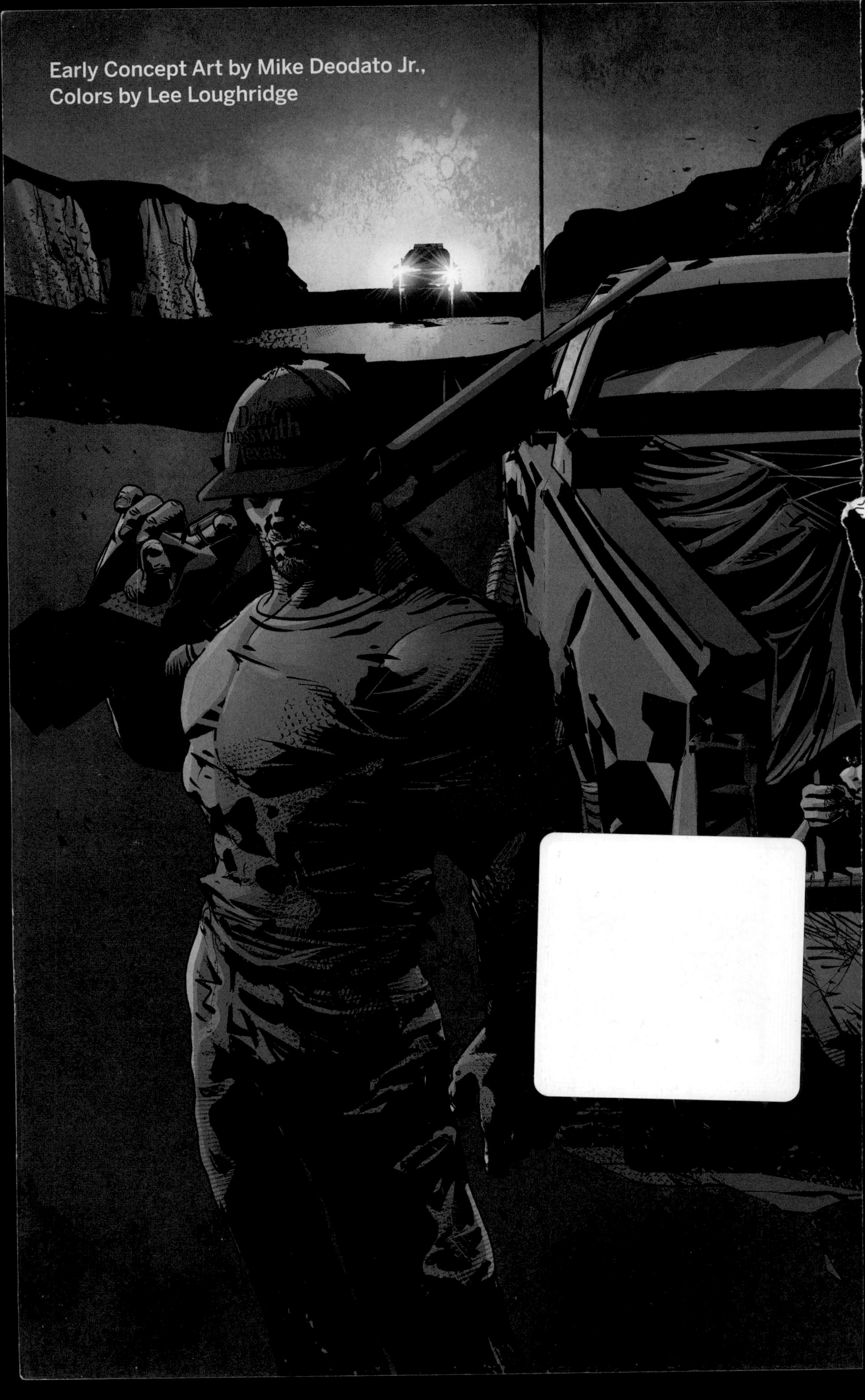
Don't mess with Texas.
Early Concept Art by Mike Deodato Jr.,
Colors by Lee Loughridge